ONE RIDE AT A TIME

LIFE LESSONS LEARNED
ON A CROSS-COUNTRY
BICYCLE RIDE

ROB LEACHMAN

ISBN 978-1-09839-490-5 (paperback)

ISBN 978-1-09839-491-2 (eBook)

DEDICATION

This book is dedicated to members of the Trans-America Cycling Fall 2017 Cross-Country Team: Chuck, Larry, Alan, Allan, Jim, Ray, Ross, Steve, Ted, and especially Bev. Thank you for playing an integral role in six-and-a-half of the best weeks of my life.

TABLE OF CONTENTS

PREFACE
"WHAT HAVE WE GOTTEN OURSELVES INTO?"

It was a question I would ask myself countless times as we worked our way across the southern United States. My wife Bev and I, each sixty years old at the time and relatively inexperienced recreational cyclists, had finally committed ourselves to tackling our long-time goal of cycling across the country, joining seven other riders and two support guides for this once-in-a-lifetime journey. Though we were nervously excited as we departed on this incredible adventure, in many respects we had no business even attempting a challenge of this magnitude. In the first few days, there were times when I felt we were clearly in over our heads, and I genuinely questioned whether we would be successful in our quest to cycle from San Diego to Florida. At a roadside ice cream stand in rural Arizona, a woman asked me,

"Are you riding all the way across the country?" I jokingly offered a response that belied a much deeper meaning, saying, "I hope so." By that time, though we had crossed one state and were making steady progress across another, I still had my doubts that this grand adventure would ultimately end in success.

We did make it all the way to St. Augustine, progressively getting stronger as we increasingly enjoyed the greatest adventure of our lives. Virtually every day for one and a half months, we woke up early, pedaled for six to ten hours, had a couple of beers and a good (and typically huge) meal, got a good night's sleep, and then did it all over again. We faced challenges even greater than we had anticipated, encountering mountains and deserts, large city parkways and isolated rural roads, bright sunshine and pouring rain, strong headwinds and even a sandstorm.

In the process, this amazing journey changed us, profoundly, and taught us some lessons about cycling that we realized could also deeply impact our daily lives.

Every few days throughout our trip, I sent members of our family a detailed account of where we had been and how we were doing. As we progressed across the country, I began to consider the viability of expanding these emails into a book-length manuscript. But I questioned whether what we had accomplished, as important as it seemed to us, was significant enough to justify the publication of our story. Then, near the end of our trip, another rider was involved in a tragic and life-altering accident, one he courageously overcame. This incident bound the team of riders and support guides even more tightly together, and it was at that point I realized that our story, and the critical lessons we learned in the process, was truly worthy of telling.

This is a story of pushing boundaries to fulfill a dream, of finding great joy in challenging circumstances, of seeing America from a most unique perspective, and of how a unique and eclectic group of individuals bonded together in ways we could never have anticipated. I am honored and excited to share that story with you.

Rob Leachman

July 2021

PROLOGUE
"YOU WANT TO DO WHAT?"

I f you tried to envision the prototypical cross-country cyclist—young, lean, athletic-looking, adventurous, risk-taker, etc.—that individual would likely bear little resemblance to me or my wife Bev. And there was little in either of our backgrounds to suggest we would one day tackle, much less complete, such a challenging journey.

Born and raised in different parts of the Midwest, Bev outside of Chicago and I near Kansas City, we grew up in the 1960s and 70s before the fitness craze began to fully take hold. As a child, I recall shopping for school clothes at J.C. Penney where we always found our way to the section with "husky" blue jeans. Though I had some athletic ability, I maintained my rather pudgy physique until my high school years, when I finally shed much of my "baby fat." As I moved on to college, where I focused on academics to the exclusion of any collegiate athletic endeavors, my weight began to stabilize at around 200 lb. on my 5'10" frame. Though I have been mostly able to maintain relatively good physical condition, I have kept that "husky" frame throughout adulthood. In other words, when one thinks of those svelte and lanky riders climbing historic peaks in the Alps during the Tour de France, my image doesn't come to mind.

As a female coming into maturity in the 1970s, Bev grew up under far different circumstances. Although she grew up in a household that celebrated sports and competition for her two brothers, like most during that generation her family simply didn't stress athletics for their only daughter, just as American society during that time placed minimal emphasis on sports for young women. There was no malice on the part of her parents in failing to push Bev toward physical activity; rather, their mindset represented a symptom of some of the cultural traditions from which American society was just beginning to evolve. Within ten years of her graduation from high school, interscholastic athletics for female students were in full bloom. That, however, did little to address Bev's naturally competitive instincts.

As a child, Bev had to find other avenues for the physical activity her body craved. Though in adulthood she has found maintaining a healthy body weight to be fairly natural, as a child she received "good-natured" ribbing for being overweight. Perhaps these seemingly related factors, a lack of organized physical activity and ridicule for being mildly overweight as a child, contributed to the active, healthy lifestyle Bev has followed through adulthood. Even fifty years later, she still has vivid memories of the childhood joy of being outside in the Indiana summer sunshine, and in particular the times she spent riding her bicycle with her friends around the small town in which she grew up. Even at that young age she required sunlight and physical activity, a visceral need that would follow her into adulthood.

After high school, Bev attended Murray State University in Kentucky where she studied Speech and Language Pathology. Having also graduated from high school in 1975, I moved on to Northwest Missouri State University where I pursued my lifelong aspiration of becoming a history teacher. Though we hadn't yet met, in our later years of undergraduate study we both began running for fitness, an activity that would in time become an important avocation for each of us and one that would lead us to run numerous half-marathons and eventually a full marathon.

Upon graduation, I accepted a position as a high school teacher and coach in a growing school district in the northern suburbs of Kansas City, Missouri. Beyond my wildest imagination at the time, thirty years later I would retire as Superintendent of that school district. During my second year in that teaching position as I was coaching football, one of the other assistant coaches mentioned that his sister had moved to Kansas City to complete her master's degree in Speech and Language Pathology at the University of Kansas Medical Center. Working behind the scenes, my fellow assistant football coach and his wife conspired to get the two of us together. Bev and I began dating that fall and were married the following August. Three years later we welcomed a son, and two years after that, a daughter.

• • •

The starting of a family made our already busy lives much more hectic. Bev was serving as a speech therapist in a nearby school district and I had continued in my teaching and coaching position. I had also completed one graduate degree in educational administration and had begun a second in the same field. Before the birth of our children, we remained focused on fitness, running three to four times each week in addition to weight training at a local fitness center. We purchased our first road bikes, long since discarded, and eventually completed an MS 150 bicycle ride for the physical challenge and to raise funds for multiple sclerosis. The first day of this weekend trek took us eighty-five hilly and windy miles through central Missouri, a distance that proved particularly daunting. As we arrived at our overnight campsite at the Missouri State Fairgrounds, we were almost too exhausted to put up our tent and genuinely questioned how we would be able to complete the next day's sixty-five-mile ride. But we did manage to put up our tent, and despite even more challenging conditions, we completed the second day's ride with surprisingly few struggles.

From this experience, we learned two vital lessons that would serve us well in future adventures. First, long bicycle rides require specific training, as being in good running shape and being prepared for hours on a bike are two different issues. Second, the human body is incredibly resilient and its ability to recover is amazingly robust. Other than training for and completing that two-day charity ride many years ago, Bev and I considered ten to fifteen miles to be a "long bicycle ride." But with running, occasional cycling, and regular weight training, we were in decent cardiovascular condition.

With the arrival of our two children, our lives were transformed in so many ways. With time more limited, the regular exercise that had been so important to us became a casualty. We ran less frequently and gave up biking and visits to the gym entirely. Like many young couples with families and developing careers, we devoted much of our available time to our children and their activities and development.

Shortly after the birth of our daughter, I accepted my first position as a high school principal, the beginning of what would be a twenty-two-year career in school administration. Because I worked at least sixty hours most weeks and continued to work on an advanced graduate degree, there was no time for exercise; or perhaps more accurately, I failed to make time. And as Bev continued to work as well and was forced to assume even more of the responsibilities related to our household and children, the bulk of her fitness time was also curtailed. Like many young couples, we were devoted to nurturing our children, advancing professionally, and otherwise simply surviving. For both of us, our fitness, and likely our health, suffered.

• • •

In time, though, our children got older and increasingly independent, and as our respective careers continued to progress and provide more flexibility, we were able to gradually resume our fitness regimen. We ran several times each week, joined another fitness club, and eventually purchased bicycles, this time hybrid bikes that could be ridden on both roads and trails. Our return to fitness was gradual, but it felt great to be back outside and to make some real progress toward getting back into shape. While Bev had maintained a fairly consistent body weight during our time of less physical activity, my weight had gradually crept upward, and as I continued to get older it became increasingly challenging to shed those extra pounds. Still, it felt great to improve my cardiovascular fitness.

Many runners and cyclists, even those like Bev and I, who are active strictly for fitness purposes rather than competitive instincts, have long-range goals or "bucket-list" items they would like to someday complete. For us, the completion of a marathon was at the top of our list, something we wanted to do in our younger years but had not, in part because of family and work obligations. As we got older and into our early forties, we decided that if we didn't reach this goal soon, we might never do so. By 1999, I had completed work toward a doctoral degree, and with a possible job change on the horizon the time seemed right for a significant physical challenge. So, we decided to begin training for a fall marathon, waiting to commit ourselves to a specific race until we were more assured we could actually complete the 26.2-mile distance. That commitment would not come until early November as we completed a brutally cold and windy 23-mile training run just three weeks before the Dallas White Rock Marathon. As assured as was possible, we registered for the race, made air and hotel reservations, and began our final preparations.

We had completed the bulk of our final training in unseasonably cold autumn weather in Kansas City. When we arrived in Dallas, though, we learned that the forecast for marathon day called for unseasonably warm temperatures with sunny skies. Bev handled the conditions well, but I struggled as the race progressed, drinking copious amounts of water (likely too much, as I would later learn) as I tried to deal with the hot and sunny conditions. But we finished, running the entire race together just as we had completed every long training run side-by-side, beginning a practice we would continue to the present as we trained for and completed various physical challenges. Although slower than we might have hoped, we had attained this long-term goal.

• • •

That possible job change did materialize for me, Bev moved into different positions within her school district, and in 2009 we both retired from our careers in K-12 education. We each transitioned quickly into higher education positions, Bev working with future speech therapists and I working to help prepare the next generation of school district leaders. I worked with graduate students in different capacities for eight years, while after two years at the university level Bev began work as a self-employed speech therapist. As our respective careers began to wind down, we each had more time to devote to areas that were important to us, including family visits, spiritual activities, and of course, fitness-related activities. And with our two children now grown and living in other states, we had fewer issues tying us to a prescribed schedule.

While various injuries curtailed much of the running I had so enjoyed, we joined the local YMCA, resumed a weight training regimen, and began taking yoga and spin classes. We purchased road bikes to utilize on rides for which our hybrid bikes were less appropriate. And we began hiking, just the two of us as well as with hiking groups. As we had all our adult lives, we gained great satisfaction from our renewed emphasis on improving our physical fitness. We were comfortable in the routines we developed, but in time, simply following a routine resulted in less motivation and ultimately, declining results. As we had learned during our preparation for the MS 150 and then the Dallas White Rock Marathon, when we had a goal, a specific physical challenge to prepare for, both of us were much more focused and driven and simply worked harder. With more time on our hands and far fewer job-related stresses to consume our attention, we had no reason not to identify bold goals and then work diligently to achieve them.

The Katy Trail is a rails-to-trails conversion, crushed limestone trail running nearly the width of the state of Missouri for 240 miles, most of it parallel to the Missouri River. Bev and I had run on different sections of the trail on numerous occasions and had ridden our hybrid bikes on parts of the trail a few times as well. We had often talked about how enjoyable and challenging it would be to ride the length of the trail, staying in old inns and hotels along the way. But time and logistical issues always seemed to prevent this goal from getting beyond the conceptual stage.

By 2013, we realized that lack of time was no longer a valid excuse and that solving logistical issues simply required creativity and a good internet connection. We decided that we would target a week in early August, a hot and humid but otherwise typically dry time of the year in Missouri. We began researching the route, realizing that the length of each day's ride would be determined as much by the availability of appropriate lodging along the trail as by the number of miles we could reasonably ride on a given day. For a ride that, with side trips, would end up totaling 260 miles, we decided we would divide the trip into five sections, averaging fifty-two miles each day, and would stay in old, restored hotels and bed-and-breakfast inns. As the trail is a converted railroad bed and thus relatively flat, we began training on a long county road that itself had years ago been converted from a rail line. Realizing our longest day of riding would be a long—for us—seventy-two miles, we gradually extended our long rides to the point that we were comfortable with our ability to complete that longest ride, as well as the entire week on the trail. Over a long, hot summer of preparation, we reinforced our belief that we worked best and hardest when we had a challenging goal in front of us.

We were nervous as we departed on this adventure, but shouldn't have been, as those five days represented one of the best weeks in our many years of marriage. Though we faced the inevitable challenges, such as nearly running out of water toward the end of our longest day and my dog-induced crash just three miles from the end of the trail, we blossomed as a result of the experience and took enormous pride in its completion.

Our Katy Trail trip taught us at least three important lessons. First, we realized that with conscious attention to patience toward each other, Bev and I worked very well together as we trained for, planned for, and completed this multi-day trip. Second, the completion of a trip like this, one that we had aspired to tackle for some time, brought us a tremendous sense of satisfaction. And third, and perhaps of greatest importance, was the realization that despite any doubts we had about what we might have been able to accomplish with our then-fifty-six-year-old bodies, we were far more physically able than we had imagined, and certainly more capable than the voices in our heads kept telling us. Though the end of this journey didn't automatically lead to a discussion about what our next adventure might entail, deep down we understood that we craved more challenges that would push us both physically and mentally.

• • •

Since Bev and I were first married, the homes in which we have lived have been filled with books, hundreds of volumes dealing with a multitude of subjects that interest us. As a result of my fascination with what we might call adventure sports or travel, we have over the years filled to overflowing an entire bookcase dealing with this topic. Climbing Mount Everest or K2, hiking the Appalachian Trail, the Pacific Coast Trail, or the Camino de Santiago, rafting through or hiking across the Grand Canyon, exploring the north and south poles, and cycling, walking, and even running across the United States are all represented by the titles in this bookcase. We never envisioned climbing Everest, trekking to one of the poles, walking across the country, or even traversing one of the major trails, because those extended adventures were likely beyond our ability levels, our financial means, or our attention spans—or, in the case of Everest or K2, our lack of desire to risk death. We weren't looking to die as a result of one of these adventures, but rather to push ourselves physically and mentally, and in the process complete journeys that had always enticed and fascinated us.

Completing a rim-to-rim hike of the Grand Canyon, however, seemed to qualify as a very tough but ultimately doable challenge. We had visited this amazing national park with our children in the mid-1990s, and I had become instantly enthralled by the magnificence of this stunning natural wonder. I was able to steal some time away from the family to hike a short distance down the Bright Angel Trail into the canyon and was fascinated by the changing scenery I encountered on my descent. The incline was very steep on this short section of trail, with countless switchbacks as I left and then returned to the South Rim. I was particularly struck by the hikers carrying large backpacks, either returning from an overnight stay in the bottom of the canyon or, more likely, completing a rim-to-rim hike. I came away thinking how fascinating but exceedingly difficult it would be to hike from one rim to the other. But, as someone in his thirties with a family and a particularly challenging job, I assumed at the time that this would likely never transcend the point of simply being another dream.

Fast forward to 2015 and we had both largely retired, with Bev doing limited private practice speech therapy while I taught just one graduate course each semester. Time was no longer an actual impediment and we had the financial wherewithal to consider a trip of this nature. The Grand Canyon, as incredible as it is, can be among the most inhospitable environments on the planet, and at times outright dangerous, an arid climate with temperatures that can approach 120 degrees. We were fifty-seven years old at the time, had no backcountry experience (particularly not in that type of environment), and questioned our preparedness to tackle such a journey on our own. Plus, there were logistical issues, most notably attaining backcountry permits and very limited campground reservations, as well as securing a shuttle for the five-hour trip from one rim to the other at the start or finish of the rim-to-rim hike. As a result, it became apparent that if we were truly interested in trekking across the Grand Canyon, we needed to find an outfitter with competent guides and the wherewithal to take care of all permits and reservations.

Bev and I have personalities that are different in many ways. As an example, I am contemplative and deliberative, needing to analyze and think through significant decisions before they are finalized. On the other hand, when Bev gets a thought she is often prone to action, figuring she can clear up any resulting residual problems later. She can become frustrated with me (sometimes for good reason) for taking too long to reach a conclusion on some pressing matter. Conversely, I can become a bit irritated by her quick-to-action strategy. Despite the minor frustrations and irritations that can occur, when working together our proclivities usually make for a pretty good team. As we had just begun to discuss the possibility of hiking across the Grand Canyon, I mentioned that Road Scholar, a travel company catering primarily to older individuals, had scheduled a five-day trip around Memorial Day that looked interesting. Interesting was enough for Bev, who quickly contacted the company, and in no time we had signed up for a trip that would fulfill a long-time dream.

We began the specific training we felt we would need to handle the rigors of the trip, particularly the two-day climb out of the canyon. The steep climb of over a mile in elevation gain in potentially brutally hot conditions could not be replicated near our Kansas City-area home, but we certainly tried. We found a local state park near the Missouri River with a hilly trail along the bluffs and hiked countless loops. Needing lightweight gear, we became popular customers of R.E.I. in purchasing packs, sleeping bags and mats, hiking poles, and a tent. We eventually completed most of our training hikes with fully loaded packs, and as our departure date neared we decided that we were likely as prepared as we could be.

After traveling to Flagstaff, Arizona, just ninety minutes from the Canyon but a five-hour drive from our starting point on the North Rim, we met the two guides and seven other hikers at an orientation meeting the night before our departure. The guides were immensely qualified and very knowledgeable, and we quickly considered ourselves to be in good hands. The seven other hikers were an interesting and eclectic group, a mixture of individuals both older and younger than us from California, Minnesota, Connecticut, and Hawaii. During our five days in the canyon, we would get to know these individuals very well. Though the food we would consume was provided by the touring company, we divided it and carried it in and out of the Canyon. With the assistance of the two guides, we would truly be self-sufficient as we completed what would total nearly thirty miles of hiking.

On our previous trip, we had seen the Canyon from both the North and South Rims, and I had taken my short jaunt along the trail below the South Rim. But as we quickly learned, observing the Canyon from either rim provided only a glimpse of the magnificence of this incredible natural phenomenon. The guides had warned us that the most challenging part of the climb would be the descent into the canyon rather than the climb out, a counterintuitive notion that proved to be accurate. After a long early morning bus ride from Flagstaff to the North Rim, which had opened for the summer only a couple of weeks earlier due to seasonal snow, we began our hike down into the canyon. Due to the much higher elevation, it was surprisingly cool and foggy as we began, making the much-anticipated vistas virtually invisible. But as we descended deeper and the fog lifted, the views became incredible, perhaps even more spectacular than we had anticipated. The North Kaibab Trail was well-worn but still rough, and at times we could peer over the railless edge and view the bottom of the canyon a thousand feet below.

On the North Rim of the Grand Canyon

As predicted, we found the steep descent to be far more strenuous than we expected, but by the time we reached the bottom of the canyon on the second day the terrain had become more level and still more varied. The hub of the inner canyon is Phantom Ranch, a location that had mystified me for many years, but which we found to be merely a collection of old but very iconic buildings. The guides had told us that the canteen at the Ranch closed to the public at 3:00 p.m. and would not reopen until after dinner had concluded at 8:00 p.m. It had been a great two days descending into the Canyon, but the lower in elevation we progressed, the hotter it became. Though we had plenty of water, the guides had been talking about the availability of cold beer at the soon-to-be-closed canteen, and that fact caused our pace during the last couple of miles to increase dramatically; that beer from the local Grand Canyon Brewing Company was among the most memorable we have ever consumed.

Though we certainly could have continued our trek after only one night at the base of the Canyon, it was so nice to take a day to explore the area, wash out our clothes, and wade into Bright Angel Creek, the closest we came to a bath or shower during our five days on the trail. But when Thursday morning came, we were ready to leave the Phantom Ranch area behind us. We hiked around half of the remaining distance to the campground for the night, a hot and barren area just off the Bright Angel Trail. After dinner, the guides led us to Plateau Point, a rock formation overlooking the Colorado River where the sites and eventual sunset were simply stunning.

We were around five miles of trail and 4,500 feet of climbing from the South Rim, and having never attempted such a steep and incessant climb under such tough conditions, we were a bit nervous as we turned in for the evening. The night was terribly hot and windless, and Bev and I both struggled to get to sleep. We awoke early, ate a quick breakfast and packed away our equipment, and were on the trail just after 6:00 a.m., hoping to make as much progress as possible before the heat began to build in the Canyon. After several miles of ascending trail, we reached the almost-vertical face of the canyon leading to the south rim. This last section of trail was very steep and challenging, but was made passable by the construction of switchbacks and thus traversable even with 30 lb. packs. Despite our prior trepidations, the climb was easier than we had anticipated and by 10:30 a.m. we found ourselves at the end of the Bright Angel Trail and among the numerous tourists milling about the south rim. The week had been tough but ultimately rewarding, and the satisfaction Bev and I and the other hikers felt upon topping the edge of that canyon was incredibly special.

Our hike across the Grand Canyon, assuredly a powerful experience but still physically doable for countless individuals, taught us several valuable lessons. First, the importance of preparation for a challenge like this is difficult to overstate. Our miles of hiking on the steepest trails available to us and our hours of working on step machines and elliptical trainers at a high resistance level or steep incline made our trek out of the canyon far more enjoyable than arduous. It reinforced the notion that with a focus toward a defined goal, we would push ourselves to even higher levels of fitness. Second, even in one of the most challenging and at times inhospitable environments available, great beauty can be found all around you. As we descended into and then climbed out of the canyon, the terrain visibly changed, sometimes simply due to the changing angle of the sun. And in some instances, we experienced views and vistas, waterfalls, native flora, and ancient indigenous home sites pointed out by the two guides that we would have likely missed if trekking on our own. And third, we enjoyed our five days of interacting with the other nine individuals in our travel party. We had never before spent such an extended amount of time with a group of people in any sort of travel situation, much less one in which showers and washing machines were unavailable, and we all slept within a small area with only the walls of lightweight tents between us. We traveled home with a sense of accomplishment, but also with a desire to tackle more and perhaps greater challenges. Maybe some of the adventures represented in the books in our travel bookcase were not as outlandish as we had once thought.

• • •

On that bookcase are at least ten books detailing the exploits of individuals who traveled across the United States on bicycles. There were books about older people riding to fulfill a long-time goal (sound familiar?), others about riders completing such rides to raise money for various charities, volumes about riders wanting to lose weight, and books about people hoping such a challenging feat would help them get over a tough breakup. There was one about an older couple riding cross-country on a tandem bicycle and another by a free-spirited man who seemingly took off on a whim. I had a soft spot for these memoirs and I read every one I could find. Early on, though, I had no real sense that I would ever do more than read about these trips, enticing though the prospect was. It was one of those "if only" dreams; if only I had the time, if only I was a better rider, if only I wasn't getting older, and so on.

Bev didn't share this dream, at least early on, and as a result she didn't read most of the adventure travel books I brought into our home. One title, though, piqued her interest. Bill Hancock is a prominent college athletic administrator residing in the Kansas City area who became the first executive director of the college football Bowl Championship Series and then the playoff system that followed it. In 2001, he was serving as director of the NCAA Men's Basketball Tournament when his son Will, media relations director for the Oklahoma State men's basketball program, was tragically killed in an airplane crash while traveling to a game in Colorado. Like many fathers, Hancock had developed a close bond with his son and was understandably devastated by this tragic loss. To deal with his overwhelming grief, the fitness-minded Hancock decided to ride a bicycle from Huntington Beach, California to Tybee Island, near Savannah, Georgia. Supported along the way by his wife Nicki, who traveled in a pop-up camper, Bill Hancock completed the 2,700-mile journey in thirty-six days. A few years later he published *Riding with the Blue Moth*, a poignant portrayal of his journey as well as his battle with grief and sadness.

Hancock's story was one of triumph over not only a major physical challenge, but more importantly over the darkness that often accompanies profound personal loss, and it resonated with Bev. This was in 2005, and we were both in our late forties. Knowing of my fascination with the challenge of a cross-country bike ride, Bev commented to me one day that if I ever wanted to take on such a challenge, she would be willing to support me much like Bill Hancock's wife Nicki had done for him. At that time in her life, Bev couldn't grasp the notion of being able to tackle such a daunting trip herself. Facing work constraints and my own sense of limitation, I never seriously considered accepting Bev's offer. At the time, neither of us could have imagined that just twelve years later we would both follow a similar southern route in completing our own cross-country journey.

• • •

In reality, that goal of biking across the United States was little more than a fantasy . . . at least, until Bev came to share that dream with me. As often happens in a relationship, when one partner has a bold thought it often languishes unless and until the other partner comes to share that idea, and then suddenly it reaches critical mass. That is what occurred with our thoughts about biking across the United States. Our Katy Trail trip had been a great experience, one that was surpassed two years later by our Grand Canyon hike, and now we needed a new goal. In time, Bev began to occasionally make passing comments about when we were going to do our bike trip, and eventually the idea took hold to the point that it would be a life disappointment for each of us if it didn't happen. With Bev now on board, things began to fall into place.

The notion of riding a bicycle for several thousand miles was daunting, perhaps a little outlandish, but seemed increasingly doable. Still, for this dream to become a reality we would have to address some significant logistical issues. First and foremost was the question of whether we would travel on our own or with a group, in essence with a travel company. We were both approaching the age of sixty at the time; not as old to us then as it had seemed ten or twenty years earlier, but old enough to be a concern regarding being stranded out on the road with a health issue. Additionally, while I could probably fix many mechanical problems with one of our bikes if needed, I am not a natural "fix-it" kind of guy, and the likelihood of having a significant mechanical issue in the middle of nowhere seemed fairly high. And finally, we had enjoyed our immersion with a group of fellow hikers during our Grand Canyon trek and similarly traveling across the country over several weeks with a group of like-minded individuals appealed to us. It quickly became clear that if we were going to tackle this challenge, we would need to do so as part of a group.

Numerous travel companies offer guided, cross-country bicycle trips along different routes and with different levels of support and amenities. Though anyone with a bicycle and a smartphone (or atlas) could chart their course across the country, with traffic, terrain, and road conditions being so critical, most follow established routes, such as those identified by the Adventure Cycling Association. This organization has identified what it calls the "TransAmerica Trail" (Oregon to Virginia), a "Northern Tier" (Washington to Maine), and a "Southern Tier" (California to Florida). Each route offers unique challenges, terrain, and cultures, and different travel companies generally follow variations of one of these routes.

As we became more serious about completing this trip, we needed to determine when we would be physically prepared to begin. Some individuals are avid cyclists who are active year-round, logging thousands of miles of riding each year. These cyclists would probably need to simply increase the length and frequency of their long rides, but for many a cross-country tour might represent just an extended, tougher version of their regular cycling schedules. At best recreational cyclists, Bev and I bore little similarity to these dedicated athletes. If we had any hope of completing a cross-country ride, we would need to train much longer, harder, and more specifically for the challenges we would encounter. As such, it made sense to seek a fall tour, allowing us to bump up our mileage through the spring and summer riding seasons. Winters in Missouri can be unpredictable, typically cold and often snowy and icy, and thus leaving roads largely unsafe for bicycles. As a result, based on our level of cycling fitness, a fall tour made the most sense. And if we wanted to complete our ride during the autumn months, the possibility of fall snow and other inclement weather in northern states suggested that a southern route was preferable.

Both now largely retired, Bev and I are financially comfortable but not wealthy, so the cost of both of us completing this trip was an obvious consideration. As we researched tour companies, we found that the level of amenities and accommodations each offered varied greatly, from nightly camping to high-end hotels and everything in between, with the cost largely commensurate with the level of "luxury" riders could expect to regularly encounter. Trips offering high-level lodging came with a correspondingly much higher cost, and apart from the financial factor, we determined that after six to ten hours of cycling each day we would simply need a hot meal, a clean bed, and a shower. Conversely, at the other end of that spectrum, some tour companies simply transported tents and camping gear to the next overnight campground, and such limited amenities obviously reduced the tour cost significantly. However, we found the notion of completing a day-long bike ride over challenging terrain, only to have to erect your tent at the end of the day, to be largely unappealing. What we sought was an affordable, supported tour with a fall start date that followed a route through southern states and included modest but serviceable lodging and meals. We weren't sure that such an option existed.

Finally, Bev identified a tour company that seemed to fit our needs. Based out of northwest Arkansas, Trans-America Cycling (TAC) was a relatively new company that followed a 3,000-mile route from San Diego to St. Augustine, Florida. As was common for such bicycling touring companies, TAC was a relatively small operation consisting of two individuals who completed all organizational and supportive activities both before and during the tour. Cross-country tours were offered each year beginning on April 1 and October 1, the latter a date we considered ideal. Shortly after discovering this company, we were able to follow their spring tour through their Facebook page, getting a little bit of the flavor of what the trip might be like. It seemed from the daily postings that the riders were making steady progress across the country, and in the process were having a great deal of fun.

We were ready, we thought, to begin making commitments to be a part of Trans-America Cycling's fall of 2017 tour. The first concrete step was to make a non-refundable deposit that would ensure we had two of the available spots that would depart from San Diego on October 1. Having grown up in a middle-class family that frowned upon the waste of money, this initial payment was significant. At this point, we hadn't shared our intentions with any family or friends, so this payment represented the first time the thought of biking across the United States had become more than a conceptual notion. With our training already underway, we clearly had some serious work to do.

• • •

Upon realizing that we hoped to complete this trip in the near future, we had started the training buildup at least a year before the anticipated start date. We felt like we had built a fairly strong base of fitness, but the physical and mental rigors of a 3,000-mile bicycle trip, including the completion of, on average, a seventy-mile ride each day, would make any level of fitness these sixty-year-old grandparents had developed simply the foundation for where we needed to be.

In fact, in recent years—or at least, since we both no longer had a daily work schedule—Bev and I had followed what some might consider a fairly aggressive exercise routine, completing some form of workout six or seven days most weeks. Typically on two days each week, we completed a tough elliptical session followed by a brief weight workout; two days of biking, either through spin classes, outdoor rides, or workouts on indoor trainers; one or two days of running, hiking, or brisk walking, either outside or on a treadmill; and one day each week we completed a yoga class. But by the time the actual tour approached, other than our weekly yoga class, we were completely focused on cycling, riding five or six days a week.

For most of the winter, we completed hour-long spin classes and other increasingly long sessions on stationary bikes. Aided slightly by watching television or listening to an audiobook or podcast, we dealt with the monotony of spending up to an hour and a half riding in one place. We longed for springtime and the opportunity to ride outside, but we were steadily building our bicycle-specific endurance. In time, as the weather improved, we were able to ride outdoors more consistently, interspersing those rides with spin classes until it became apparent that high intensity, hour-long sessions of this nature were not providing the type of saddle time and training that would best prepare us.

We began receiving periodic correspondence from Trans-America Cycling, and some of those emails confirmed the notion that we needed to prepare for "hills" that would begin on the first day of the tour. We would eventually learn that the tour guides had not overstated the early challenges we would face. Still, it was clear we needed to prepare for long and steep climbing, something made much more difficult by the relatively level Midwestern terrain that surrounded us. Though we were able to fit in a week of riding in the Colorado mountains, almost all our preparation would be completed on the plains and short hills of Missouri.

We scouted the area for the longest inclines we could find, and when we found one we often rode repeated climbs and descents to simulate what we might face after leaving San Diego. These workouts improved our riding condition, but didn't really come close to adequately preparing us; to truly prepare to bike up (and down, as we would discover) mountains, one must climb mountains, and they just weren't available to us.

One lengthy incline we located close to where we live became a gauge for how our training was progressing. Parallel to one of the runways of Kansas City International Airport, we found an isolated road that included several hills, the longest a steady 4-5% incline for almost a mile. The first time we cycled on this road, the springtime weather was cool and strong headwinds met us as we climbed that longest hill. It was a brutal, disheartening experience, with the incline and incessant wind causing us to stop midway. The realization was downright frightening: if we couldn't climb this hill, long by Missouri standards, how could we possibly navigate the real mountains we would encounter in California? We returned to this hill time and again as our preparations continued, at times completing multiple repeats as we continued to build our climbing endurance. Our last trip up this hill, just a few weeks before the beginning of our cross-country tour, was virtually effortless. It wasn't necessarily a sign that we were ready, but rather that we had made a great deal of progress.

Though we had placed a financial deposit to ensure our spot on the trip, we still had our trepidations, subtle doubts that we would be ready to go when the tour left San Diego on October 1. Our grown children were aware that cycling across the United States was a potential feat that interested us, but we hesitated to tell them about our plans. For me, it has always been rather irksome to hear people proclaim what they were going to accomplish, with their achievement level never getting past the proclamation stage. I didn't want to suggest to anyone, even our children, that we were planning to ride across the country in the coming fall unless we were reasonably sure we could actually do so. Though Bev shared some of my feelings of skepticism, she was much more ready to let our family know what we were planning. So we compromised, agreeing that we would tell our son and daughter of our plans once we had completed a fifty-mile ride.

Before a new airport was opened almost fifty years ago, travelers flew into and out of a terminal on a patch of land just across the Missouri River from downtown Kansas City. Now a commuter airport, the facility had over time become a popular route for cyclists and runners due to the largely flat, 3.75-mile road around the runway. On a hot and sunny mid-July day, we rode around this oval thirteen times, stopping every few laps for food and what they call in the Tour de France, "natural breaks." The three-and-a-half-hour ride became more monotonous than physically challenging, which it really was not, and just like that we had reached the "magic" 50-mile mark we had arbitrarily established.

We separately told our daughter and then our son and daughter-in-law that we were leaving in around two months on a bicycle ride across the country. Their respective responses were interesting and not necessarily unexpected. At the prospect of hearing that their sixty-year-old parents planned to complete such a journey, many grown children might react with a dose of skepticism, or concern, or even a lack of interest. Our children responded with feelings of support, excitement, and a little bit of amazement. They weren't surprised, and at no time did they express any doubt that we would be successful. In effect, they had more faith in our ability to do this than we had in ourselves. Their support was gratifying.

Over the next two months, we continued to extend the length of our long rides, reaching seventy miles on a five-and-a-half-hour ride three weeks before we were scheduled to depart from San Diego. We were riding five or six days each week and preparing for the tour consumed us, taking virtually all our energy and attention. What equipment would we need that we didn't yet have? How many sets of cycling jerseys and shorts would we need to take? What rain gear? Cold weather gear? What "street clothes" would we need? At last, our plane tickets were booked and our bikes were shipped to be reassembled in San Diego. We might not have been ready for what lay ahead, but we were as ready as we were going to be. And ready or not, this adventure was about to begin.

CHAPTER 1
SEEMS LIKE A LONG WAY
TO FLORIDA

As our flight edged its way from Kansas City to San Diego, our minds were engaged in a continual tug-of-war between excitement and nervousness. In my mind, nervousness was clearly gaining a distinct advantage. It was the Friday morning before the Sunday start of the tour, and all of our preparations were long completed, leaving little to be done except to think about what was ahead of us. Our bicycles had been shipped ten days earlier to a San Diego bike shop for reassembly, waiting to be picked up (we hoped) the following day. Our clothing and equipment had been carefully selected and packed away, and thousands of miles of training rides were now behind us. As we checked into our hotel, for the first time in months we had virtually nothing we needed to do, yet so much to ponder.

The Ocean Villa Inn, overlooking the beautiful Ocean Beach section of San Diego, presented a distinctive vibe that could be characterized as a combination of "bohemian" and "retro." One could imagine that decades earlier this was a very upscale establishment, a property that still offered stunning views of the ocean from our balcony. Between our balcony and the ocean was the San Diego River Pathway, the paved trail that would serve as the first ten miles or so of our cross-country route. Every time we stood on the balcony, enjoying the ocean breezes and endless vistas, the view of the trail in the foreground brought us back to the overriding purpose of our trip. We had important business to take care of.

Once settled into our hotel room, we ventured out to explore the beachfront and the surrounding neighborhood. Both having been born and raised in the Midwest and over a thousand miles from any ocean, Bev and I had in recent years developed an affinity for beachfront settings. Though neither of us has much of a connection to water sports, we both have come to love the beach while seldom actually getting in the water. We traveled to Daytona Beach almost yearly during this time, finding great joy in running along the wide Atlantic Ocean beaches. Conversely, this trip to San Diego represented one of the relatively few times we had been in close contact with the Pacific Ocean. After walking along the beach and out onto the Ocean Beach boardwalk, we found a nearby restaurant with a rooftop deck and sat under the shade of an umbrella as we enjoyed beers and an appetizer. It was hot on this late-September afternoon, but the breezes coming off the ocean were cooling and the views were magnificent. Hard as it was, we tried to relax and enjoy the amazing setting.

Since registering for this tour with Trans-America Cycling several months earlier, we had received a great deal of correspondence from Larry and Chuck, the two individuals who together comprise this unique travel company. (Throughout this narrative, I refer to

Larry and Chuck as "support guys," a term used to describe two individuals whose roles were too broad to refer to them as merely "guides" or any other more formal designation.) Though we had seen photos on the company webpage, we hadn't met them and knew little about these two people who would play a huge role in any success we might experience over the coming forty-six days. As we entered the hotel parking lot in the late afternoon, we noticed a van, a pickup truck, and a large trailer, all bright white with "Trans-America Cycling" emblazoned on the sides of each. Larry and Chuck had just arrived after having driven from their base of operations in Northwest Arkansas. We introduced ourselves to these two gentlemen, who we would soon find to be very interesting, supportive in so many ways, and to us absolutely indispensable.

· · ·

The coming together of these two personalities to form Trans-America Cycling was an almost serendipitous process. Born in the St. Louis area, Larry eventually found his way to Arkansas to work for the Walmart Corporation, headquartered in nearby Bentonville. With a great interest in history, particularly the Civil War, he eventually gravitated to teaching, and at the time our cross-country tour began Larry had recently retired as a middle school Social Studies teacher.

Having begun my career in education as a high school history teacher, continuing as a student of the Civil War, and having toured almost all of the major battlefields of that conflict, I considered myself to have some authority on the subject. One day well into the tour, Larry and I were having one of our numerous discussions about various Civil War topics. I mentioned that I had spent two days walking the Gettysburg battlefield and had on numerous occasions watched the Ted Turner movie based on that battle, as well as completed several readings of *The Killer Angels*, the book on which the movie was based. Responding nonchalantly and with no discernible boastfulness, Larry commented, "Yeah, I was in that movie."

A bit stunned, I asked for more information. Larry offered that in his younger years he had been very active in Civil War reenactments, and he was one of the thousands of reenactors who traveled to Gettysburg to participate in the filming. Taking part in Pickett's Charge, arguably the most pivotal action of the entire war, he modestly told us that in his many viewings of the film, he had been unable to pick himself out of the countless participants in the battle. I suggested that I felt I had immersed myself in the Gettysburg experience by completing a detailed tour of the battlefield, only to find that Larry had actually "fought" in the battle. As our conversations continued, I would learn that Larry had published multiple historical novels about the Civil War, basing his writing on his review of numerous diaries and other first-hand accounts.

Chuck had grown up in a small town in Kansas, and through the course of his working career he gravitated to computer support positions. Like Larry before him, he ultimately settled in Northwest Arkansas after accepting a position with Walmart, providing software support for specific divisions within the corporation. As they were preparing to begin offering cross-country tours, Chuck retired from his primary career. With his knowledge not only of cycling but also his appreciation for good literature, movies, wine, and a variety of other areas, we similarly found Chuck to be a unique and interesting individual.

Larry and Chuck of Trans-America Cycling

Both avid cyclists, Chuck and Larry were active in their local riding community, but only knew each other in passing. A few years back, Larry decided to devote his summer break to completing a bicycle ride along a northern route across the United States. When Chuck learned of this plan, the two decided to tackle this journey together. Riding unsupported and carrying all of their equipment and supplies, they completed their cross-country trek, gaining invaluable experience and accumulating countless stories.

From this trip came the decision to form Trans-America Cycling. As we gathered in San Diego to begin our tour, we didn't realize ours would be only the third tour they had led. As I reflected partway through the trip, I realized it was fortuitous that we weren't aware of their relative inexperience leading such complex ventures. Had we been aware we might have shied away from selecting Trans-America

Cycling for our tour, which in retrospect would have been a significant mistake.

• • •

Buoyed by the two-hour change in time zones, we woke up particularly early on Saturday morning. On this last day before the beginning of the tour, we had three important tasks to accomplish: most notably, to pick up our bicycles, attend the orientation meeting at which we would meet all the other riders, and then get a good night's sleep. We would be able to check only two of the three off our list, finding deep sleep to be largely elusive. After breakfast, we walked along Ocean Beach before it became crowded, which it did on this beautiful Saturday afternoon in Southern California.

Wanting to ensure sufficient time for our bikes to make it to San Diego and then be appropriately reassembled before the start date of the tour, we had shipped them to a bike shop located a couple of miles from our hotel. I was a bit nervous about this entire process for a variety of reasons. After experiencing knee and back soreness during and after long training rides, I had completed a professional bike fitting, a process that had largely alleviated those pains. The reassembly of my bike to those exact specifications could not be guaranteed. Simply tearing down a bicycle, repacking it, and shipping it almost 1,500 miles naturally raised the possibility of damage, and as we had shipped two bikes that possibility was multiplied. Packages can get lost in transit, and though they are usually found eventually, that process could take considerable time. It was Saturday, the tour was starting on Sunday, and as such, we had no time to wait for one or both of our bikes to be located, transported, reassembled, and picked up. As a result, when we had dropped off our bikes to be shipped, we felt a combination of sadness at missing these bikes, which had been such an important part of our lives for the past six months or so, as well as trepidation that there might be missteps in the multi-step process before we finally picked them up at the San Diego bike shop. Luckily, when I called a few days before leaving Kansas City, the helpful folks at Performance Cycle had confirmed that both of our bikes had arrived and would be ready to be picked up as promised.

Looking at Google Maps, it appeared we could walk around a mile and a half on the trail before getting off and walking around a mile on a commercial street to get to the bike shop. On this warm and sunny Saturday morning, we took off on the same trail we would follow the next day, walking leisurely as we dodged the occasional biker, runner, or dog walker. It was a truly beautiful day, no doubt typical San Diego weather, and we enjoyed our walk on the trail. As we exited the trail, though, we had to navigate a very hectic interchange under Interstate 8, already extremely busy on this Saturday morning. It was a bit nerve-wracking to walk through that intersection and then onto an extremely busy major street. Admittedly at this point still novice cyclists, we had done almost none of our many training rides on busy city streets, and besides, a hectic traffic day in Kansas City might represent a light day in this Southern California city. As a result, as we were walking the mile or so from the trail to the bike shop, we were pondering how we were going to navigate those same issues with our bicycles.

We finally reached the bike shop, a bit concerned about the potential hazards of getting back to the hotel. As we entered the store, standing just inside the entrance were Larry and Chuck. They had transported another rider to pick up his bike, a request we hadn't thought of making. They both greeted us and quickly offered to transport our bikes and us back to the hotel. This would not be the last time these guys would assist us in dealing with a logistical issue, this a relatively minor one compared to what we would face in the coming weeks. Meeting them was fortuitous and was but another example of everything falling into place as we prepared to tackle this major challenge. As I reflected afterward, it was another sign that we needed to trust the process and ourselves, and that we would complete this cross-country trip successfully.

We picked up our bikes, which had been reassembled in a very satisfactory manner, and loaded them onto the bike rack on the back of the Trans-America Cycling van. Our ride back to the Ocean Villa Inn was our first opportunity to get to know Chuck and Larry, as well as the other rider, Alan from Scotland. After we unloaded our bikes at the hotel, Bev and I quickly changed into our riding gear and took our bikes on a short ride on the adjacent trail to make sure they had been reassembled appropriately. As we were leaving the parking lot, we noticed Larry talking with a couple of other individuals we assumed were riders. As we passed them, alluding to the official tour start the next morning, I wryly commented, "We decided we needed a head start." (We probably did.) They laughed, and we quickly determined that our bikes were working well and fitted appropriately.

• • •

Except for Alan from Scotland and of course Chuck and Larry, we had not formally met the individuals who would comprise our "family" for the next forty-six days. As we nervously gathered in the hotel's breakfast room that afternoon for our first "team meeting," which would occur each evening before dinner for the remainder of the tour, Bev and I waited anxiously to meet our fellow riders. There were no formal introductions, so we would piece together the general biography of each rider over the next few days. We received the set of Adventure Cycling Association maps that we would sequentially use until we reached St. Augustine and the handbook of general tour guidelines and comprehensive course information detailing each day's route. Larry largely ran the meeting, and we experienced for the first time the meticulous approach this former middle school teacher applied to the preparation for the tour. As we would find out later, most of the riders had previously participated in large tours, though none as long or extensive as this one. Bev and I had not, and as a result, much of what was shared in this initial meeting was new to us. In my nervous state, much of the information seemed to blur, and my recollection of much of the meeting remains oddly foggy.

Through the meeting, we were able to begin putting together who we would be riding with for the next one and a half months. Though the ages of athletes (and make no mistake, these guys were athletes) can be hard to judge, we surmised that several riders were younger than our sixty years, a couple were close to our age, and a few were older. As Bev had previously confirmed, she would be the only female rider, something that seemed a more daunting factor at the time than it would become as the tour progressed. As I commented then, and as I still believe, the fact that Bev was the only female rider said virtually nothing about the overall female population, but a great deal about Bev's drive and fortitude. From the start, the other riders were respectful of Bev as the lone female, but otherwise seldom treated her as anything other than just another rider. Though I would never attempt to speak for Bev and don't profess to understand the perspective of any female athlete, I suspect that being treated like "just another rider" by her male counterparts would constitute a supreme compliment. For Bev's part, as the only woman spending a month and a half interacting almost exclusively with a group of men, she had to learn how to act and how to flourish in such a unique setting. While I know she missed the company of other women, it seemed that Bev handled this challenge so well that, at least to everyone else on the tour, the fact that she was the only woman was truly a non-issue.

Among the riders was Ray, a recently retired physician from Minnesota who had the distinction of not only being the oldest rider, but also the only one to ride a recumbent cycle. A longtime avid and accomplished cyclist, Ray had eventually found that riding a traditional upright bicycle placed too much strain on his neck. He had prolonged his cycling career by transitioning to a recumbent cycle that allowed him to sit in a chair-like seat and keep his head and neck in a neutral position. Then there was Ross, who we would find to be the best pure cyclist on the team, and who had also recently retired from a technology management position in Oklahoma. Early in the tour, Ross mentioned in passing, and with no boastfulness, that before the cross-country tour his riding mileage for 2017 was over 12,000 miles. Based on his riding the first days of the tour, we had little reason to doubt this passing claim. A third rider, Jim from Illinois, was a military retiree who had come to cycling relatively late in life. But his descriptions of training rides in central Illinois, as well as his yearly completion of the RAGBRAI tour, a famous and often raucous annual ride across the state of Iowa, spoke to his devotion to the sport.

Two riders from Ohio, Steve and Ted, were related by marriage and were riding as an informal team, each dedicating his respective ride to a selected charity. Steve, who had just retired from a position as a health auditor, checking the cleanliness and biological safety of food processing facilities, was raising funds for digestive disease issues (think colon cancer and related conditions) through the Cleveland Clinic. Though healthy himself, Steve's family had been greatly impacted by the disease. Ted was a retired air traffic controller who was raising funds in support of individuals with Williams Syndrome, a condition with symptoms not unlike those of Asperger's Syndrome. Ted and Steve had a nephew with that condition. By the time we reached the Atlantic Ocean, these two would be the source of countless laughs and good times.

Finally, the only two non-American "team members" (as Trans-America Cycling referred to us in Facebook updates) were rooming together on the tour and were ironically named Alan and Allan. Scottish Alan, as we would refer to him to distinguish between the two, was older than he looked but a few years younger than us, and was a structural engineer from Scotland. The other Allan was the youngest team member, and as we would find, the strongest rider, and worked in law enforcement in his native Denmark. Most of the riders had grown children, but Danish Allan was the only one with school-aged youngsters back at home.

So for the next month and a half, we would spend a good part of each day with this eclectic group of riders, sharp and well-educated, most of them very accomplished cyclists and much more experienced than Bev and me. As we departed the breakfast room at the Ocean Villa Inn that Saturday evening, we had no way of knowing just how much we would come to enjoy the company of these guys, and the highs and tragic lows we would experience together.

As we sat in the meeting, however, the magnitude of what was ahead of us began to sink in. The next morning we were leaving on a bicycle trip across the United States, a notion that had previously seemed impossible, and that in the recesses of our minds still did. We had worked hard to prepare, and we were probably as physically ready as we could be. But we sensed that, severe as they might be, the physical challenges might be surpassed by the mental ones that accompanied the daily grind of long rides, most of which approached the previous longest ride we had ever completed. With this adventure scheduled to begin in only eighteen hours, I continued to seriously wonder if we weren't in over our heads.

• • •

After the meeting concluded, Bev and I decided to head out for an early dinner. We walked a couple of blocks from the hotel and found a tavern with a largely uninhabited outdoor patio, choosing a large table overlooking the sidewalk on this gorgeous Saturday evening. We ordered a couple of burgers and beers and settled in for what we anticipated would be a quiet pre-ride dinner. Before our food arrived, we noticed Ray and Jim walking up the sidewalk. We invited them to join us, and were soon getting to know two of our fellow riders. Shortly thereafter Scottish Alan joined us, and suddenly more than half the team of riders were having dinner together. It made for an enjoyable evening, but talking with these three cyclists brought focus to our limited experience in advance of this cross-country excursion. Jim talked about his long rides with his training group across the plains of central Illinois and his yearly tours across Iowa as part of RAGBRAI. Alan shared tales of traveling to Europe to climb some of the iconic peaks made famous by the Tour de France. Perhaps most impressive was Ray, a decade older than us, who had ridden his recumbent cycle all over the country and spoke of regularly participating in "Ride the Rockies," the annual multi-day tour of the Colorado mountains that featured tens of thousands of feet of elevation gain. These guys weren't boastful in the sharing of these stories, but the conversation was simply symptomatic of the degree to which cycling played a central role in their lives. To Bev and me, riding our bicycles was simply one of several activities used to stay in shape, and we had selected this trip, which was beginning to seem more and more outrageous, to meet a long-time goal and to provide some focus to our conditioning. As we returned to our hotel after a pleasant dinner, my trepidation had not been diminished. With what we thought might be a short and fairly easy ride ahead of us the following day, we settled in for what, at least for me, would be a fitful night of sleep.

• • •

I could faintly hear the rhythmic sounds of the nearby ocean as the ancient air conditioning unit in our rustic hotel room cycled on and off. It was around 11:00 p.m., and in ten hours or so we would leave on a forty-six-day, 3,000-mile cross-country bicycle trip. And as I struggled to sleep, a relentless stream of questions kept flowing through my mind, none of which I could answer with any clarity, at least not yet:

Could two sixty-year-old grandparents, recreational cyclists at best, actually make it from San Diego to St. Augustine, Florida?

Had we trained enough? Was it possible to train enough to be ready for what we would face over the next one and a half months? How could we possibly ride an average of seventy miles a day, day after day, when our longest ride, at least in the last twenty-five years, had only been seventy miles? What were we thinking?

Would we be able to get along with the other seven riders and the two support guys? Would they get along with us?

With thirty-six happy years of marriage behind us, after such an arduous and challenging journey, would Bev and I still be together to celebrate our thirty-seventh anniversary? Past adventures had served to bond us together even more strongly, but we had never taken on a challenge approaching this one.

How would we handle the rigors of the mountains? The desert? The cities? The monotony of interminably long and boring stretches of nameless roads? Would we be strong enough physically? Mentally?

And finally, though not a conscious issue as we prepared to begin this journey, perhaps the most important question facing us was, how would this experience change us? How would we be different after forty-six days of the most arduous physical challenge of our lives and after seeing the broad stretch of this country in one of the most up-close and personal ways possible? In the end, that was the real question.

Bev was lying in the bed next to me, seemingly asleep, though I suspect she was facing some of those same trepidations. We had completed every long training ride together and had numerous discussions about how we were progressing. But we had avoided the blunt conversations about the doubts that would be natural for any sane person in our position, getting ready to ride a bicycle across the United States. Still, those doubts were there, we both had them, and for me, the many questions facing us were simmering just below the surface, keeping me from the sleep I needed so desperately.

Whether we were ready or not, the answers to our many questions, along with the many life lessons we would learn along the way, would begin to appear the next morning as we began the greatest adventure of our lives.

• • •

Waking up particularly early on this important first day of the tour, I tried to quietly make a cup of coffee in the little coffee maker in our hotel room while Bev finished what I hoped had been a good night's sleep. After a quick breakfast at the hotel, we packed up, got dressed (donning the "Trans-America Cycling" jerseys we were asked to wear on this first day), and proceeded to what would become known as "the trailer." Larry drove a pickup that pulled a cargo trailer in which was placed spare bikes, extra equipment, the plastic bins we had each been given for storing our extra bike supplies, and most importantly our luggage. In our pre-tour correspondence, Larry and Chuck had emphasized that each rider could utilize two carry-on sized pieces of luggage with a combined weight of fifty pounds. Packing these two small suitcases with everything we anticipated needing for the next one and a half months had been a bit stressful, picking and choosing what we would be taking. And on that first day of the tour, it was similarly stressful as Larry and Chuck weighed each piece of luggage. We weren't sure what the guys would do if anything was overweight, but we didn't want to take the chance of having to leave a critical piece of clothing or equipment in a trash dumpster at the Ocean Villa Inn. We came to understand and appreciate Larry's attention to ensuring that no piece of luggage was over-weight, as he and Chuck lugged these suitcases at the end of each ride so they were in our hotel rooms when we arrived. Luckily, none of our small suitcases exceeded the weight limit, and anyway, we would soon realize we didn't need much of what we had brought to San Diego.

Departing from Ocean Beach in San Diego

With all the logistical issues completed and our luggage stored in the trailer, we all rode the short distance to Ocean Beach, where we would dip our *back* tires in the Pacific Ocean, a traditional symbolic gesture for riders beginning a cross-country trip. (We hoped that in forty-six days we would dip our *front* tires in the Atlantic.) After countless photos of individual riders (and of Bev and me together) dipping their tires in the water, and then a large group photo, we were ready to begin what we thought would be a relatively easy thirty-two miles to the small town of Alpine, an opportunity to ease into the rigors of the tour. Much to my surprise, this ride, one of the shortest of the tour, would severely test our resolve and cause us to question whether we had any chance of coming close to completing this cross-country ride. The route was a combination of urban trails for the first ten miles or so, then streets through commercial and then residential areas of San Diego, and then finally, the last third or so on a road bordering Interstate 8 leading up to Alpine. Larry led us on the complicated series of trails that took us to the first SAG stop, where Chuck was waiting with water and snacks. Though we didn't appreciate it at the time, these SAG stops (the acronym for "Support and Gear") would in time greatly help to motivate us as we progressed through long rides. After eating a banana and a granola bar and topping off our water bottles, we headed on toward the next stop. It was by now an early Sunday afternoon in San Diego, and though it was warm, we were nervous and excited enough to not pay close attention to weather conditions. After the second stop, as Bev and I were largely riding by ourselves, we noticed the urban terrain progressively becoming more bucolic, with less traffic and far fewer businesses.

Around twenty miles into the ride, we began to experience the "hills" the support guys had warned us we would encounter on this first day. We started climbing; not especially steep, at an incline that ranged from 3% to 5%, but relentless. Among the hills near our Missouri home, there are some that are very steep, but none that are particularly long. In other words, you could complete a hard climb and eventually reach the top, after which you could then catch your breath as you descended. But on this warm Sunday afternoon, this "hill" just kept going upward. At first, we were only a little concerned, and I joked that "Even Everest has a summit." But by all appearances, this mountain did not. We kept pedaling, with me in front and Bev right behind me, and around each corner, we expected at least a little momentary relief that came from a downhill section. But it never came.

This was hard—much harder than we had anticipated—and far beyond the conditions for which we had prepared. (As we reflected afterward, with a destination called *Alpine*, we should have anticipated the terrain we would encounter.) As the climbing continued, and as we got hotter and more tired, we began to wonder whether we would be able to make it to the hotel on this first day of a forty-six-day tour. Both of us panicked a little and began to press, which made the climbing even more difficult. Added to these challenges, about a mile from the finish Bev started to experience stomach cramps that at one point caused her to have to stop and bend over the front of her bike. About the same time, I was starting to experience some rather severe heartburn, making us possibly the two most pitiful people in Southern California that afternoon. At the last SAG stop, I had consumed some snack foods I had never eaten during a ride, and all of a sudden those snacks began to wreak their revenge. As we reflected after the ride, both our stomach issues were probably exacerbated by the dehydration we were likely experiencing on this warm October afternoon.

As we were stopped on the side of the road, a local cyclist rode by and asked if we needed any help. (We lied and said we didn't.) We spoke briefly about what we were doing, our cross-country tour (the remaining 2,970 miles seemed like the distance to the moon at this point), and he asked where we were stopping for the day. When we told him the Ayers Inn in Alpine, he gave us a big smile and said, "Well, that's just up ahead." Locals are notorious for giving inaccurate estimates of distances (though we have found cyclists to be far better at this than many in cars and pickups), but sure enough, after climbing another quarter mile or so, we rounded a corner and were suddenly in Alpine, California, our destination for the evening. We were the last to arrive, as we would be most days, but we didn't care. As we got to our room for the evening, Bev was spent, I was still a little sick, and the dominant thought in my mind was simply, "If this is what this trip is going to be like, I don't know if we're going to be able to make it."

• • •

When we arrived at the Ayers Inn, located alongside Interstate 8, Bev was exhausted and I was little better, so we sat on some patio chairs as we tried to determine the protocol on this first actual night of the tour. As we would quickly determine, Larry typically arrived at each hotel before any riders, checked into each of the rooms, hauled all of the luggage to the rooms, and then distributed keys or key cards as riders arrived. As we sat out on the patio on what would under normal circumstances be considered a beautiful afternoon, it took us a little time before we could concern ourselves with where we needed to go and what we needed to do; we were in a sort of survival mode at this point. We eventually got into our room, and some cold water and a shower did wonders to raise our spirits, though my heartburn was a continuing concern. As we'd had little "real food" since breakfast, Bev suggested that we get some late lunch.

As we were unfamiliar with the area, our food options seemed limited. Next to the hotel was a Carl's Jr., virtually identical to the Hardee's restaurants in the Midwest and not particularly known as a health food outlet. Still feeling some gastric discomfort, I questioned whether eating would be beneficial, but hoped that it would. As we scanned the burger-laden menu, the healthiest choice seemed to be an item called the "Charbroiled Chicken Club." After all, what better treatment for heartburn and indigestion than a sandwich with bacon and melted Swiss cheese? But it had been a tough day, and I was hungry, so I ignored my instincts and dove in. It would take a while, but I would eventually come to realize the folly of this food choice. We went back to the hotel and I was soon experiencing not just heartburn but also nausea and chills, the beginning of what I thought was possibly a little bug. The day had started well enough, but the last third had been more grueling than we could have imagined, causing both of us to doubt our ability to get out of California—much less ride all the way to Florida. And now I was getting sick. As I lay in my bed in Alpine, California, fearing I would be unable to ride the next day on a route that was longer and tougher than the one we had experienced today, my emotions were running rampant, with none of them particularly positive.

As this was the first day of riding, the team began to settle into a routine that would be followed for the next forty-six days. At 5:00 p.m., all riders would meet with the two support guys to discuss any logistical issues and in particular to highlight the route for the following day, the location of SAG stops, any particularly treacherous sections or scenic sights, and the location of the hotel at the end of the ride. After the meeting, the group would travel—on foot, when possible—to a local restaurant for dinner, which was provided by Trans-America Cycling as part of the tour package. Still confined to the hotel room, I stayed back while Bev attended the meeting and then walked with the group to a Chinese restaurant, where she got take-out food to bring back to the hotel room, ordering what she thought was the best dinner for a queasy stomach. I was able to eat most of it and began to feel a little better.

When our kids were little and we visited Bev's parents, and when the grandchildren inevitably whined when asked to do something, their grandma would half-jokingly tell them to "buck up." After we finished our dinner in our hotel room, Bev and I had a frank and honest conversation about what had occurred earlier in the day and what we needed to do going forward. The last third of the ride had been brutal, and jacked up on nerves and impatience, we had made it much worse than it needed to be. We agreed that in the future, when faced with a tough ride—something which was inevitable, and which would occur as soon as the following day—we needed to try to relax, find the easiest gear needed, and take our time, stopping to rest or drink water as needed. We agreed that while we didn't want to dawdle, we had all day to get to our next destination. And contrary to what we had allowed ourselves to experience on this first day, we needed to have fun. Even when in distress, including on the particularly difficult rides, we absolutely needed to find enjoyment. Regarding my stomach issues, I offered that just like their grandma had told our kids, I needed to "buck up." Unless I felt a lot worse when we left the hotel the next morning, I would ride and see how the day developed. In many respects, this conversation was pivotal for us, and in some ways set the tone for the remainder of our tour. And it was so uncomplicated, the notion that we would take our time if needed and try to find enjoyment in our daily rides.

· · ·

We woke up the next morning feeling a little better, and after breakfast we began a fifty-one-mile ride that would include almost 5,000 feet of climbing. As we left the hotel, we had no idea how the day would progress, but we were anxious to see what lay ahead. As we made a left-hand turn onto the same road we had followed for the latter part of the previous day's uphill ride, we were faced with a smooth, wide shoulder, but the same steady incline. What was different, though, was our attitudes. We found an easy gear and simply took our time, being greeted by other riders as they passed us and stopping every mile or two to take a drink and catch our breath and then get back to climbing. We suddenly found that this route, actually far more challenging than the day before, was seemingly doable. After several miles on Alpine Boulevard, we merged onto Interstate 8, the first time either Bev or I had ridden on an interstate highway. The shoulder was wide and allowed us to keep a good distance from fast-moving traffic, and though we were still climbing, it was actually better and safer riding than we had been experiencing. Still, having tractor-trailer rigs pass us going faster than the listed speed limit of 75 mph was rather daunting at first. In time, though, we just put our heads down and continued to climb and put miles behind us.

The support guys typically set up SAG stops every twenty to thirty miles, and on this fifty-one mile day there would be two. The first was at a scenic overlook pull-out just off of the interstate. As we exited the highway and approached the riders gathered near the two Trans-America Cycling vehicles, for the first time I began to take in the splendor of the terrain that surrounded us. With our concentration focused on riding along the interstate, we had largely paid attention to asphalt, highway lines, and fast-passing vehicles. But from this picturesque overlook, we focused on the scenery for the first time, and it was magnificent and vast, with mountain vistas extending west to San Diego and south to Mexico. After lounging for perhaps fifteen minutes and consuming some snacks and replenishing our water, we headed back out to continue our climb. Though we would come to realize that this ride was significantly more challenging than what we had experienced the previous day, we were doing amazingly well. And enjoying ourselves.

In time, we exited the interstate and moved onto "Old Highway 80," a well-maintained road with a good shoulder that continued to climb, though now with occasional short downhill sections. We ultimately rode into Pine Valley, a nice little town that I can assuredly state we would have never visited were we not on a cross-country bike ride, and one that was noteworthy mainly for its picturesque location in what we would learn were the Cuyamaca Mountains. The second SAG stop was located in the parking lot of a little hamburger joint called "Frosty Burger." As part of the tour package, Trans-America Cycling provided breakfast (typically the breakfast offerings of the hotel in which we were staying), dinner, and snacks throughout the day. If anyone wanted a traditional lunch, assuming a restaurant or convenience store was available, it was his or her responsibility. By the time Bev and I had arrived, most of the other riders were sitting around shaded outdoor tables, either eating or waiting for their Frosty Burgers. As we had both experienced varying degrees of stomach issues the previous day, we were a bit concerned about eating either the wrong food or too much of any food. But with the smell of hamburgers on the griddle wafting through the air, we decided to sample some of the famed (at least to TAC cross-country riders) Pine Valley cuisine. Bev and I shared a hamburger, a vanilla milkshake, and a regular Coke, all items that, in our older years, we seldom if ever consumed. In a setting that would be less than memorable under any other circumstances, we savored these items.

Sated with food that would never be recommended by sports nutritionists, we continued toward our destination for the evening in Jacumba Hot Springs. The elevation wasn't high enough to impact performance, but it was hot and dry, and the long uphill sections made for a challenging afternoon. We eventually topped the last hill and began a long gradual downhill. After two days of incessant climbing in hot conditions, this extended descent—steep enough to preclude the need for pedaling, but not particularly fast or technical—was a glorious ending to what, for Bev and me, had been a relatively strong bounce-back day.

Focused on the ride, we had at first paid little attention to the white SUVs emblazoned with large green diagonal stripes that we had seen with increasing frequency since leaving Pine Valley. These U.S. Border Patrol vehicles became increasingly ubiquitous as we approached our destination for the evening, which was only a few hundred yards from the U.S.-Mexico border. As we descended the last few miles into Jacumba Hot Springs, we rode alongside the border wall to our right, occasionally passing Border Patrol vehicles parked on the hills overlooking the border. Our view of the wall, with border guards patrolling the area and with hills and dwellings of Mexico just beyond, made for a surreal sight, one that before had simply been an abstract notion. Our contact with the border would continue off and on for the next two weeks.

• • •

Jacumba Hot Springs was like many of the small border towns we would encounter: hot, dusty, and at first glance, economically depressed. There was a post office, a small number of businesses that didn't appear to be open, a school, and a handful of houses. But as we rode down the secluded highway, taking in the sights of this second stop on our tour, we saw Chuck ahead and to our left, waving us into the parking lot of an adobe-looking structure that was like an oasis in this arid part of California. At the end of the second of two tough days, we needed a shower, a clean room, a good meal, and a beer. The Jacumba Hot Springs Resort and Spa provided this and more. The last to arrive, we walked down an outdoor walkway to our room and talked briefly with several of the other riders, most of whom had found the bar and were lounging in this shaded area overlooking a large, spring-fed swimming pool. Covered with a combination of sweat, road grime, and sunscreen, we each needed a shower as we entered a surprisingly nice room, and as I took my turn the warm water had a restorative effect after a long day.

Clean and revitalized, Bev and I made our way to the bar for a couple of well-earned beers for me and a glass of wine for Bev. We would find as the tour continued that a cold beer put a nice cap on almost every day of riding. After a quick team meeting in the area overlooking the swimming pool, we had a memorable meal in the hotel restaurant, which like the inn itself was surprisingly good. Seeking unique fare when available, Bev had a dish called Hopi Lamb Stew and I had Pasta with Bison Meatballs. After this filling dinner, we excused ourselves to return to our room. In this isolated location on the Mexican border, we had no cell coverage and the Wi-Fi was spotty at best. But the satellite TV was excellent, and we were able to watch the second half of the Monday Night Football game as our hometown Kansas City Chiefs came back to defeat the Washington Redskins. Yes, it had been a good day.

• • •

As we left Jacumba Hot Springs early the next morning, we had no notion that this day would provide one of the most harrowing experiences of the tour, followed by a setting that brought forth a surreal sense of spirituality. We departed this sleepy little hamlet early in an attempt to miss some of the brutally hot temperatures that were anticipated at the end of this long seventy-mile day. As we climbed out of Jacumba Hot Springs, we encountered cool temperatures and some light rain. Once we had climbed out of the valley in which we had stayed, we would again merge onto Interstate 8 for a long descent into the desert that bordered the Imperial Valley, which would be our home for the next two days. At our team meeting the previous evening, Larry had stressed that on the long downhill on the interstate we might encounter winds. We certainly did.

As recreational cyclists, we had little experience on long downhills, particularly fairly steep, curving descents that continued for several miles. Like most activities, cycling downhill involves skill and confidence, both of which are gained from experience. As such, the discussion of a long downhill on an interstate highway had created in us some apprehension, but as we merged onto the shoulder of I-8 we were simply anxious to get to the bottom safely. After traveling a mile or so, we came to a sign informing us that there would be 6% downhills for the next seven miles. Already beginning to experience the effects of the increasingly strong crosswinds, that sign foretold the challenge that faced us. We have traveled yearly to Colorado, and these descents were comparable to the mountainous sections of I-70. And like on I-70, there were "runaway truck ramps." Freaking out a little, I hoped they wouldn't be needed as runaway "bike" ramps. Outweighing Bev by at least seventy pounds, I more quickly gained momentum on the downhill and soon got ahead of her, trying to keep an eye on her in the mirror on my sunglasses while watching the road ahead. Not wanting to put too much distance between us, I stopped with a great deal of effort on the descent. When she caught up with me, we tried to discuss the conditions, a nearly impossible conversation given the howling winds. This long descent on Interstate 8 wound its way down through a canyon, with cliffs rising on each side that concentrated the winds into stiffer and more unpredictable swirls. As we stood on the side of the road, two other riders stopped briefly before proceeding. We soon continued down the mountain with the wind increasing in intensity, at one point almost knocking me off my bike. We ultimately rounded a curve and came to some signs indicating "road construction ahead," and contemplated what else we could encounter on what for us was an increasingly terrifying ride. As I stopped and waited for Bev, I noticed that some of the road construction signs mounted on springs were bent backward by the strong winds. I was honestly concerned the wind would knock us off our bikes, rather frightening under any circumstances, but especially on an interstate highway with fast-moving traffic to our left and steep drop-offs to our right. As I stood with my bike on the side of the shoulder, it was at times challenging to stand up against the swirling winds. When Bev arrived, she asked me what I thought we should do and I quickly told her I didn't think we should go on, instead riding to the bottom of the mountain with one of the support guys who were still behind us. Bev concurred and quickly sent a text message to Larry. In the meantime, we saw Chuck approaching and waved for him to pull over. As he opened the door on the van, the strong wind caught it, wrenching the hinge and damaging the door to the extent that it would need to be repaired. After telling Chuck what we wanted to do, with great difficulty we loaded the bikes on the rack and rode in the van down the mountain, passing the other riders who were spread over several miles.

Everyone else made it down the mountain largely unscathed, though Danish Allan sustained some cuts and scrapes on his legs when he was hit by a wind-blown construction sign. The other seven riders would have some stories to tell about their ride through the canyon on Interstate 8, and I was proud of them for their fortitude. As for Bev and me, as we exited the van at the location of the first SAG stop, we had absolutely no regrets regarding our decision. At our orientation meeting three days earlier, Larry had told us there would be times when it was determined (either by us as riders or by the support guys) that conditions were unsafe for riding. In my mind, this had been one such time for Bev and me. We had tackled this tour for the challenge, not to put ourselves in danger, and our experience on that long, windy, winding downhill highway had done just that. We were relieved to be off the interstate and on level ground.

● ● ●

We knew that as we crossed the country, we would experience changing climates and terrain, but seldom would ten or fifteen miles result in such an abrupt transformation. As we had climbed out of Jacumba Hot Springs that morning the weather had been cool and cloudy, conditions that, with the harsh winds, continued on the long descent through the canyon. But when we exited the van at the site of the SAG stop, a gas station just outside of Ocotillo, California, we found sunny skies, little wind, and much warmer temperatures. We were just outside the Imperial Valley, and this section of Southern California was largely barren and desert-like. The contrast was amazing.

After eating some snacks and replenishing our water, as we prepared to leave the SAG stop I heard Bev say, "I've got a nail in my tire." There's a scene in the movie "Sixteen Candles" in which the characters Farmer Ted and Samantha are sharing deep thoughts while sitting in a junk car in the auto shop of their high school during a high school dance. (Bear with me here.) Risking his reputation "as a dude," the geeky Ted sheepishly shares, "I've never bagged a babe." In the world of recreational cyclists, a corresponding admission might be, "I've never fixed a flat." And with a nail in Bev's back tire, both of us could make that admission. We had taken bicycle maintenance classes and I had watched countless YouTube videos on how to change a tire tube, but neither of us had ever fixed a flat on our own because we had simply never had a flat tire out on the road. It's a little amazing that in all of our riding, collectively logging thousands of miles on roads and trails, we had never had to deal with this issue. We could probably attribute this to a combination of luck and the sealant we always placed in our tire tubes. Being the solid support guy that he was, Larry jumped in to guide and assist me through the process, and soon we were ready to continue on the route.

We had about thirty miles or so to the next SAG stop, and as we rode on a sparsely traveled highway we seemed to travel farther and farther away from civilization with virtually no traffic and seemingly no inhabitants. We were truly in desert conditions, with sand and scrub brush and little else. With the nearby mountains of northern Mexico on the horizon, this was some of the most memorable scenery through which we had ever ridden. It was a truly surreal and almost mystical setting, barren but incredibly beautiful, and when we stopped, with no traffic and no wildlife, the silence was amazing. This was the memorable kind of experience we were hoping for when we decided to tackle this tour. In time, we would find that the stunning vistas and sensations, even those that passed quickly, far outshone any challenges we encountered.

We eventually entered the Imperial Valley, and as we approached the city of Calexico we began to see more and more farms and other signs of civilization. As we entered this small city, we noticed a significant increase in traffic and a surprising police presence. Not having studied the map beyond the actual route, we didn't realize at the time that Calexico was the location of a major border crossing into Mexico, specifically into the city of Mexicali, which was just a few blocks away. Riding with two other riders, we struggled to follow the route, which had been altered due to road construction, and ended up asking one of the many police officers for directions. We eventually made our way to the second SAG stop, which was located just outside of a 7-Eleven in this hectic little city. After consuming a sandwich and sharing a large iced tea from the convenience store, we headed out for our destination for the evening, a Best Western hotel in Brawley, California.

Though the distance from the last SAG stop to the hotel was only around twenty-two miles, the combination of heavy traffic, sunny skies, and temperatures in the low nineties made for a challenging ride. There was a particularly tricky "diamond cloverleaf" intersection with Interstate 8 that we nervously navigated. We finally made our way to the hotel and we welcomed the air conditioning, shower, and clean bed in another surprisingly nice establishment. Once we had taken our bikes to our room, while Bev showered, I walked a couple of blocks to a convenience store and bought a six-pack of Blue Moon beers and a small bag of Cool Ranch Doritos. Beginning a routine we would follow with few exceptions all the way to the Atlantic, I brought the beer back to the room, placed it in the freezer section of the little in-room refrigerator, and then took a shower while Bev washed out our riding clothes. By the time we had both finished getting cleaned up, the beer was particularly cold, and at the end of this hot and challenging day those icy cold beers and salty snacks seemed to revitalize us. After the team meeting, we walked to a nearby Chinese restaurant where Bev and I both had huge portions of a salty dish with different kinds of seafood and vegetables.

It had been a day of shifting emotions, progressing from fear to amazement to simply persevering. But at the end of this seventy-mile day, we had made it safely and were in good spirits. The doubts we had experienced on the first day's climb were behind us, and after making a safety-first decision on today's ride, we had begun to feel ourselves getting into a routine. Perhaps for these inexperienced sixty-year-old riders, completing this cross-country trip might be feasible after all.

• • •

We left Brawley early that Tuesday morning, our last full day in California with a hilly ride of eighty-seven miles to Blythe. In arid temperatures into the nineties, this would also be the longest ride Bev and I had completed . . . at least thus far. The first part of the day, however, was pleasant, with flat roads, nice, wide shoulders, and relatively cool temperatures and light breezes. We rode through huge Imperial Valley farms, the ever-present irrigation sprinklers creating occasional rainbows as we rode by. It was a good start for what would be another tough day.

In time, we started to climb and eventually reached the first SAG stop on the edge of the Imperial Sand Dunes Recreation Area, a huge area of dunes maintained by the Bureau of Land Management. As we climbed a long hill leading to a pull-out area where Chuck and Larry had set up the support stop, we were fascinated by our surroundings, with sand dunes as far as we could see in any direction. As we had entered the area, signs warned about drifting . . . sand. In fact, as we sat at the SAG stop taking in the surreal images, a truck drove by plowing sand off the highway just as similar plows removed snow from roads back home in Missouri. On a trip in which we must have had over a hundred SAG stops, each one greatly appreciated, this was among the most unique and memorable.

We left the support stop and were soon out of the dunes, though the southeastern California terrain remained stark and barren. Then we turned a corner and, for the first time since leaving San Diego, encountered significant headwinds. The most popular direction for cyclists crossing the United States regardless of the route is from west to east, and a significant reason is the predominance of supportive westerly winds. In other words, typically a rider heading east would more often than not have the wind at his or her back. The effect of wind, positively or negatively, can be profound. As an example, on a flat road, a tailwind makes a ride feel downhill, while conversely, a headwind makes it feel like you're pedaling uphill. A headwind on an uphill section becomes doubly impactful. But contrary to the historical predominance of tailwinds behind riders moving in the same direction as we were headed, this would be the first of many days in which we would experience challenging winds in our faces.

We rode alongside the Chocolate Mountains, not really mountains but rather large hills with an interesting dark brown color. At the team meeting the previous evening we had been warned that we would encounter what the support guys called "bunny hop hills," fairly short ascents of a few hundred yards that would be followed by a corresponding descent. Larry had suggested that this stretch of road would "drive us nuts," and he was so correct. We would climb a short hill, long enough to be challenging, and once over the top head downward and then repeat the process over and over for the next thirty miles. This would be challenging and frustrating under any circumstances, but this was a fairly heavily traveled two-lane highway with a constant stream of tractor-trailer rigs, a 65-mph speed limit, and a very narrow shoulder. On the steepest downhills we were going maybe 25 mph, and less than half that on the inclines, so typically trucks and other vehicles had to either pull over into the left lane or wait to pass us if there was oncoming traffic. For the first few miles, it was a bit harrowing to be out in the middle of nowhere with vehicles of all sorts approaching us from behind. But we had to get to our hotel in Blythe, and as a result, we had no choice but to trudge on and trust that the drivers of those vehicles would take care not to hit us or force us off the road. We came to a road sign that said, "Dips Next 7 Miles" and later another that said, "Dips Next 5 Miles." We came to realize that "Dips" was in California the official name for "bunny hop hills." So, for thirty miles, and with the wind largely in our faces, we went up and then down, up and then down, a ride that certainly took us out of our comfort zone, but which in time we simply got used to. Bev would share afterward that it was this stretch of road, challenging as it was, where she felt she had "found her legs," as she put it. By the time we were riding on flat roads that day, she had come to realize that physically, she could handle pretty much whatever we would face as we progressed across the country.

Shortly after noon, we passed through a Border Patrol checkpoint where every vehicle traveling in the same direction we were headed (NW) had to stop and be subject to inspection. The support guys had informed the agents that several bike riders would be passing through. As a result, the two agents waved us through (evidently middle-aged cyclists in form-fitting gear on relatively expensive bicycles didn't fit into their targeted demographic), but we got a good look at the setup and at the dog that was employed to check each vehicle that passed through. The support crew had set up the second SAG stop just past the checkpoint, available should any rider have any difficulty as they passed through (none did). As we lounged in the limited shade provided by Chuck's van with the shed-like pass-through structure of the checkpoint in the foreground, we ate peanut butter sandwiches and other snacks at the second very unique and memorable SAG stop of the day.

We experienced more "dips" for another twenty miles or so until the terrain leveled off as we headed into Palo Verde, the location of the last SAG stop of the day at a roadside convenience store. It was getting past mid-afternoon, and in this arid environment with temperatures rising well into the nineties, it was extremely hot. Chuck had discreetly set up the support stop around a picnic table in the shade of the store, and it felt good to get out of the baking sun. Bev got the bold idea of getting a "Slushee" in the convenience store, so I got one too, mango-flavored. On that terribly hot day, the sensation that came from the first sips of that icy drink would be difficult to describe, the incredibly cold liquid cooling our bodies just a bit. Then the brain freeze hit, and after the brief headache subsided, we enjoyed one of the more memorable drinks of the entire trip.

We were a flat twenty miles from our hotel, a Super 8 Inn in Blythe, California ("First Sunrise in California"). Though it was incredibly hot, after the bunny hop hills, hectic traffic, and headwinds we had experienced, the ride from Palo Verde to Blythe was rather pleasant. We caught up with Ted a few miles out and together arrived at the hotel at around 4:15 p.m. It made for a long, hot nine hours on the bike, but we were eighty-seven miles closer to our ultimate destination. And Bev and I had completed our longest single-day ride.

After a quick team meeting, Larry and Chuck drove us to a Sizzler Steakhouse, a restaurant chain that hadn't been available near our hometown for many years. We had ridden more than nine hours, battling headwinds, high temperatures, and frustrating hills, and since breakfast at the hotel had subsisted on peanut butter sandwiches, granola bars, bananas, and other snacks. My smartwatch indicated that I had burned over 4,500 "active calories," and though the accuracy of those measurements can be suspect, I knew we had worked hard all day. In other words, the entire group was hungry.

For me, a member of the middle class living in middle America, it had been a long time since I had been really, truly hungry—not simply desiring food because the clock suggested it was time to eat, or because some food item sounded tasty, but genuinely needing nourishment. On this night I was absolutely famished. As we lined up to place our orders, Bev and I were at the front of the line (perhaps not coincidentally), and after finding our large table we quickly made our way to the extensive salad bar, where I piled my plate so high I left a trail of lettuce and vegetables as I made my way back to our table. I pride myself on exhibiting good manners, and I would typically never begin a meal until everyone around us had been served. But at the Sizzler in Blythe, California, all of that went by the wayside as I began inhaling my salad while some of the other riders were still in line to place their orders. Bev and I each ordered a large steak and a baked potato, which we also consumed without waiting. After most had finished their meals, one of the other riders mentioned that he had noticed an ice cream machine on the other side of the salad bar, so of course we had to have ice cream sundaes. For those with a refined palate, a steak, potato, and salad at the local Sizzler Steakhouse doesn't qualify as gourmet cuisine, but on this occasion, no five-star meal would have been more appreciated.

Bellies full, we returned to the hotel to get situated for the next day's ride. Afterward, we tried to watch a TV show but could barely stay awake until it ended at 9:00 p.m. This cross-country cycling, we were learning, was tiring work.

•   •   •

In four days we had crossed California, the first of the eight states on our cross-country route. After experiencing such doubt and apprehension on the first day, we had relaxed and settled into an increasingly comfortable routine. That routine was basically: rise, eat breakfast, pack, check bikes, ride, get settled into the hotel, find a nearby convenience store for beer, shower, wash out cycling clothes, attend the team meeting, eat dinner, prepare for the next day, sleep . . . and then do it all over again. Though we were on the most amazing journey, we were living a rather spartan existence, and we were feeling surprisingly good about it. Just four days in, though there were thirty-eight more rides in the next forty-two days, we were coming to believe that completing this tour was increasingly possible . . . and might be even more satisfying and enjoyable than we had anticipated.

LIFE LESSON #1
Listening to your ego instead of following your instincts and intuition can get you into a lot of trouble.

"Rule your mind, or it will rule you."

—Horace

When Bev and I hurtled down the mountainside interstate highway in California, our speed and momentum building as we continued, we felt the swirling and gusting winds blow us all over the shoulder of the highway. On only the third day of our cross-country bike trip, we had already found ourselves in a precarious situation, justifiably fearful for our safety. As we approached a stretch of road construction the extent of which we didn't yet know, we stopped for the last time and had difficulty standing upright with our bicycles. It was eerily reminiscent of the footage you might see of wind-blown CNN correspondents reporting on an approaching hurricane.

As Bev and I stood there pondering our options, my instincts told me we shouldn't continue our ride down the mountain and any logical person with our experience and skill level would have likely reached the same conclusion. But as we were being blown around on the shoulder of Interstate 8, logically knowing we should stop, divergent questions continued to work their way into my thought process. What would the other riders or the support guys think about us (i.e., me) if we skipped this part of the route? If we called for assistance and rode in a vehicle down the remainder of the mountain, wouldn't that mean we had failed? Could we then honestly say we had ridden our bikes across the country? Was this a moment of truth that would end up defining our entire cross-country tour?

In this potentially dangerous and incredibly stressful situation, knowing full well we needed to stop, I still doubted myself based on how this might look to other people, subconsciously considering putting ourselves in danger simply for the sake of appearance. Though with Bev's agreement my instincts and conscious intellect eventually prevailed, on that wind-swept interstate highway my ego was clearly exerting itself.

There are countless definitions of the term "ego," some from the Freudian psychoanalytical world and largely beyond my level of understanding. The *Merriam-Webster Dictionary* lists as synonyms of "ego" such words as conceitedness, pompousness, pridefulness, vainglory, and swelled head. At a deeper level, Deepak Chopra suggests, "The ego is our self-image, not our true self. It is characterized by labels, masks, images, and judgments." It's like a force in our heads that wants to control us, but which will ultimately never allow us to be happy or satisfied.

I similarly prefer to view the impact of the ego from a more metaphysical perspective, and I see that playing out the strongest in matters of life happiness. When the ego is in charge, life can never provide enough for us to be happy; we're never good enough to meet whatever nebulous standards we're shooting for, we can't allow ourselves to be shown in a negative light, and if something goes wrong (and it always will), it's the fault of somebody or something else. All too often, the ego can be a powerful and even overpowering force. I believe that in each of us, there is a still, small voice providing infinite guidance if we are willing and wise enough to listen. The ego as I'm describing it is virtually the opposite, a loud and obnoxious voice in our subconscious mind demanding to be heard and seldom if ever having our best interests in mind. I am by most measures a rational and fairly intelligent person, but on this cross-country trip there were numerous instances when my conscious intellect struggled to keep that ego voice in check.

In the days following this truly frightening episode on the wind-swept California interstate, I thought a lot about my barely-subconscious reluctance to call for assistance and interrupt our ride, all despite the preponderance of evidence suggesting that on that day, riders of our ability and confidence level had no business continuing. There are undoubtedly countless ways an out-of-control ego can impact lives, causing individuals to take actions they consciously know are not in their best long-term interest. Such as the many instances in which people purchase houses (or cars, or clothes, or whatever) they know they can't afford simply because of the appearance that owning such material items might provide them. Or individuals who remain in esteemed jobs, doing work they loathe simply because of the prestige such positions provide. But then when those same folks work up the courage to pursue an occupational change to something more in line with their true calling, that same voice in their heads tells them they'll never succeed in their new endeavor, or they won't make enough money, or their family and friends will no longer like or respect them.

Viewed by the rational mind, these ego-driven thoughts make little sense, though when the ego is in charge the rational mind takes a back seat. But as Eckhart Tolle suggests, "The . . . ego is actually afraid of your consciousness." In other words, to regain control, the rational, conscious mind must take charge, and to accomplish that it simply must be active. Though like most people I have struggled with this form of ego, I have found that by simply pausing and thinking logically and rationally, more often than not I can reach the conclusion that is truly in my best interest and not what feeds the ego lurking in the recesses of my mind. This isn't rocket science (or brain surgery, for that matter), but simple awareness of one's thought processes can be immensely powerful.

That day when I stood with my bike along a mountainside interstate highway, struggling to remain upright while consulting with Bev regarding our options, although my ego flooded my mind with bizarre thoughts and questions, my rational mind was able to prevail, logically realizing that, for the two of us, continuing would make no sense. We lived to ride again, and the value of our tour was, in our minds, not diminished in the least.

CHAPTER 2
BUT IT'S A DRY HEAT . . .

How many people can say they have ridden a bicycle across an entire state, any state? As we woke up in Blythe, California, ready to enter Arizona, we realized what we had accomplished. The challenge, though, was that we still had seven more states ahead of us, most of which would take us more time to cross, and some that would be even more challenging. California had been a mixture of terrains and emotions, and we were ready to cross the Colorado River that served as the border with Arizona.

On this fifth day of the tour, we had completed four rides, each difficult in its own way and more challenging than the one that had preceded it. We were adapting well to the rigors of these tough, hot daily rides, but we probably needed a bit of a respite. In planning the route, the support guys had realized this need would likely exist. Of the forty-six days of this cross-country trip, four were designated as "rest days," and it was too soon to schedule a day of no riding. So they did the next best thing, scheduling what they called a "partial day," what would end up being the shortest day of the tour: a quick 22-mile jaunt from Blythe, California to Quartzite, Arizona. And though we experienced some unanticipated detours, it was a really good day.

Given the short route, we left the hotel later than usual on what would be a beautiful California then Arizona autumn day. Though particularly short, the route into Arizona had some slightly complicated turns, so the plan was for Chuck to lead us from the hotel to the only SAG stop of the day. We departed as a group and made our way to a pedestrian bridge across the Colorado River. Many years ago, Bev and I with our children had rafted the upper portion of this commanding river and then saw its awesome power up close during our Grand Canyon hike. As we walked our bikes across this narrow walkway, we hardly recognized this waterway, its width and flow at this point on its descent into Mexico doing little to distinguish it from many other rivers. But it did represent our exit from one state and our entrance into the next, so we stopped for numerous photos and then proceeded on our way.

About half the route on this short day was scheduled to take place on a section of Interstate 10. But as we approached the merger point onto the interstate, Chuck received a phone call from Larry, who had driven ahead to set up the SAG stop in a rest area off the interstate. Larry indicated that on the way to the rest area he had encountered a short patch of road construction that eliminated the shoulder on which we would be riding. Even in a construction zone with reduced speed limits, the notion of riding a bicycle in the traffic lane of an interstate highway made virtually no sense. So, we backtracked a quarter-mile or so to a truck stop and waited while Larry made his way back, picked up Chuck, went back to the hotel to pick up the other vehicle, and then picked up the nine riders and their bikes and transported us to the rest area located beyond the construction zone. Trans-America Cycling's detailed planning generally made for a well-oiled machine, but critical issues such as a short amount of road construction couldn't be reasonably anticipated. Though our brief twenty-two-mile day had been further shortened by around five miles, the waiting actually made the ride take longer than originally planned. But as we lounged outside the truck stop, waiting to be shuttled around the road construction, I heard complaining from none of the riders; we knew these issues would inevitably arise.

Once riders and bicycles were loaded into the two vehicles, we quickly made our way to the rest area on I-10, where Chuck quickly set up an impromptu support stop. By this time it was still just late morning, and with only twelve miles or so to the next hotel, no one was particularly anxious to get moving. But we were soon on our way, riding on the shoulder of the interstate for several miles until we exited onto Dome Rock Road, an isolated two-lane road that would take us into Quartzite, our first Arizona destination. Despite the arid and at times desertlike terrain, the temperature wasn't oppressive and there was little traffic, making our shorter-than-expected ride rather pleasant. And with the namesake "Dome Rock" looming in the foreground, it was a scenic ride as well.

Our lodging that night was at another Super 8 Motel, not particularly large or luxurious accommodations, but with air-conditioned rooms, showers, clean beds, and of considerable importance on this day, a laundry room. Of particular excitement, when we arrived at 12:30 in the afternoon our rooms were already available. On longer days, such as the two that had preceded this one, getting to the hotel later in the afternoon made for some hectic times after a tough ride, trying to get settled and showered in time for the team meeting at 5:00 p.m. To be able to get into a hotel room early in the afternoon was an absolute treat. This short ride and extended hotel time would be beneficial to all of us in anticipation of the next two day's rides of ninety-six and ninety-four miles, the latter taking us through Phoenix.

This was our fifth day of riding and the seventh day since we had left home, and though Bev had done an admirable job of hand-washing our cycling clothes, she decided it was time to do some real laundry. With a laundry room available and more downtime than we'd had in a week, Bev set about doing a couple of quick loads. While she undertook that chore, I went looking for some sort of convenience store where I could find the crucial combination of beer and lunch.

According to Google Maps, the closest convenience store appeared to be in a truck stop located about a mile from the hotel. Despite the increasing, early afternoon Arizona desert heat, I set out on foot toward a large Love's Travel Stop at the bottom of a long downhill heading toward the downtown section of this small town. Hot, dry, and barren with minimal development, especially on the outskirts of town where our hotel was located, Quartzite reminded me of Radiator Springs, the fictional town in the Disney movie "Cars," with long stretches of rocky, barren land interspersed with an occasional business or museum or flea market. The small town was known as a retirement haven for RVers in the winter months and hosted large gem and mineral shows during those peak times (not surprising, given the name of the town). But on this hot afternoon in early October, not much seemed to be happening. The 24 oz. Corona "tall boys" and Subway sandwiches were a treat when I got back to the hotel.

Not even a week into the tour, routines were already being established, and with a little more time available on this shortened day we were able to reflect on how things were going. We were getting to know the other seven riders in the group and were increasingly enjoying their company. Groups and pairs had begun to form, and each day the same riders tended to ride together. There was some competitiveness, though nothing extreme, and some of the riders we might see at the first SAG stop of the day and then not see again until the team meeting later that evening.

Bev and I quickly fell into a rhythm and became like our own little group. As we had done on every long training ride leading up to the beginning of the tour, we rode every mile together and came to an unspoken agreement that if one of us wasn't able to ride for whatever reason, neither would ride. As we sensed we would require more time on the road than any of the other riders, we tried to leave as quickly as possible in the morning. We established a steady but sustainable (for us) pace as we began each ride, and within the first several miles each rider would pass us, exchanging brief pleasantries before continuing toward our next destination. We would typically see at least some of them at SAG stops, but otherwise, we were more often than not the last two riders on the route, as well as the last to arrive at the hotel at the end of the ride. We didn't want to waste time and wanted to get to the next hotel as quickly as possible, but we really weren't in any hurry. As we had learned in a tough lesson from the first day, we needed to relax and take as much time as was necessary, and the pace of the other riders was of little influence on the two of us as we proceeded across the country. In the process, we did our best to fully grasp and enjoy the experience.

A major part of that experience was the countless number of locals with whom we came into contact. And there were some memorable ones, almost all of them kind and welcoming people. Sure, there were some instances to the contrary, such as the young man in an old pickup who angrily flipped us off, evidently incensed at having had to wait behind a large truck as we climbed a long hill on a shoulderless highway, causing him to be fifteen seconds or so later in ultimately getting to his destination. Most likely, deep down we were just the recipient rather than the cause of his anger. And then there was the business in Calexico which had plastered on an entire wall wording that included "Hitlery Clinton." I couldn't read the rest of the writing, but I suspect it was less than flattering.

But for every less-pleasant experience, there had been multiple positive ones, such as the older Latino highway worker whose stop sign had delayed us before we reached a stretch of road construction outside of Brawley, California. He asked me with a stern face whether we had a "pass," intimating that we wouldn't be allowed to proceed without this required permit. This instantly befuddled me until this highway worker broke into a wide, toothy grin. That smile sustained me for the next several miles. Then there was the Native American father we met in Manzanitas, California, a hamlet barely large enough to be called a town. We had stopped to regroup on the long descent into Jacumba Hot Springs and soon noticed this distinguished gentleman walking out of a small candy store. As he walked toward us and his car, we struck up a brief conversation. He asked us where we were headed and seemed genuinely interested in our cross-country tour. He told us he was traveling back to his home in Arizona and that he always stopped at this little shop to get a box of chocolates that his daughter particularly liked. He spoke with unabashed pride about his daughter, a straight-A student and an accomplished musician in the school band. We said it sounded like his daughter deserved a box of special chocolates and he wished us luck on our journey. As evidenced on our trip across the country, it seems the positive people in this world aren't outnumbered by the negative ones, just outshouted.

After an early team meeting, the support guys drove us to a nondescript restaurant called Taco Mio for an excellent platter of Mexican food, tacos, enchiladas, and a large burrito, all smothered in a rich red sauce. As we would find in the coming weeks as we made our way across Arizona, New Mexico, and Texas, there were a lot of similar meals in our future, in part because they were authentic and good but also because, in some of the remote outposts in which we would stay, such fare was all that was available.

•   •   •

With a long, hot day ahead of us, we left Quartzite at an early 7:00 a.m., riding through the still-slumbering town in surprisingly cool temperatures. The route took us around twenty miles on Interstate 10 and then the remaining seventy-six or so miles on U.S. 60, a usually lightly traveled highway that would take us to Wickenburg, Arizona, our destination for the evening. The rolling hills of the interstate passed fairly quickly before we exited onto the highway that, over the next two days, would take us into Phoenix. On this still-cool morning, and with minimal shoulder but even less traffic, it was a scenic ride to the first SAG stop located in the tiny town of Brenda. Chuck and Larry had set up the stop in a little pull-out area, over which loomed a huge saguaro cactus (which quickly gained the moniker of the "big-ass cactus"). A photo opportunity ensued, and we spent more time posing in front of this towering succulent than we did consuming water and nourishment. A long day still ahead of us, we soon left the big-ass cactus behind and proceeded down the highway.

The "Big-Ass Cactus"

It was a rather monotonous ride, with pretty but consistent scenery and relatively little traffic. Then, in the late morning, we began to notice a huge uptake in the number of vehicles on this two-lane highway. There was a narrow and inconsistent shoulder, and an inordinate number of the added vehicles were tractor-trailer rigs. At times traffic moved slowly, occasionally stopping and starting, and our proximity to this string of huge trucks was at times unnerving. Such heavy traffic on a late Friday morning made little sense, as the highway we were on took a more circuitous route to Phoenix while the nearby Interstate 10 provided a virtually straight shot into the city. At the next SAG stop, we learned that tragically a bad accident had closed all eastbound lanes of the interstate while several who had been severely injured in the crash were airlifted to nearby hospitals. In time, the interstate reopened and traffic on U.S. 60 was soon back to normal. With some climbing but little changing scenery, the remainder of the ride into Wickenburg was hot and a little boring. A break in the monotony occurred about twenty miles from the hotel when Bev got her second flat tire. It was hot and terribly dry, and a flat was not the kind of excitement we were looking for. But no longer a flat tire virgin, with Bev's help I was able to get the tube changed and was pumping it back up when Chuck pulled up to provide some final assistance and get us on our way. Hot and a little frustrated, we relished the last ten miles of downhill riding into Wickenburg and then the ride to our hotel, located on the far outskirts of town. With ninety-six more miles behind us, Bev and I had completed yet another longest ride of our lives.

We stayed that night at a Quality Inn, which although not luxurious was nice and roomy. Bev and I had four bags and two bikes, which always took up quite a bit of space. The last two nights we had stayed in Super 8 Inns, which provided clean and appreciated lodging but with smaller rooms. With our bikes and bags, it was at times challenging to navigate the rooms which, like all the rooms reserved by TAC, had two beds. We were always able to make things work, but it was nice this evening to have extra room to spread out.

The support guys drove us to an Italian restaurant called Quory's, where Bev and I each had a huge portion of Chicken Parmesan and a couple of glasses of wine. After a long, hot day, we were ready for a good, large meal, and this didn't disappoint. As we were leaving, Larry announced that it was Chuck's birthday and to celebrate he was taking everybody to Tastee Freeze for ice cream. It was a nice ending to an oddly satisfying day, and my milkshake tasted particularly good. Before beginning the tour, I hadn't had a milkshake in years, my aging metabolism unable to keep pace with such high caloric treats. But over the next few weeks as we traversed the country, for both Bev and me there would be many, many milkshakes. In the meantime, we returned to the hotel to nervously prepare for the next day's ride, a long, hot, and hectic route to and through Phoenix.

• • •

The routine each morning was for the trailer to be opened by the support guys at the time they had announced at the team meeting the previous evening. This trailer, which was pulled behind the pick-up driven by Larry, fulfilled a critical role as we progressed from one location to the next because in it was transported everybody's luggage. The predetermined trailer opening time was based on the length of the day's route, the forecast for the day (especially if it would be cold in the morning or hot in the afternoon), and the anticipated time for the sun to rise, as the support guys wouldn't allow anyone to leave in the dark. In many respects, the trailer opening time was the mechanism Larry and Chuck utilized to regulate when everyone departed in the morning. I always suspected that if they didn't follow such a routine and procedure, some of the riders on our tour might have slapped a headlight on their handlebars and departed the hotel at 5:00 in the morning. Our route that Saturday would approach our longest thus far, and given the traffic and congestion we might encounter, it would likely be the longest day of riding. Luckily, breakfast at the hotel started at 5:30 a.m. that day, so the trailer was opened at 6:30 a.m., right as the sun was rising. The route was complicated, a combination of rural and suburban highways, urban trails, and commercial and residential streets. The plan was for groups to form at the first SAG stop and then stay together for the remainder of the ride. As Bev and I anticipated we might be the slowest to the first stop, we were concerned about being left behind when the groups departed.

As a result, we left the hotel just after 6:30, right during the transition from darkness to light. As we departed Wickenburg it was unseasonably chilly, probably in the low fifties, an odd juxtaposition from the hot temperatures and arid conditions we would encounter later in the day. As a result, starting that day we were cold, and our initial discomfort was heightened by the route taking us downhill for the first few miles. It quickly warmed up, and in time the rural terrain transitioned into the seemingly continuous retirement communities of suburban Phoenix. The first SAG stop was in the parking lot of a Walmart in Surprise (the spring training home of our hometown Kansas City Royals), and in time we departed as a group to cross the geographically huge city. The route included multiple turns and some heavily traveled thoroughfares, so after six days of largely riding on our own, we welcomed the opportunity to ride as a team.

Two of the other riders had navigational devices onto which they had downloaded the day's route. (We had a paper map that depicted this complicated and nearly 100-mile route in a section the size of a postcard.) As the devices provided turn-by-turn directions, we were more than happy to let either of these two riders lead. From the Walmart we passed through commercial areas, already hectic on this warm Saturday morning. We then turned into a residential area, and almost miraculously the traffic and noise suddenly disappeared. Other than the desert-friendly landscaping around the attractive homes we passed, we could have been in virtually any city in the country.

In time, we turned onto the first of a series of trails we would follow for around fifteen miles, taking us to the other side of the city. The trails followed irrigation canals and drainage ditches through parks and between different neighborhoods. These very well-maintained trails allowed us to bypass some of the most heavily traveled streets, but also caused us to miss much of the scenery of Phoenix. I for one welcomed the trade-off. The second SAG stop was at a prominent Greek Orthodox Church. It was terribly hot, and as the afternoon seemed to drag on we began to wonder if this church actually existed (not really) when in the distance we saw the dome of a huge building. Sure enough, we exited the trail and there were Larry and Chuck with food and much-needed water.

Appropriately, given the setting alongside a Greek Orthodox Church, the support guys had set up the tables and folding chairs along the sidewalk in the only shade available, under a grove of olive trees. Though minimal, the shade those olive trees provided was much appreciated. For the fifteen miles or so as we rode along the urban trails, we had traversed areas almost totally devoid of trees, the sun in the cloudless sky bearing down on us through the late morning and early afternoon. And it was hot, with temperatures in the mid-nineties. As we rode in these hot and dry conditions, I had experienced an odd phenomenon I had never before noticed to this degree, even when we hiked along the floor of the Grand Canyon. The temperature was high, the sun was intense, and I knew we were working hard as we rode as a group on the urban trails, and I was no doubt sweating profusely. But as I got off my bike at the SAG stop, I noticed that my jersey was completely dry. At the end of the day, as I ended the tracking of the ride on my Apple Watch, the readout indicated the relative humidity had been 8%, which was incredibly dry—especially to someone who had spent sixty summers in the hot and humid Midwest. As they say, it's a dry heat, but if you're not careful conditions like that can dangerously trick you into not drinking enough liquids. So, drinking some cold water in the shade of an olive tree made for a memorable setting.

We still had around forty miles to our destination for the evening, and the heat was continuing to build. The prescribed route called for us to leave the trails and follow commercial and then residential streets as we made our way to Apache Junction, the location of our hotel for the evening. Still riding as a group, as we started to prepare to leave the SAG stop I noticed two of the riders having a focused conversation as they studied Google Maps on their phones. They suggested that if we continued following the trail, we could cut off several miles to the next SAG stop and avoid traffic in the process. Though there were some examples in which the TAC guys had altered the route for purposes of safety and the availability of lodging, we were following a route that had been identified and refined over time by the Adventure Cycling Association, the organization that had developed and printed the maps we were following. In other words, the route hadn't been established by some guy at home on his computer, but rather by a large network of individuals who had traveled and studied available routes and identified those that were safest and most efficient. As a result, some healthy skepticism was likely in order when someone indicated he had identified on the fly a better and quicker route. There was some disagreement among some of the riders; not arguments, but rather a frustrated desire to end this long, hot day a little quicker. The support guys reiterated what they had told us at the initial orientation meeting, that each day they would recommend a route but that it was ultimately up to each rider to determine how to get to the hotel at the end of the day. In other words, they seemed to be suggesting that it was up to us if we wanted to try to find a quicker route. As the discussion continued, and as the afternoon continued to get hotter, I offered that whatever the group decided to do, we needed to get going.

In time, the group tacitly decided to take a chance that the trail would continue and would reduce the length of the route. All went well for a mile or so until the trail suddenly turned from asphalt to gravel—not a good sign—and eventually, the trail came to an end behind the Wrigley Mansion, a Phoenix landmark. It wasn't surprising and was mildly disheartening, but with nowhere to go we sheepishly turned around and rode back to the location of the SAG stop to resume riding on the original route. We were lucky in many ways because this detour had only added two or three miles to our route. Though we were beaten down a bit by the heat and long day, no one really complained.

Riding along congested city streets as a group, we eventually made it to the final SAG stop of the day, located in the shade of a large tree in beautiful Papago Park in Tempe, near the campus of Arizona State University. As we sat eating snacks and replenishing fluids, groups of college kids cavorted around us, playing softball or listening to music or having a picnic. It was an almost serendipitous setting, realizing we still had around twenty-five miles of riding ahead of us. But it was a beautiful location nonetheless, with all the necessary amenities (i.e., shade and a bathroom).

We soon regretfully left this idyllic setting, the group breaking into multiple groups for the final push to the hotel. Bev and I rode with a trio of other riders led by Ross, who naturally led the group given his cycling experience and Garmin navigational device. From the park, we crossed beautiful Town Lake and rode onto the Arizona State campus with Sun Devil Stadium looming to our right. We soon left Tempe, and on a very hectic road we entered Mesa, a suburb that seemed almost endless. Riding in heavy traffic on this four-lane parkway, we passed retail areas, industrial parks, and the Chicago Cubs spring training complex and stadium. We eventually made our way back into residential neighborhoods as we approached Apache Junction, and it felt like we were on a ride that would not end. But with Ross leading the way, we made one last turn, and to our delight at almost 5:30 p.m. we rolled into the parking lot of the Best Western Apache Junction Inn. Relatively speaking it was a nice hotel, but after eleven hours of riding, any room with air conditioning, a shower, and a bed would have been appreciated. It had been another tough but ultimately satisfying day.

After a delayed team meeting, we walked a short distance to a nearby Village Inn restaurant where we had a nourishing and filling if nondescript meal. As the restaurant was known for its pies, the support guys sprang for dessert for everyone. (I had French Silk pie . . . exceptionally good.) After dinner, we walked back to the hotel while talking with Ross, who we hadn't previously had the opportunity to get to know. We told him we were from the Kansas City area and he responded that he had grown up in western Kentucky. Bev suggested that she was familiar with the area because she had done her undergraduate work at Murray State University in Murray, Kentucky. Even in the darkness as we continued to walk, we could sense Ross brighten up, and he asked Bev when she had graduated. When she responded that she had finished her degree in 1979, Ross shared that he had also graduated from Murray State that year and had attended from 1975 to 1979, the same years Bev had attended. In 1975, Murray State had perhaps 1,200 freshmen enrolled, and the notion that some forty-two years later two of those "Racers" would find themselves among the nine cyclists riding together across the country was astounding to all three of us. As we continued walking to the hotel, I happily took a back seat as this computer major and speech pathology major reminisced about the good old days in Murray, Kentucky. Over the coming weeks, there would be many stories shared between these two Murray State alumni.

• • •

To enjoy the experience more fully, Bev and I were making a concerted effort to focus on each day's ride, striving to avoid worrying about the next day's route until the current ride was completed. Sure, we knew when the rest days were on the calendar, and by listening to the other riders we knew when particularly long days were coming up. But otherwise, we tried as best we could to experience the tour as it came, to live in the moment as much as possible.

Due to the length of the ride, that Saturday evening's team meeting was held at 6:00 p.m. These gatherings to discuss the next day's route and logistical issues were usually led by Larry, and perhaps tapping into his middle school teacher persona, he typically approached these meetings with a blend of humor and attention to detail. As he discussed the next day's route to Globe, Arizona, it was clear that he had dropped the "happy-go-lucky" demeanor he often exhibited. As he described the route for the next day, a relatively short ride at fifty-seven miles, he stressed that the ride would be particularly challenging in the fifteen miles between the first and second SAG stops. He talked about steep inclines and downhills with little or no shoulder on two-lane sections of the highway, blind corners with no shoulder, a tunnel with no shoulder. This section was still on U.S. 60, a heavily traveled scenic thoroughfare that would likely be hectic even on a mid-October Sunday. He shared that on a previous tour, a rider had traffic so backed up that the Arizona Highway Patrol asked them to get him off the road. While I can't speak for the other riders, Larry had my attention.

Bev asked if we had the option of starting that section of the route and then, if we weren't comfortable or felt unsafe, be picked up by one of the support vehicles. Larry responded that if someone was truly in trouble, he and Chuck would find a way to get to them, but that there were sections of the route where this would be very difficult, with no shoulders and very few pull-out areas. He also told us much of this section was isolated with no cell coverage, so there might be no way to get in touch with the support crew. As a result, he stressed that he and Chuck might not realize that someone had had difficulty until they were particularly late getting to the second SAG stop. In other words, a rider who started the route would most likely have to ride to the next SAG stop. Unspoken but understood, at least by Bev and me, was the notion that those unsure if they were ready and capable probably should skip that section of the route.

While we didn't decide to complete this bike tour so we could ride in a pickup truck, we also knew our limits given our cycling experience, skill level, and confidence. As we listened to Larry discuss the challenges presented by this section of the route, it became clear to both Bev and me that while we might have liked to test ourselves on this section, there was a huge risk that we would soon find ourselves in peril, creating challenges not only for the two of us but also for the support guys and potentially even the motorists passing us. We talked it over after the meeting and quickly came to the same conclusion. The next morning, we told the support guys that we had decided we would bike from the hotel to the first SAG stop, bypass the middle and most treacherous section, and then ride again from the second SAG stop to the hotel in Globe. They didn't disagree with our decision and told us there had been riders on each of their tours who had reached the same conclusion. We appreciated their attitude, and deep down I hoped we had made the right decision.

We left the hotel in Apache Junction on a surprisingly cool fall morning, riding on the Old West Highway until we merged onto U.S. 60, the same highway we had followed the entire distance from Quartzite to Phoenix. In this part of Arizona, the highway was called the "Superstition Freeway," a moniker we hoped had no hidden meaning. In time, the largely flat road began to turn upward and we were soon climbing into the little town of Superior, the location of the first

SAG stop in the parking lot of a large convenience store. After the other riders had left and headed up the mountain, we loaded our bikes onto the rack on Larry's truck and started driving to the next SAG stop.

If anything, when Larry had described the potential challenges of this section of the route he had perhaps undersold how challenging and treacherous it would be. Shortly after the SAG stop the highway took a distinctly upward turn, the pitch steep and continual. After reaching the outskirts of town the road started to narrow, presenting the tight turns we had anticipated. We came to the shoulderless tunnel Larry had described and noticed one of our riders walking his bike as close to the side of the tunnel as possible while cars and trucks passed through at a surprisingly high speed. Luckily just past the tunnel was a small parking area, allowing Larry to pull his pickup and trailer off the highway. When the rider walked up with his bike, he indicated that he had been brushed by a passing vehicle as he rode through the tunnel. Visibly shaken, he told Larry he wanted to ride with us to the next SAG stop.

We continued up this long, steep incline, not as curvy as we expected but an unrelenting uphill with virtually no shoulder in most places and with traffic moving faster than we might have anticipated, given the terrain. Within a couple of miles, Bev and I looked at each other in agreement that we had clearly made the correct decision to bypass this section of the route. The downhills were as steep as the inclines, with similar shoulders, steep drops, fast vehicles, and little room to ride.

I had personally been a bit reticent about our decision to not ride this section, feeling a mixture of guilt and a bit of disappointment that we wouldn't experience this challenge like the rest of the team. But by the time we made it to the little village of Claypool and unloaded our bikes at the second SAG stop, those feelings had been fully replaced by relief that we had been wise enough to make the right decision for the two of us. All six of the other riders made it over the mountain safely, though later that evening one pulled me aside and told me, "You guys made the right decision," suggesting that at one point his riding partner had nearly fallen off his bike into the lane of traffic. On subsequent offerings of this tour, Trans-America Cycling revamped the route to avoid this section.

After a quick sandwich in Claypool, we rode the ten miles to the Day's Inn on the outskirts of Globe, Arizona. It had been a short day, made even shorter by our ride in a support vehicle through the middle section of the route, and we made it to the hotel before Larry, who generally drove ahead and checked into the rooms. Sitting in the air-conditioned comfort of the lobby as we waited, it was another opportunity for Bev and Ross to reminisce some more about life in the late 1970s in Murray, Kentucky.

That Sunday represented one of the "rider's choice" evenings, and there were multiple dining options within a short distance of the hotel. After the team meeting, Bev and I crossed the highway to a little Mexican restaurant called Irene's, where we each had a huge combination platter and a couple of bottles of Corona. Shortly after we sat down a couple of other riders came in, and then three more, and then the two support guys, and eventually all eleven of us were sitting around enjoying our food, and more importantly each other's company. We had only been on the road a week and we had already gelled into a pretty cohesive team.

• • •

As we prepared to leave Globe on the ninth day of the tour, there was a sense of excitement in the air. For starters, the forecast called for a westerly wind, the expected tailwind that had been virtually nonexistent since leaving San Diego. Of more importance, though, was that at the end of this hot, seventy-six-mile stretch into Safford, Arizona we were scheduled to have our first rest day. Each of the nine riders was tired, and many of us were dealing with various aches and pains, not the least of which were the saddle sores that resulted from six to ten hours of riding every day. I knew my behind needed a little recovery time. (We were using a product called "Chamois Butt'r"—a name I always found particularly clever—to keep our rear ends from being rubbed raw. Others used the same product, as evidenced by the rider who shared one evening, "Man, that stuff is saving my ass.")

With a light wind at our backs to begin the day, most of the route took us through the San Carlos Apache Reservation with some formidable uphill sections and some long downhill stretches, all with stunning rock formations providing majestic vistas on either side of the road. The first SAG stop was in the little town of Peridot, with the support guys set up in the parking lot of a grocery store. Bev and I had driven through different Native American reservations in the past, but this was the first time we experienced one in such an up-close-and-personal manner. On this Apache reservation, with its proud tribal heritage and traditions, there were some newer buildings like the grocery store and post office and the numerous health centers that we passed as we traversed the reservation. But as we rode through the heart of this Apache nation, we also saw ever-present poverty and squalor. And though everyone we encountered on the reservation was pleasant and friendly, an almost palpable sense of sadness seemed to permeate the region. Despite the intense sunshine we were experiencing, it felt as though a sad cloudiness had descended over this proud people.

The second SAG stop was at a neat little rest area in the town of Bylas, still within the reservation. It was a very hot and dry day, and the shade offered at this early afternoon stop was both needed and appreciated. Tribal police and a large number of cars were present as we rode into the parking lot of the rest area. We later learned that the funeral of a popular paramedic who had been a prominent member of the tribe was being held in a nearby community center. As we sat under the shade, getting ready to make the final push to the hotel on this sizzling Monday afternoon, an older woman with a cane walked up and sat down at a table nearby as she waited for a bus that would take her to her home. She was very friendly and open, talking about the young man who had tragically died and sharing information about her tribe and the reservation. She shared with Bev a story about how she had assisted a bicycle rider who was struggling as he passed by her place of residence, ultimately staying in touch with this individual after he returned to his home. Her pride and sense of tribal independence were evident as she informed us with no sense of arrogance, "We allow white people to ride through the reservation." In short order, her ride arrived, and as she began to make her way to the bus she very nonchalantly wished us well. We would have liked to have heard more of the countless stories from her decades on the Apache reservation.

As we left Bylas for the next twenty-five miles to our hotel, we noticed that the wind at our backs was beginning to kick up, a consistent tailwind that allowed Bev and me to maintain speeds that consistently exceeded 20 mph on this largely flat stretch of highway, a good speed for the two of us. We were riding through the Gila Valley, though we didn't realize until later that our route was adjacent to the Gila River. We noticed a different-looking cotton plant in huge fields along the highway and didn't grasp what we were seeing until we entered the little town of Pima. We learned that Pima cotton, one of the finer and rarer forms of the plant, was a staple of the area, though the town was named for the cotton rather than the other way around.

Knowing virtually nothing about cotton, I would never again look at Pima cotton bath towels or bed sheets in the same way.

Ten miles or so earlier, we had started to see small signs advertising "Taylor Freeze" (kind of like Tastee Freeze, only not). We began seeing these signs every mile or so, and then every half-mile, and the ad campaign was clearly working its charm on us. By the time we reached Pima, where this ice cream-focused fast-food joint was located, we needed a milkshake. Bev stayed outside with our bikes as I went in and ordered, and as I waited for our milkshakes, one of the workers asked, "Are you riding across the country?" I responded only half-jokingly, "I hope so." So she took my photo with a Polaroid camera and then placed it on a wall at the back of the dining room. Looking at the display, it was obvious that this restaurant had been a popular stopping point for cross-country cyclists. And based on the quality of the milkshakes, Taylor Freeze was a worthy stop. Riding the tailwind that would continue to be a rarity on this trip, and fortified by the energy boost from a couple of thick chocolate shakes, we quickly made our way to the Best Western Desert Inn in Safford, Arizona, which would blessedly be our home for the next two days.

• • •

As we pulled into the hotel parking lot we saw Larry, who was distributing room keys as each rider arrived. He told us he had something else for us and handed us what appeared to be a greeting card. Through the week and a half we had been on the road, I had provided members of our family with several email updates detailing our progress and experiences, and we had exchanged text messages and occasional phone calls. As a memorable example, during a long day in California (the "bunny hop hill" day) in the middle of nowhere, we had received a text message from our daughter-in-law Kassie with a video of our granddaughter Edie, in which she couldn't stop giggling.

It was another boost to get us through a tough ride. Getting mail in Safford, Arizona, however, was a surprise. After taking our bikes to our room, we opened the envelope to find a nice card of encouragement from our daughter Annie. Our appreciation for her thoughtfulness would be hard to overstate, a tangible link to our "regular life."

After completing long bike rides, every day for nine days, the notion of having a day of no riding was amazingly satisfying, though by the end of the rest day I was starting to feel a little antsy and oddly anxious to get moving again. But in the meantime, we enjoyed the notion that there was virtually nothing we had to do. After arriving at the hotel, I walked to a nearby convenience store for a couple of tallboy cans of beer (Dos Equis this time), and then, because we had no ride tomorrow, we had another beer with dinner. After dinner that first night in Safford, Bev and I walked the half-mile or so to Walmart and picked up various supplies we needed. We went to bed at our usual early hour (Bev rarely made it past 9:00 p.m., and I was almost always asleep by 10:00), but the realization that we could get up the next morning and just hang out was so enticing. Life was incredibly good.

At the team meeting the previous evening, Chuck had indicated that he would help anyone who showed up the next morning with cleaning and lubing their bike chains. We have already established that I am not a master bicycle mechanic (or any level of bike mechanic, for that matter), but I have certainly cleaned and lubed my share of bike chains. But with Chuck's expert guidance, we learned what a cleaned and well-lubed chain actually looked like. In the understated but fully informed manner that we were coming to appreciate, Chuck stressed that taking some time to keep your chain in really good condition could make the entire ride so much easier and more enjoyable. I had never really thought about issues related to dirty chains, but this idea resonated with me. (You know you're immersed in a bicycle tour when chain maintenance takes on an almost philosophical bent.) For the remaining five weeks of our trek across the United States, whenever I began to feel a little roughness or hear a little rattling coming from the chain or derailleur, at the end of the day I took some time and cleaned and lubed my chain, and when I worked on mine I cleaned and lubed Bev's chain as well. And with well over 2,000 miles remaining on our tour, that small investment of time yielded more dividends than we probably realized.

The remainder of the rest day involved laundry, a trip to the one bike shop in town (I bought two tubes and an extra tail light and got a little excited in the process), a leisurely lunch, and a matinee movie. In a dark little multiplex theater tucked in the back of a largely vacant strip mall, on a day the sunny temperature was back above ninety, Bev and I saw "The Mountain Between Us," a film set in the Rockies in which two survivors of a plane crash try to survive in an environment of snow and freezing temperatures. And likely coincidentally and not as a designed special effect, the theater was positively frigid.

As we were walking to the theater, Bev and I discussed our progress thus far and both agreed that we were a little surprised we didn't feel more physically "beat up." We both were experiencing some numbness in our hands that isn't uncommon, given the constant pressure that comes from leaning forward onto the handlebars. I was starting to have some soreness in both of my arms, minor pain that would soon subside. And I was starting to experience a little saddle soreness, but without going into unwanted detail (which would be any detail at all), antibiotic ointment and the aforementioned Chamois Butt'r were serving to keep that problem from getting out of hand. We could ride all day, rest and refuel, and be ready to begin the routine all over the next morning. We were finding that our sixty-year-old bodies were far more resilient than we could have imagined.

Safford is a town that we would drive through quickly under most circumstances, if at all. But for our first rest day and our last full day in Arizona, it fit our needs very well.

• • •

As we left Safford early the next morning, we quickly realized what a difference two days can make in terms of riding conditions. Whereas we had flown into Safford with a stiff wind at our backs, as we left town and prepared to begin climbing into New Mexico, we found the wind had shifted to almost directly in our faces. Though steady, the climbing we would encounter was seldom particularly steep, but the headwind made the seventy-eight-mile route even more challenging. It was a long, tough, and rather boring day, but not without its highlights. It would be our last day to be surrounded by mesas, buttes, and other formations on either side of the lightly-traveled highway, reminding us of the set from a 1950s Western movie.

The second SAG stop of the day was in the restored and historic village of Duncan, the only town of any sort we passed all day. It had a neat little downtown area with a butcher shop and little market that the proprietors were working hard to keep going. Bev and I had a grilled ham and cheese sandwich at Hilda's Restaurant and Market, a clean little business which, except for a couple of other riders who came in while we were there, was devoid of customers during what should have been the busiest time of the day. But the service was quick, the sandwiches were good, and the three ladies working there (including, we assumed, Hilda) were very nice.

We took our sandwiches to where the SAG stop had been set up in a little park area, enjoying what limited shade was available on this sunny east Arizona afternoon. As we ate our lunch, we looked over to see a disheveled, rather husky young man and his dog ambling toward us. With a dark navy blue t-shirt and a pair of jeans his belt was struggling to maintain at his waist, this friendly guy offered in a rather loud voice, "Anything you guys need?" Larry was still there, and as the leader of the group, he responded that we were all fine. "You need me to run a power cord back here?" the guy responded with a huge smile dominating his face. "No, we're good," Larry said respectfully, but while struggling to maintain a straight face. As the young man turned to head back in the direction from which he had come, he stressed that if we had any problems, he was the man to contact. As he strode off, we noticed that on the back of his t-shirt in large yellow letters was the word "Security." Duncan was a nice little town, and I think we were all comforted to know that its safety was in good hands.

It was a pleasant little break, but our day was only half over and the headwinds had already begun to take a toll. After leaving Duncan the highway began to flatten out, and a short time later we came to a large "Welcome to New Mexico" sign. After a week and a half of riding, we had crossed our second state. At that point, we also passed another milestone—crossing from the Pacific to the Mountain time zone, in the process "losing" an hour on what was becoming a longer and longer day.

We were riding on U.S. 70, a well-maintained, two-lane highway with good shoulders, and on this day there was very little traffic. We were able to focus on the scenery, at one point riding past a huge longhorn bull on our side of the fence who eyed us as we ambled by. He apparently didn't find us particularly enticing, but a couple of riders behind us said this huge bull started running alongside them before trying to jump the fence back into the field. This rather benign event was significant primarily because it was the most exciting, or perhaps the only exciting, occurrence on an incredibly long and monotonous stretch of highway.

For the last twenty-five miles or so the highway was incredibly flat and straight, and on a ride we were quite honestly wanting to end, that straight, flat road was beginning to mess with our minds a little. We would ride and ride, thinking that perhaps there would be a curve, or a hill, or anything just over the horizon, but there was only more straight and flat road. About ten miles from our destination, Bev spotted the buildings and houses of Lordsburg, New Mexico in the distance. But like in an old cartoon, we kept pedaling and pedaling, and the town seemed to get no closer. It was like an oasis in the middle of the desert (and it kind of was) that for a seemingly long time we just couldn't reach. But we did eventually, though we were exhausted by the long day and the incessant winds. Lordsburg isn't large, but working our way through town to our hotel just off of Interstate 10 was a bit challenging. When we got to the hotel, we had a message informing us that for unstated reasons there would not be a formal team meeting before dinner, but rather that we would walk to a nearby restaurant at 6:00 p.m. After quickly showering, we made it to the lobby of the hotel only to find that two riders were still out on the route. These unexplained late arrivals were rare, but for the support guys they were nerve-wracking, causing concern that there had been an accident or some other mishap involving the missing riders. The last seventy miles to Lordsburg had all been on the same highway, so it seemed unlikely these two guys had made a wrong turn. Then, as we were walking to the restaurant and one of the support guys was preparing to leave to search for the missing team members, the two riders turned the corner and rode into the hotel parking lot (to a standing ovation, no less), having gotten just a little lost as the route wound through Lordsburg. We joked a little, but everyone was relieved that all had finished the ride safe and sound.

We continued to the restaurant for the evening, a nice establishment called Kranberry's Chatterbox Café. It had been many miles and only a few snacks since our grilled ham and cheese sandwiches in Duncan, so Bev and I were famished. We had huge helpings from the salad bar, and then, because we had noticed that they had soup, we had a bowl of Green Chile Corn Chowder. For our main course, we each had a large chopped sirloin steak with mashed potatoes and gravy. Speaking for myself, it was a massive amount of food . . . and I quickly ate every bit of it.

It had been a tough day, one of the most difficult so far, and I was a bit down because I had gotten so tired fighting the headwind for virtually the entire ride. But as all nine riders discussed the day's ride over dinner, the consensus quickly developed among even the most seasoned riders that this was one of the toughest days in terms of wind that most had experienced. Knowing this didn't make us any less tired, but at least we weren't so tired alone.

• • •

To our relief, the next day's ride was a little shorter (sixty-two miles), the temperature was a little cooler, and the wind wasn't particularly strong and generally hit us from the side. From the hotel we merged onto I-10, which we followed for about forty miles. The interstate had a 75 mph speed limit and an endless stream of large trucks, but with a wide shoulder, we made good progress, though the scenery became rather boring. A few miles outside of Lordsburg we came across Ray, the recumbent bike rider, standing aside his bike on the side of the shoulder. He had touched the back wheel of the rider he had been following and had fallen, and in the process had cracked the stem that held his handlebars. Our destination for the evening was Deming, New Mexico, a small town with few if any cycling services, but the following day we would enter Las Cruces, a good-sized college town, and there were likely several reputable bike shops available. But recumbent bicycles are rare, and replacement parts are even rarer, so it was unclear when he would be able to get back on the road, at least with the bicycle he was used to riding.

Ray seemed unfazed, and told us he was okay and was waiting for the support guys to pick him up, which they did shortly thereafter. A short time later the support van passed us with Ray in the passenger seat and his broken cycle sadly strapped onto the bike rack. But by the time we got to the only SAG stop of the day in an interstate rest area, Ray had already ordered a replacement part that would be shipped overnight and arrive at our hotel in Las Cruces the next evening. He was being set up to ride a replacement bike, a regular non-recumbent version that, unlike the cycle he had been riding, put far more pressure and friction on his rear end. We were so impressed by the unflappable resilience Ray showed in dealing with what could have been a serious blow to his tour; we (and especially he) hoped his behind would show the same level of resilience.

Just before the SAG stop, we had passed a sign on the interstate indicating that we had crossed the continental divide, relatively low at 4,500 feet. From Lordsburg, we had been climbing at an almost imperceptible incline toward this high point, but at least in theory the rest of the ride should be downhill all the way to Florida. At least in theory. With unexciting scenery and most of the route on the interstate, this moment was the highlight of another rather monotonous day of riding. About ten miles beyond the rest area we were given the option of either remaining on the interstate or completing the ride on a state highway. Tired of the relative tedium of I-10, everybody chose this alternate route, which represented the last twenty miles of the day.

Crossing the Continental Divide, near Lordsburg, New Mexico

As we approached the exit onto the state highway, we noticed a billboard advertising a Dairy Queen, so of course we stopped for milkshakes. I was burning thousands of calories every day, but I (mistakenly) sensed that I was maintaining my rather husky level of weight. While I was burning lots of calories, I was also ingesting massive quantities of food. We had learned long ago that we needed to eat while on the road to avoid "bonking," or running out of fuel. At each SAG stop, I typically had a granola bar of some sort, a banana or some other type of fruit, and around lunchtime, I would also quickly consume a peanut butter and jelly sandwich. The support guys tried to cater to the whims of individual riders, so if there were items that particularly appealed to me I didn't hesitate to help myself. I developed a taste for little bags of "Sweet and Salty", containing M&Ms, peanuts, raisins, and sunflower seeds, which were probably 250 calories each and incredibly tasty. There were days when the thought of one of these little bags was like the carrot drawing me to the next SAG stop. And then there were the milkshakes. It was suggested that if you lose weight on a trip like this, you're probably not eating enough. As a result, for one of the only times in my adult life, I wasn't the least bit concerned about my calorie consumption.

The road ended at the entrance to the parking lot of our hotel for the evening, a Comfort Inn in Deming, New Mexico. We got into our rooms just after 2:00 p.m., and it was a luxury to arrive so early in the afternoon. Following our routine when possible, I went in search of a convenience store that sold beer (kind of like our penchant for milkshakes). I got for each of us a large can of Corona and a bag of Cheetos, further adding to our calorie count for the day. We were able to lounge around the hotel room until the team meeting at 5:00, after which we walked to Benji's (with a chili pepper representing the "j" in the logo), a tiny restaurant that offered Mexican and American fare. Bev had an order of chicken fajitas and I had a huge chicken-fried steak with mashed potatoes and gravy. (After all, I didn't want to "bonk" while walking back to the hotel.) Tomorrow would be a longer day at eighty-seven miles, and the trailer was scheduled to open at 7:15 a.m. to get us on the road shortly after sunrise. Back at the hotel, we were both in bed and asleep by just after 9:00 p.m.

• • •

So many of the people we had met seemed interested in what we were doing. As an example, when we stopped at the Taylor Freeze on our way to Safford, Arizona and I was waiting for our order, a man passing through with his family started asking me some very detailed questions about how far we rode each day, where our trip would conclude, how much training we had done before the start of the tour, etc. I was more than happy to answer his questions, and when after he thanked me and walked out to his car, he came back with even more questions, I was equally happy to try to address them. His queries seemed to arise out of more than just general curiosity; if, as I suspect, a cross-country bike trip was a long-held goal of his, I hope he can someday fulfill that dream. Many people were just generally supportive, such as the greeter at the Walmart in Surprise, Arizona who was almost spiritual in offering her best wishes on our travels. Many asked how far we were going. Bev most often responded to these questions, and her response that we were riding to Florida typically brought forth reactions of mild disbelief. (We weren't sure if that disbelief came from the notion of how far we were planning to ride . . . or that Bev and I were the ones doing the riding.) But by far the most memorable reaction came in the parking lot of that same Walmart in Surprise. A young man in an older, rusted-out car drove by and stopped, and likely thinking we were just riding our bikes around the area asked, "Where are you guys riding to?" When one of the riders responded that we were riding to Florida, this young guy paused for a second and then said, in a loud voice, "You're shittin' me!" There were times when pondering what we were hoping to accomplish that, internally at least, I had a similar response.

• • •

The next morning, day twelve of the tour, we again left the hotel fairly early, facing an eighty-seven-mile route to Las Cruces, our last stop in New Mexico. For the first time since leaving San Diego, we began our ride under cloudy skies. Combined with light breezes and possibly the best riding surface we had thus far experienced, it made for a very pleasant morning. At the team meeting the previous evening, Larry had told us with a wry smile that the first SAG stop would be at "the saddest rest stop ever." We thought he was joking, or at least exaggerating, but while we were glad to reach the first stop, we found that he hadn't overstated the sad state of this "rest stop." It was truly pitiful, with a fenced-in area of about a half-acre of dirt on which had been placed six concrete picnic tables. There were no trees, no grass, no shade, no restrooms, basically nothing but these barren tables set among the dirt. We soon departed, hoping to get in as many miles as possible before the blessed clouds broke up (they never really did all day; we even got a few drops of rain).

The highlight of the day was passing through Hatch, New Mexico, the self-proclaimed "chili pepper capital of the world." It was a neat, interesting little town, and we wished we had more time to explore the little shops and establishments in the downtown area. The Hatch chili peppers were the focal point of this town, and we began to smell the peppers as we approached the city limits. Downtown Hatch was the location of the second SAG stop, and the atmosphere of this stop was a vast improvement over the saddest stop we had experienced twenty-five miles earlier. We had found that we rode best when we had a more formidable lunch beyond the snacks offered at the SAG stops, so Bev and I walked down the street to the Village Market. This little market had a deli section that offered all kinds of Mexican food, as well as some scrumptious-looking barbecued ribs, none of which seemed particularly fitting given that we still had thirty miles to ride that afternoon. We opted instead to share an order of chicken tenders. Not particularly optimal biking food, but they were good nonetheless.

After leaving Hatch, we sensed a noticeable change in the terrain and vegetation—more grass, and just a greener feeling to the countryside. We were riding alongside the Rio Grande River, which was, at this point on its path to the Gulf of Mexico, less spectacular than we had anticipated. We started to pass by huge groves of pecan trees lining both sides of the highway. We didn't know much about the horticulture of pecans and still don't, but we were struck by the pools of water standing among the pecan trees. "Flood irrigation," it is called, and it was fascinating to see in this arid part of the country.

Riding on largely flat roads on this cooler, cloudy day, we made our way to the outskirts of Las Cruces, our destination for the evening. Las Cruces was much larger and busier than we had anticipated, but with little difficulty, we navigated the main road through the city and reached our hotel, a La Quinta Inn. Despite the long eighty-seven-mile day, we were able to get into our rooms by 3:00 p.m. I walked across the street to a convenience store for a couple of tall Coronas, and they were a nice reward following what had been a really good day of riding. Dinner was at a Cracker Barrel Old Country Store, a chain of down-home restaurants with standard American fare. It was the first time one of the European riders had ever been in a Cracker Barrel, and with the visual assault one received upon walking into the "country store" and then viewing the huge menu, he seemed just a bit overwhelmed.

• • •

The following day we were scheduled to leave New Mexico, our third state, and we were anxious to pass another milestone as we rode toward El Paso. The idea of reaching Texas was enticing, but we would soon view that former republic as the state that seemingly would not end.

LIFE LESSON #2
A clean chain makes the ride go a lot smoother.

"Rest when you're weary. Refresh and renew yourself, your body, your mind, your spirit. Then get back to work."

—Ralph Marston

O n the day we traveled alongside the Pima cotton fields on our way to Safford, Arizona, the site of the first rest day of the tour, despite strong tailwinds the pedaling wasn't as easy as I might have expected. It was our ninth consecutive day of riding, and though we hadn't yet encountered any rain, we had dealt with some very dry conditions made worse by strong winds whipping up dust and grime. The lubricant that was designed to make the bike's drive train turn smoothly also acted like a magnet for the dirt and muck a cyclist inevitably encounters. Unless dealt with appropriately, that mixture of dirt and lube works to gum up the chain and other components, making pedaling progressively more challenging.

Like many cyclists, I didn't pay enough attention to matters of bicycle maintenance, a lapse that was less critical when we were just riding a few miles on infrequent occasions. And let's face it—for the recreational cyclist who completes an occasional leisurely ride, a gunky chain is more of a nuisance than a critical issue. But on this tour, we were riding six to ten hours each day, which throughout the tour would result in millions of pedal strokes and a similar number of revolutions of the drive train and chain. Under these conditions, not only is there a greater opportunity for gunk to form, but the effect of that often-unseen buildup also seems to increase exponentially. And with each pedal stroke, the effort required imperceptibly increases. The cycling gets harder and harder until it gets so bad that the roughness in the chain can be felt with each stroke. The cyclist is forced to put forth more and more effort and often doesn't even realize it.

At the team meeting in Safford, Chuck informed us he would be available the next morning to assist all riders interested in cleaning their chains. At the prescribed time on that rest day, all nine riders showed up in the parking lot, ready to complete this seemingly mundane maintenance task. I thought I had a grasp on the fundamentals of cleaning and lubing a bike chain, but after about three minutes of this tutorial, I realized I knew relatively little. With Chuck, the sage cyclist and support guy, watching over me, I used a shop rag to clean the built-up grime off of the revolving chain. After a while, I asked him if he thought the chain was sufficiently clean to begin applying fresh lube. Making a quick glance, he recommended that I spend more time removing deeply embedded grime from the chain, suggesting that, "It'll pay off down the road." So I did just that, and as a result the drive trains on our two bikes were probably as clean as they had been since they were new. The next morning, as we departed this small Arizona town, the smoothness and relative ease with which we could travel down the highway was particularly noticeable. Time devoted to this mundane task had made our ride much easier.

• • •

From my perspective, a gunky, gummed-up, and poorly maintained bike chain is a fitting metaphor for what so often happens in our lives. Like the cyclists who believe they are too busy riding to take care of critical little tasks like cleaning their chains, so many of us seem too busy to take care of ourselves, such as dealing with the constant stress that often unknowingly wreaks havoc on our minds and bodies. With the constant pressures of our careers and other issues resting on our shoulders, life so often leaves us beaten down. Like the cyclists who seemingly lack the time to keep their chains clean, the common response of so many of these stressed-out people is to simply put their heads down and work longer and harder, causing the stress to build up at an even faster pace. At the same time, their mind is in constant overdrive pondering problems (real, perceived, and anticipated), sleeping far less than what is optimal, and then feeling guilty about not devoting sufficient attention to family members and issues. It's a spiraling pattern so many have experienced at times in their lives; I know I have.

Originally published in the late 1980s but still incredibly relevant today, one of the most eloquent discussions of this issue was presented by Dr. Stephen Covey. He refers to the seventh and last habit in his famous book, *The 7 Habits of Highly Effective People,* as "Sharpen the Saw." He uses the metaphor of a woodcutter who had struggled for hours to saw down a large tree, with his saw getting progressively duller and the cutting process getting slower and more difficult. When a passerby asks him why he doesn't stop to take a few minutes to sharpen his saw, and thus make the job go much easier, the woodcutter responds that he doesn't have time to sharpen the saw, because he's too busy trying to cut down the tree. Sound familiar, at least metaphorically? Covey describes how essential it is for everyone to address or renew the physical, spiritual, mental, and social/emotional dimensions of their nature. What is particularly critical, Covey suggests, is that appropriately addressing this habit of self-renewal is so important, it enhances our effectiveness in all aspects of life.

What all of this looks like is different for each individual, but one factor is typically common to all of us: it takes time we don't believe we have to spare. I finally internalized and applied most of the lessons I have learned regarding "self-renewal" after the point in my life when they were most needed, times when, despite outward appearances of success and competence, it often seemed like my life was more about simply surviving than about striving to reach lofty goals. For me, with a career that was increasingly consuming me, sitting in front of the television and watching largely mindless programming provided little benefit beyond a momentary distraction. When I was able to watch TV, I was typically doing work on my laptop computer, thinking about work-related issues I was facing, or often dozing off. Going on short, intense, and harried vacations with my family, though memorable and enjoyable, seemed on a deeper level to serve little purpose beyond providing a brief diversion from the pressures of life and career. At the most stressful times in my career, I seemed to be devouring myself from the inside out. I knew it was unhealthy, but I lacked the knowledge and ability needed to truly do anything about it. And even if I had possessed that knowledge base, I likely would have considered my common sixty-hour weeks too hectic to allow time for such activities. In essence, I was too busy cutting wood to keep my saw sharpened. As a result, like many of the individuals who serve as a school district superintendent, though I was still a relatively young man and, in many respects, at the peak of my abilities and effectiveness in that position, when I had the opportunity to retire, I did so—and in the process, sought a second rewarding but less-stressful career.

That less-stressful second career was as a part-time administrator and instructor at a nearby university, and though there were definite challenges, compared to my past positions I felt like I was now on a permanent vacation. The work was stimulating and rewarding, but I suddenly had more time for activities I wanted and needed to complete. I had previously struggled to find time for exercise, often considering it just one more item on my to-do list when I was able to carve out such time. With more available time, I not only exercised more, with more running, more hiking, more biking, and more time spent in the gym, but just as importantly, I also found renewed joy in those activities. When I went running along a favorite trail or rode along a scenic road, I started to again find enjoyment and satisfaction in completing these strenuous activities, all in addition to the obvious health benefits I experienced. With Bev having completed her own career transition, we soon were planning long bicycle tours and adventure hikes, activities that would have been time-prohibitive just a few years earlier.

And then, as I was recovering from a cancer-related surgery and struggling as I tried to deal with the inevitable mind-racing issues related to such a diagnosis, I began incorporating meditation into my daily life. I initially struggled to maintain focus for five or ten minutes, my "monkey brain" jumping from one negative branch to the next. In time, though, by focusing on either my breathing or a mantra, I was able to calm my mind, an effect that seemed to extend beyond the fifteen minutes of practice I was eventually able to regularly incorporate into my morning routine. What had at first seemed like such frivolous use of precious time was actually having a positive effect. Unfortunately, during those decades when I could have most benefited from a regular practice of stillness, I likely would have considered it impossible to eke out even a quarter of an hour from my hectic daily schedule.

Similar to meditation, in a simplistic but oh-so-challenging strategy that for me fits firmly into the categories of "work-in-progress" and "easier said than done," in my later years I have experienced the benefits of conscious mindfulness, of trying to live in the moment. In 1994, Jon Kabat-Zinn published a book advocating mindful meditation with the simple but powerful title of *Wherever You Go, There You Are*. Some might consider this title and respond with a "well, duh," but how often are our minds focused on events and destinations that bear little resemblance to the physical location and situation in which we find ourselves? Kabat-Zinn offers that "[Mindfulness] wakes us up to the fact that our lives unfold only in moments. If we are not fully present for many of those moments, we may not only miss what is most valuable in our lives but also fail to realize the richness and depth of our possibilities for growth and transformation." Excessive focus on what has happened in the past or what might happen in the future acts like an over-lubed bicycle chain on a dusty, windy day, building up emotional gunk in our psyches that not only decreases our effectiveness but over time serves to zap so much of the joy out of our lives. As Ferris Bueller so famously proclaimed, "Life moves pretty fast. If you don't stop and look around once in a while, you could miss it." For me, focusing on the past or the future instead of remaining mindful of the present moment has no doubt resulted in the buildup of more than my fair share of emotional gunk. But when I consciously focus on the here and now, I find my life to be far richer and more enjoyable.

Which brings us back to the need for regular cleaning and lubing of a cyclist's bike chain, a need that seems to increase the longer and harder one rides and the more adverse the conditions become.

Taking the time to clear the gunk and grime from the drive train, whether or not you feel like you have enough available time to do so, will make those tough rides so much smoother. Kind of like dealing with the challenges of life.

CHAPTER 3
MILES AND MILES OF TEXAS

"Be careful what you wish for," as the adage suggests.

We had been looking forward to tackling Texas, a geographically huge state that would for us consume over two weeks and more than 1,000 miles, representing around one third of the tour. Our excitement as we entered Texas would be surpassed by our joy when we finally left it fifteen days later.

But first, we had to get from Las Cruces to El Paso, a largely rural route that would consume almost half of the seventy-mile day. We left Las Cruces on a cool Saturday morning, riding in largely rural areas that would gradually become more urban. For the first time since leaving San Diego, we saw groups of other cyclists, a welcome sight on this gorgeous day, though we weren't sure if they were predominantly from Las Cruces or El Paso, both college towns. We had a brief but interesting interaction with a young female rider from El Paso at the first SAG stop, a triathlete preparing for an upcoming Ironman competition. Facing her own amazing challenge, she was nonetheless fascinated by what we were doing and peppered the riders at the stop with questions about our cross-country journey.

We continued toward El Paso, and as the terrain became more suburban we passed from New Mexico into Texas, an unheralded milestone due to the lack of any state boundary signage on the largely unmarked road on which we were riding. But it wasn't long until we turned onto a busy thoroughfare and it became clear we were in El Paso, the traffic rather intense even on this Saturday morning. As the heavily-traveled road intersected with Interstate 10, riding became a little nerve-wracking for a brief time until we reached the second and last SAG stop of the day in the parking lot of a Walmart. El Paso was much larger than we had anticipated, with a population of around 700,000 in this city on the Mexican border, and the level of traffic we were experiencing was probably what we should have expected in a city of this size.

After a quick lunch at a nearby Chick-Fil-A, we were ready to push on to our first hotel in Texas. The route was complicated, with numerous turns that took us through commercial and industrial areas, so we were glad to be able to ride with Ross and Ray. By the time we left a little after noon, the traffic had eased and our hilly route through the heart of the city provided a rather enjoyable ride. We passed near the Sun Bowl, home of the University of Texas-El Paso Miners football team and the annual December football bowl game. We rode through the UTEP campus and even on "Glory Road," a stretch of road through the campus honoring the historically-integrated men's basketball team at Texas Western University, as UTEP was known at the time. Texas Western won the NCAA title in 1966 with a barrier-breaking, all-black starting lineup. We also traveled through the downtown section of the city, which like many urban areas was a combination of hip new businesses, newer structures, and run-down old buildings. We rode through an industrial area that ran parallel to the Rio Grande River, which serves as the boundary between El Paso and Ciudad Juarez, a city in the Mexican state of Chihuahua. In fact, we passed under the bridges that serve as the points of entry between the two countries, looking up to see the line of vehicles waiting to enter Mexico.

By this time, Ross and Ray had gone ahead and we still had around twenty miles of well-defined route to get to our hotel for the evening. We have never ridden our bicycles through Mexico, but I suspect the next ten miles or so were very similar to highly-populated areas of that country, the Latino influence was that strong. Though the road signs were all in English, the signage for many businesses was written in Spanish, and as we passed the many markets and restaurants in the area, the aromas of tortillas and various spices were pungent.

In time the suburban environment became more rural, and after a long and hot but good day, we finally made it to the little town of Clint, Texas and our hotel for the evening, a Best Western in a remote area just off of Interstate 10. After a quick beer run to an adjacent truck stop (Dos Equis this time), we quickly got settled and cleaned up in time for the team meeting. Afterward, we walked next door to a restaurant called Mamacita's, yet another in a long string of Mexican restaurants we experienced. Bev had steak tacos and I had sirloin tacos (not sure of the difference), and both were authentic with large portions. Paying for alcoholic beverages at dinner was usually the responsibility of each rider, but this evening Larry indicated that the margaritas at Mamacita's were particularly good, and as a result, TAC would provide one for any interested rider (most expressed their interest quickly and enthusiastically). The restaurant didn't have enough of the regular stemmed margarita glasses, so they brought them out in large Mason jars. As a result, these drinks were excellent . . . and huge. It was a good ending to a good day, and as we walked back to the hotel it was dark enough to see the twinkling lights of Juarez, Mexico in the distance, its size dwarfing its smaller adjacent sister city of El Paso. Little did we know at this feel-good moment that the next day would be one of the most challenging of the tour, a ride we at times genuinely doubted we would be able to complete.

• • •

Weather forecasts cause different reactions for different people. Tornadoes, severe thunderstorms, ice storms, heavy snow, and other such forecasts catch the attention of most people. For cyclists riding from west to east, one of the more alarming forecasts is for strong easterly winds. At the team meeting that Saturday evening in Clint, there had been a brief discussion about a forecast for strong winds. But we had dealt with fairly consistent headwinds for the past two weeks, and the thought process among many of us was along the lines of, *How much worse could it be than what we had been experiencing?* (Not long after leaving the hotel the next morning, we found that it could be a lot worse.) But before turning in for the night, we watched the weather forecast for West Texas, and the strong wind warnings suggested gusts of 40 to 60 mph—strong enough to at least impede forward progress, if not blow riders off their bikes. But it had been a long day, and we were tired, so we did our best to postpone our worry until the next morning.

As was typical, I woke up early on that Sunday morning, around 4:00 a.m. and looked out the window to see a large, illuminated flag being blown almost horizontal; the El Paso weather guys had unfortunately been all too accurate. When we took off from the hotel at around 7:30 a.m. with seventy-two miles ahead of us, we found the winds weren't nearly as strong as we had feared, though they were directly out of the east/northeast. So, we started with a little relief, a sensation that lasted for about eight miles. The headwinds stepped up in velocity as the morning progressed, eventually reaching a steady 15 to 20 mph with gusts of 30 to 40 mph. This was brutal and exhausting, and at times it was a struggle to simply stay on the bike. Just as we thought things couldn't get much worse, we rounded a turn in the road and up ahead saw what looked like clouds of sand. As we approached, we realized we were in fact riding into a sandstorm, with the strong wind driving the gritty sand right into our faces. It would take days for the irritation in our eyes to diminish; in the meantime, we were completely miserable, questioning just how much of these conditions we could take. The first SAG stop was at the twenty-six-mile mark near the tiny town of Fort Hancock, Texas, and we were so beat up by the wind and sand, it seemed to take everything we had just to reach that point. (For fans of the movie *The Shawshank Redemption*, Fort Hancock was the point where the fictional Andy Dufresne crossed over into Mexico after his daring prison escape.) Chuck and Larry had set up the support stop at a wide spot on this isolated road, and Larry sheepishly expressed his regrets for not being able to do anything about the conditions. There wasn't much conversation among the riders at the SAG stop, everybody realizing the wind was simply an obstacle no one could control but everyone would have to overcome. The second and last SAG stop was around twenty-eight miles away, and Bev and I agreed that we needed to set a goal of simply getting to that stop. Deep down, I pondered whether, if the wind continued blowing from the same direction and with the same force, we would have the strength to make it to Sierra Blanca, our destination for the evening.

Riding into a West Texas sandstorm

So, we plodded on. Mercifully, we experienced no more sandstorms and the wind began to decrease in intensity; still a headwind
and still gusting, but not quite as strong. We were able to make it to
the next SAG stop without any major problems (though I did see a
little rattlesnake curled up along the side of the road). Even with the
diminished wind, it was still a challenging ride, but we were now able
to take in some of the scenery of the countryside from a road that, in
spots, was just a few hundred yards from the Mexican border. The Rio
Grande still served as the border in this area, there was no discernible
border wall, and the mountains and countryside of Mexico could be
easily seen in the near distance. We were riding through a very economically depressed part of Texas, and though I have never been in
the northern part of Mexico just across the border, I suspect that the
houses in that area a short distance from us were run-down, and some
likely dilapidated and on the verge of collapse. In other words, if my

hunch was correct, economic conditions a few hundred yards away, in what some Americans consider a third-world country, were not much different than what we were seeing in this part of West Texas.

We made it to the second SAG stop just off I-10, and with our immediate goal met we quickly replenished our water and consumed some needed calories. It had gotten warm in the middle part of the day, but we had begun to notice the sky getting darker as we prepared to leave the support stop. We had battled headwinds and sandstorms and were exhausted, and with eighteen miles to the hotel for the evening, it looked like we might for the first time on this trip experience some steady rain. As we left, we soon realized we were in a very hilly, almost mountainous area. Sure enough, we started to climb on a not particularly steep but rather long and steady incline. As we were climbing the first long hill it started to rain—not hard, but steady, just enough to be challenging; or as another rider suggested, enough to be a "pain in the ass." It had been a little cool when we started the day many hours earlier, so we had brought jackets, which we quickly put back on. The ride from the SAG stop to the hotel took around two hours, and it rained around an hour and a half of that time. The climb was tough, and would have been challenging on any day, but was made worse by the rain and the difficulties we had faced earlier in the ride. We were exhausted and, quite frankly, ready to get off the bike. The road leveled out as we approached Sierra Blanca, and in time we were riding into this little town that was probably prominent at one time, but now consisted of a couple of convenience stores, a couple of restaurants, and a motel.

The motels in which we had been staying were relatively nice, probably better than we might have expected. But the support guys had warned us that some nights, the lodging might leave something to be desired, simply because in isolated areas there were no better options. This was one such night. The "Inn" where we were staying had likely been a nice, prominent motel decades ago, but its best days were clearly in the past. Still, the shower worked well and we were able to get a good night's sleep, both of which were of extreme importance. When you've been beaten up by the elements and are particularly exhausted, your standards in lodging tend to become less discerning.

Other than a Subway restaurant in a convenience store, the only reputable restaurant in Sierra Blanca was a little place called Delfina's. On Sunday afternoons, this restaurant closed at 4:00 p.m., but Larry was able to talk the owner into staying open until 5:00. So, when we got into our room we quickly showered and then walked the half-mile or so to the restaurant. When we entered the front door, we noted the very standard diner décor and furnishings, but also the pungent smells of fresh-fried tortillas and house-made salsa (green and red, both with different levels of intensity). This was genuine Mexican food, and it was authentically outstanding. As we left, we thanked and applauded the owner for staying open later and taking such good care of us, and in return, she did a little dance for us. It was yet another interaction with some really nice people.

Given the elements and conditions we had encountered, it would have been all too easy for Bev and me to have simply quit in the middle of this tough day, and in an earlier place and time, we might have done just that. But we had not, and given all we had overcome the day ended up being oddly satisfying.

• • •

With a short thirty-two-mile ride to Van Horn ahead of us, we didn't leave Sierra Blanca until 10:00 a.m., though I was characteristically awake long before sunrise. Trans-America Cycling included in the cost of the tour breakfast and dinner each riding day, and typically the morning meal was provided by the hotel. But when hotels didn't provide a complimentary breakfast, the support guys provided items like instant oatmeal, fruit, juice, pastries, and other items. So around 7:00 a.m., I walked over to a nearby convenience store for a couple of large coffees for us to have with our impromptu breakfast.

Because of the sand and rain the previous day, everybody's bike chain was dirty, gritty, and in need of some serious cleaning. At 8:30 a.m., Chuck and Larry got out the bike racks so everyone could complete this needed work. Chains cleaned and lubed and bags packed and loaded in the trailer, we left Sierra Blanca, traveling on an outer road adjacent to Interstate 10. Though the route was a bit hillier than we had expected and a headwind was still present (though nothing like we had experienced the previous day), the short route made for a pleasant ride. As we rode, we topped a hill and saw in the distance two riders engaged in conversation. As we got closer, we realized that our teammate Jim was talking to a short and compact individual who wore a protective vest like those often worn by construction workers. We glanced up at I-10 above us and noticed this guy's bicycle loaded with panniers full of gear. We introduced ourselves to Tim from Louisville, who was riding on the interstate as part of his east-to-west ride across the southern tier. We had completed around 1,000 miles of our tour and had 2,000 ahead of us. Tim had just the opposite numbers, and in fact could quote to us the exact number of miles we, and he, still had remaining. Tim was a talkative and very interesting guy, likely anxious to simply have someone to converse with about his journey. He was completing an individual cross-country ride to raise funds for the Louisville Hotel, of which he served as director. He explained that this hotel, the only one of its kind in the United States, was split between a shelter for abused women and a hotel for the general public. He indicated that he had found the interstate highways to be straighter and a little less hilly than much of the regular Adventure Cycling Association route, so he had decided to ride almost exclusively on those major thoroughfares (though through most of the country, doing so was illegal). Most of the riders in our group stopped to talk to Tim, the first cross-country rider we encountered.

We reached the only SAG stop of the day at an on-ramp to the interstate. We refueled there, because the first three miles or so of the eight remaining miles looked to be a long and steady incline on the last stretch of interstate on which we would be riding for the remainder of the tour. (Unlike Tim from Louisville, Larry and Chuck were sticklers for following highway laws.) Now much stronger than when we had left San Diego over two weeks earlier, we were able to navigate that considerable incline with little difficulty and then enjoyed a long, steady downhill into Van Horn, five miles of wide shoulders, gentle curves, and the wind whistling through our helmets. Particularly after the brutal seventy-two miles of the previous day, this had been a pleasant and enjoyable ride.

Van Horn, Texas had the feel of a ranching town, but one with an evolving economy that increasingly relied on travelers headed east or west along Interstate 10. After a short day, we were anxious to get to our motel for the evening, an Econo-Lodge. All things are relative, and in recent years Bev and I had tended to avoid what we considered lower-end motel chains like this one, preferring a little nicer accommodations when we traveled. But after our spartan lodging of the previous evening, we were anxiously looking forward to enjoying a nicer room, even in a chain of motels we didn't typically utilize in our regular lives. And the Van Horn Econo-Lodge met our needs wonderfully, with more space, good Wi-Fi, clean lodging, and a good breakfast. Life was good.

The routine we'd established over the previous two weeks had included my making a beer run in search of tall-boy cans of the best brew I could find. But Bev had been wanting some good red wine, her beverage of choice back home, so as she was washing out our cycling clothes I went in search of a nice bottle. Google Maps led me to a small liquor store a half-mile away, and as I walked into this garage-sized establishment I sensed that the selection might be limited in this beer- and whiskey-dominated store. I spoke with an elderly lady who was sitting near the cash register, and when I told her what I was looking for, she responded, "I'd love to have your business, but the grocery store has a better selection." I said, "Well, you've been awfully nice and I would rather buy it from you." She smiled, and an older gentleman sitting in the corner chimed in, "Ah, she ain't as nice as you think," causing an even bigger smile to cover her face.

I thanked these two good people and headed across the street in search of the aforementioned grocery store with a more expansive selection of wines. The supermarkets we tended to patronize back home were more like big-box stores, but this was maybe a third of that size. I quickly found what the aisle sign pronounced as the section of "Fine Wines," expecting an impressive variety, but soon realized that the "Fine Wines" aisle was also the aisle for canned fruits and vegetables, as well as various other types of items. Locating the small section I was looking for, I sought a nice Cabernet, Merlot, or Zinfandel. Bev and I are not (I hope) "wine snobs," but we have each developed a relatively refined palate in differentiating the quality of red wine. And as I was particularly proud of how Bev had been handling the rigors of the tour thus far, I wanted to find her an especially nice bottle to enjoy on this extended afternoon in West Texas. From this limited assortment of "Fine Wines," I selected the most expensive bottle in the store; the price, $6.95. Evidently like "nice" motel rooms, "Fine Wines" is a relative term. But as we drank this budget Cabernet from plastic cups in our motel room, the wine seemed to grow on us.

At the SAG stop that morning, Bev had been talking about how she was missing cooking and reflected on what meal she might want to create if she were back home. She suggested that she would like to cook a meal with a really good small beef filet steak, like what she often purchased from a little butcher shop near where we live. Larry overheard her comment and stated that as a result of what Bev was craving, we would have dinner at a steakhouse later that evening. (I'm confident this restaurant selection had been determined long ago, but it was a fun touch nonetheless.) So, after our team meeting, we walked a couple of blocks to a nice restaurant called the Van Horn Cattle Company, likely the finest eating establishment in the entire town. Bev and I each had a bacon-wrapped filet, cooked perfectly, and we agreed that it was the best meal we had had thus far on the tour. As we were leaving to walk back to the motel, Larry joked that everybody could thank Bev for the choice of restaurants.

The next day we were beginning a challenging stretch of particularly long days that were necessitated in this part of the state by the remoteness of the area and the distance between lodging options. We had reached a point where we weren't particularly anxious about these long days, but simply considered them necessary steps in getting to our ultimate destination in Florida.

• • •

There are a lot of unexpected logistical concerns that go into the planning of a tour like this one, issues that most people would likely never consider. One such issue dealt with sunrises and time zones. For the previous several days leading up to our short day to Van Horn, we had been leaving fairly early, often by 7:00 a.m. But those days we had been in the eastern part of the Mountain Time Zone, and yesterday we had crossed into the western portion of the Central Time Zone. So, as we departed Van Horn for what would be a tough eighty-one-mile day, we left relatively late at around 8:15 a.m., shortly after the sunrise at 8:00. As we left town there were some light headwinds, but we were otherwise making good progress. After about ten miles, we came to a sign that said, "Road Construction Next 25 Miles." Yikes! We weren't sure what the road construction entailed and whether we would need to make any detours. But what we encountered was freshly laid asphalt, rough and bumpy and not yet sealed. We wouldn't have to make any detours, but because of the road construction, we would experience two hours of constant, bone-jarring terrain, which with the slight headwinds contributed to what would be another exhausting day.

Still, the day wasn't without highlights. As we were leaving the motel that morning, the support guys had suggested that the men might want to stop at the Prada store to pick up something for their wives. This didn't make much sense, as we were deep in West Texas, seemingly far from any population that might support such a high-end store. We didn't think much more about this comment until we noticed a group of cars clustered around what from a distance looked like a shed-sized structure. As we rode up, we realized that the signage suggested this was a Prada store, and through the glass storefront we could see racks of shoes and handbags, evidently typical Prada fare. We learned we were around fifty miles from Marfa, a famous artsy little town, and "Prada Marfa" was a contemporary art installation designed as a conversation piece; it sure got us talking. The next day we would pass by a similar installation, the "Marfa Target" store. But on this rather boring stretch of very rough road, stopping to take photos was a respite from the challenging monotony. The other highlight, such that it was, occurred at the turn-off into a rest area where the first SAG stop was located. Larry had told us to look for the "fork in the road" to direct us to the SAG stop. As we exited the highway, though I didn't think much of it at the time, I noticed in the middle of the road a plastic fork placed on a paper plate; this was the "fork in the road." Cheesy, sure, but when you're fighting exhaustion and boredom while on the bike for eight hours you welcome any comic relief you can get.

During the nearly two and a half weeks we had been on this tour, I had at times struggled to determine, other than on the obvious uphills and downhills, whether we were climbing or descending. Chuck had several times made the passing statement that "The gears don't lie," meaning that if you had to shift into an easier gear and you weren't riding into a headwind, you were going uphill. But on this day, I was sure we had been riding on a largely flat road since leaving Van Horn. At the last SAG stop of the day, I made a passing comment that I was surprisingly tired and that I didn't know why. One of the support guys responded that we had been climbing since leaving Van Horn; not at all steep but for the most part continuous. I wasn't any less tired, but at least I better understood why.

Bev and Rob outside of Fort Davis, Texas

We had twenty-eight miles remaining to get to our destination for the evening, Fort Davis, Texas, and though I had been unsure earlier, as we left the SAG stop this time, there was no doubt we were climbing. It was beautiful country, a mix of open range and pasturelands, but predominantly a highway cut through rock outcroppings as we climbed through what were known locally as the Davis Mountains. It had been a long day and it was a hot afternoon, so this stretch of highway was particularly tiring. Then, just as we needed some relief, we topped the climb and began a long and steady fourteen-mile descent. It was never steep or dangerous, but riding through farms and ranchland without having to pedal was a welcome treat. Bev and I were becoming better descenders, but it was at times frustrating to have to slow down when we came to metal cattle guards that occasionally covered the entire road.

In time, we entered Fort Davis and made it to our hotel for the evening. With the late start and eighty-one-mile day, it was approaching 4:00 p.m. by the time we checked into the Hotel Limpia. The town of Fort Davis was named after a military establishment that had been dedicated to Jefferson Davis, the future Confederate President who at the time was serving as U.S. Secretary of War. Larry, history enthusiast that he was, had let us know that he and Chuck were planning to take anyone who was interested to tour the Fort Davis National Historic Site. But because the site closed at 5:00 p.m., they would be leaving the hotel at 4:00. We would have liked to tour the fort, but after a grueling day, we were more in need of a shower and a beer.

Of the forty-five or so hotels and motels we stayed in throughout this tour, the most memorable was the Hotel Limpia. Originally built in 1912 as a summer retreat for cattlemen of West Texas, but now fully restored with period furnishings, this hotel had charm, beauty, and character, and we would have loved to stay more than one night. We entered the lobby and picked up our room key, then carried our bikes up a narrow winding staircase to our second-floor room. It was a bit of a struggle to navigate the staircase, but when we opened the door into our room, it was as if we had been transported in time to a century earlier. The windows were draped with thick golden curtains and the beds were flanked by huge walnut headboards and matching footstools. It was a beautiful room, made modern by the flat-screen TV and exceptionally good Wi-Fi coverage.

We quickly showered and went in search of a place to get a beer or a glass of wine. We asked the nice lady at the front desk where we might get a drink, and she smiled and replied that the only place in town was connected to the hotel, the Blue Mountain Bistro, but that the bar didn't open until 5:00 p.m. As the team meeting had been moved to 5:30, we might be cutting it a bit close, but it was the only bar in town. We killed some time by walking around the small downtown section of Fort Davis and then toured the gardens behind the hotel. A little before 5:00, we walked into the restaurant only to find that Steve and Ted had the same idea. I had a couple of cans of a very good local pale ale and Bev had two glasses of Pinot Grigio, two drinks being our limit given that the next day was scheduled to be one of the longest days of the tour. But we particularly enjoyed spending some time getting to know our two riding mates from Ohio.

The team meeting was held in a beautiful side porch/sunroom in the hotel, and then we all returned to the Blue Mountain Bistro for our second exceptional dinner in a row. (I had one of the house specialties, Beef Bourguignon, which was outstanding, with tender chunks of beef and a rich, red wine sauce.) Thanks to the beautiful accommodations, good beer and wine, and an excellent meal, we thoroughly enjoyed our brief stay in Fort Davis, Texas.

●   ●   ●

A rite of passage for cyclists is riding their first "century" ride of 100 miles in a day. Along with one other rider in our group, this would be our first such ride (actually 108 miles). Most riders prepare for their first century by training specifically for that ride, tapering their mileage and then resting in the days before the big event. Our "resting" day had been the tough eighty-one-mile ride from Van Horn to Fort Davis, and we would follow our first 100-mile day with an even tougher 90-mile ride the following day. Even though the 108 miles would be ten miles longer than Bev or I had ridden to that point, we weren't particularly intimidated by the distance. Perhaps we were a little naïve, but we were simply in a groove. We had handled every long day thus far in the tour with little difficulty, and our confidence had steadily increased since leaving San Diego. We sensed that this would be an excruciatingly long day, but not one we couldn't handle, and in both respects we were correct.

As we began our ride, I experienced the most amazing, almost spiritual sensation I would have on the entire tour. As we left Fort Davis, the weather was cool and a light breeze was blowing. Bev and I both had on light jackets, the sun had just risen and was hidden behind some beautiful clouds, and our view of the horizon in the east over some small mountains was simply stunning. About two miles outside of town I stopped to take a photo, one that could never do justice to the beauty we were experiencing, and I commented to Bev about how this was such a magical morning. As we continued riding, I was struck by a profound sense of gratitude for the opportunity to experience this tour. The tears were short-lived, but I realized that we didn't *have* to ride 108 miles today; rather, we had the *privilege* of doing so in this stunning setting. The twenty-three miles to the first SAG stop in the town of Alpine represented one of the most beautiful sections of the entire tour; mostly downhill, still cool, and on winding roads slinking through and around the small mountains through which we were riding. At that first stop, the support guys provided a variety of donuts and pastries, a tradition they had started on this particularly long day. Needing calories and never wanting to turn down complimentary food on this tour, I had a chocolate éclair, something I hadn't consumed in years. A beautiful sunrise, a long downhill stretch on a cool morning, and now a chocolate éclair . . . it was a great start to one of our longest days.

Though long, the ride was largely uneventful, on an isolated highway with a decent shoulder, rolling hills, and not much in terms of memorable scenery. The second SAG stop was in the small but historic town of Marathon, where the support guys had set up in the shade of a group of trees lining the highway. There was a nice little coffee shop where Bev and I ordered a couple of sandwiches and large glasses of iced tea, a special treat in the middle of our first hundred-mile ride. We were soon joined by two other riders, and sitting in the air-conditioned comfort of that little café made leaving Marathon, Texas more challenging than we might have anticipated. But it was after 1:00 p.m., and we still had fifty-five miles remaining on the route to Sanderson, our destination for the evening. Those miles were tough, a long slog that entailed simply grinding out mile after mile against a light headwind. Feeling bone-tired, as exhausted as we had been since leaving San Diego, we finally rolled into Sanderson a little after 6:00 p.m. As we rode into the parking lot of the hotel, we fist-bumped Steve, the other rider who on this day had finished his first century ride. Steve is a great guy, and it made a nice memory to share this moment with him . . . but we were tired.

The Outback Oasis Motel, our home for the evening, had seen better days but was a bit of a tropical oasis in the rather barren West Texas terrain through which we had been riding. It had a sort of 1950s vibe, with rooms that were uniquely and a little haphazardly decorated. But our room was clean, cool, and on an evening when sleep would be at the top of our to-do list, the beds were comfortable. In other words, this motel, which was no doubt the nicest within fifty miles in any direction, met our needs quite adequately.

As several riders didn't arrive in Sanderson until nearly an hour after our typical 5:00 meeting time, that meeting and dinner were both pushed back an extra half hour. To make sure we appropriately celebrated our first century ride, while Bev cleaned up I quickly walked (or at least as quickly as I could, considering how tired and sore my legs were) across the highway to a convenience store for a couple of tall cans of Dos Equis. We were sore and exhausted, but the support guys had warned us that the route the following day, a ride of ninety miles to Comstock, Texas, would actually be more challenging than this day's 108-mile route. It was a daunting thought, but we would soon find that their prediction was more than accurate.

Sanderson is a small town, and on previous tours the riders and support crew had dined at an establishment called—honestly—"Dairy King (and Mexican Food Too)." Larry was almost always the first of the two support guys to arrive in the town in which we would be staying, and he typically went ahead and informed the folks at the selected restaurant for the evening the number in our party and when we might be arriving. But when he went to check in at the restaurant, he learned that, for health reasons involving the owner, the "Dairy King" had closed. He scurried around and was able to locate another restaurant a short distance away. So, after the team meeting, we loaded into the support vehicles to be shuttled to the new restaurant: a small, two-person operation a mile or so down the highway. Bev and I prepared to ride in Chuck's support van, which with various coolers and boxes of food could be challenging to enter, especially when climbing into the back seats. As I tried to propel myself over a large cooler and into that back seat, the quad muscles in my thighs cramped, causing me to have to stop and try again. But with needed food on the horizon, I was ultimately able to awkwardly make it to the back of the van.

The restaurant had little discernible signage, but as we perused the menu it was obvious it specialized in a blend of Mexican and traditional American cuisine. Bev had a huge pork chop and I had another large chicken-fried steak. As we were finding in these nondescript restaurants, the food was both tasty and very filling. While we were preparing to leave, somebody mentioned that our server, a pleasant-looking young woman, was "packing." I wasn't sure just what it was she was packing until someone pointed to the handgun in a holster on her belt. We were in Texas after all, and this was a two-person operation on a secluded highway; nonetheless, this was the first time we had been served by an armed waitress (at least that we knew of). Alan from Scotland, who seldom hesitated to question these rather peculiar American customs, got the waitress to proudly pose for a photo.

A spiritual sunrise, our first century ride, and now eating a pork chop and chicken-fried steak served by a pistol-packing waitress; this had been a truly memorable day.

• • •

Still sore from our 108-mile ride, we left the next morning at 8:00 a.m. for what we anticipated would be at least an equally tough day. And it was, and then some. We rode almost the entire day on U.S. 90 on a rough chip-and-seal surface, so it was a bumpy ride all day. And it was hilly, with long uphill stretches followed by long descents, sort of like much longer versions of the "bunny hop hills" we had encountered in California. As the day continued, the winds blowing right in our faces began to increase in intensity. Climbing hills is always tough, but one can typically look forward to being able to catch a break on the downhills. As we made our way toward Comstock, our destination for the evening, the wind blew so hard that after struggling up a hill, we actually had to pedal on the downhill as well. With the rough roads, it made for yet another especially challenging day.

As we were climbing one of these countless hills, I heard a clanging sound from my back wheel. I quickly stopped and realized that I had broken a spoke, and as a result my rear wheel was "out of true" and wouldn't turn, rubbing on my caliber brake pads on every revolution. We weren't sure what to do, so we checked our phones to call one of the support guys and found we had no cell service. We were stranded in the middle of West Texas on the side of a sparsely traveled highway. I thought we were four or five miles from the next SAG stop, so we started to walk our bikes. Quickly realizing this was not a viable solution, particularly in cleated cycling shoes, I released my rear brake caliper, wrapped the broken spoke around another spoke, and started riding to the next SAG stop. After crawling along for about three miles with only front brakes and a wobbly rear tire, we saw Larry's truck coming toward us. We told him what had occurred, and he quickly loaded our bikes onto his pickup, and we were soon on our way to the SAG stop. We would luckily be in Del Rio the next day, a town large enough to have a reputable bike shop where we could get the spoke replaced and the rear wheel adjusted.

At the SAG stop, Larry pulled out a bike he thought would fit me best, no doubt the nicest bicycle I had ever ridden. Working quickly, one support guy transferred my seat to the new bike while the other strapped my bike onto the rack on Chuck's support van. Because the next SAG stop was only twelve miles away, Chuck took off to set up for the arrival of the other riders. It was then that Larry realized the pedals on his bike weren't compatible with the cleats on my shoes and that my pedals were still on my bike, which was strapped to the back of Chuck's van. So reluctantly, we loaded the two bikes onto Larry's truck and traveled the short distance to the next SAG stop, where my pedals were quickly transferred to the bike I would be riding for the next couple of days.

The location of SAG stops was well thought out, typically selected in advance by the support guys based on the distance from the last stop, preferring that riders not travel more than thirty miles before getting water and food. But occasionally, stops were shorter distances apart because of historical sites or points of interest (such as the "big-ass cactus"). Today was such a day, and the second SAG stop was located at the "Judge Roy Bean Visitor Center" in the now-tiny town of Langtry, Texas. In the late 1800s, Bean became a saloon-keeper in West Texas, and with the nearest court some 200 miles away, he soon established himself as the local justice of the peace ("the law west of the Pecos"). The legend of this historical character grew as he was portrayed in movies and on television, perhaps most notably by Paul Newman in the "based on fact" 1972 movie, *The Life and Times of Judge Roy Bean.*

This section of U.S. 90 was isolated, and Langtry was actually located on a side road. But the Judge Roy Bean Visitor Center was impressive, with a nice (air-conditioned) museum and little theater and various restored buildings, including Bean's saloon/courtroom. It made for a nice diversion on a long, rough, and windy day, an impressive historical site just a few miles from the Mexican border.

We still had around thirty miles to go before we'd arrive at the Comstock Motel, and with the rough road and a couple of stops, it would take us over four hours to get there. By now, the wind was blowing directly in our faces at a steady 15 to 20 mph with gusts much stronger, and the long uphill sections and the wind-impeded down-hills, coupled with fatigue from the previous few days, made this last section for Bev and me one of the most challenging of the entire tour. The ninety-mile route from Sanderson to Comstock was completely devoid of services (restaurants, gas stations, etc.), so one of the very few highlights was crossing the bridge over the Pecos River. By this point in the tour we had crossed more rivers than we could remember, but this one was different. First, though we weren't sightseeing—at least initially—we would later realize that the river was geologically impressive, a wide ribbon of water flowing through the deep canyon it had slowly carved out over time. Second, the U.S. 90 bridge over the Pecos was a long, narrow, and impressive two-lane span of well over a quarter-mile. But the narrowness created issues for two tired cyclists like Bev and me, the latter riding a very nice bike but one I had never been on until a couple of hours earlier. On the bridge, there was a very narrow shoulder and the guardrail lining the edge of the pavement was just a couple of feet high. As we descended a short hill and observed the imposing bridge ahead of us, we experienced a little bit of panic. With the wind howling through the canyon, and with occasional large trucks meeting each other on the two-lane road, we pondered the possibility that we might be forced or even blown off the bridge. In retrospect, there may have been some irrationality in our concerns, but in our tired state they felt very real. As a result, we did something that was likely illegal, given the signs suggesting that pedestrians were prohibited; we walked our bikes across the bridge. Luckily, there was no other traffic on the bridge as we tried to quickly get to the other side of the river. Once on the east side of the Pecos, we walked down a path to an observation deck to get a good look at what we had just crossed and the flowing river at least a couple of hundred feet below it. It made for an impressive photo opportunity.

We still had around ten miles to the motel, and with the wind and ongoing fatigue it seemed that this most difficult day would never end. I was exhausted, and knew Bev was as well. On one of the longest uphill sections, perhaps a mile long, we had been riding off and on with a couple of other riders. I looked back to see the three riders behind me strung out, fighting the wind to get up this long incline. I thought the two riders closest to me were the other two team members, and that Bev was much farther down the hill. I stopped to wait for her to catch up with me, which she did fairly quickly, as Bev was in reality the rider closest to me. On perhaps the toughest day in the toughest week of the tour, I realized just how much stronger Bev was becoming as we worked our way across Texas.

Around 6:00 p.m., we finally turned into the parking lot of the Comstock Motel, a small, quaint, but clean establishment. Just after getting off our bikes and even before we received our room keys, the support guys handed each of us a bottle of beer. Larry and Chuck, realizing how tough this day had been, took an atypical step and bought beer for all the riders; it was a nice and appreciated gesture. For dinner, we walked across the highway to the J & P Bar and Grill, a dive-looking establishment with the most prominent signage being a large, hand-painted piece of plywood extolling highway travelers to "Eat Here." While it could boast the first services on this highway for ninety miles, Comstock was yet another really small town, and we were fortunate a rather notable restaurant was available. Some periodical had recently proclaimed that the J & P Bar and Grill had the second-best "roadhouse food" of any such establishment in Texas. Though we had a frustrating wait to get our food (evidently such noteworthy fare takes a little extra time to prepare), my cheeseburger and Bev's "Stoner Burger" (a large burger with fried cheese sticks under the bun, something I couldn't imagine her ever ordering in her regular life) were both very good. We walked back to the motel, exhausted but anxious to watch our Kansas City Chiefs, who were playing on Thursday Night Football. We learned the next day that the game had

had an incredible ending; we wouldn't have known otherwise, as we were both sound asleep long before that thrilling finish.

• • •

After riding almost 280 miles in the past three days, most of them into a stiff headwind, we needed a break. Though the next rest day was still four days away, we were all excited that we were facing another "partial" day, a short thirty miles into Del Rio, Texas, another city on the Mexican border. When we left Comstock a bit later than usual, the highway was wet and the air was full of mist, making it challenging to see very far into the distance. The headwinds were still blowing, making this short ride a little more difficult, but everybody was excited to get it finished. After a quick SAG stop, we found ourselves on the outskirts of Del Rio. It was the first town of any size we had passed through since leaving El Paso almost a week earlier, and it was nice to get back to civilization (which at this point meant fast food restaurants, a Walmart, and a bike shop). Our hotel for the evening was a Ramada Inn, one of the nicest and most full-service hotels in town. With laundry facilities, a pool, an exercise room (which we never even tried to find), a bar, and a restaurant, this was a great place to spend a partial day. When we rode into town before noon, our rooms weren't yet available, so we stopped at a Chick-Fil-A for a quick lunch. We soon received a text from Larry and were in our room by 1:00 p.m., a happy development the likes of which would be difficult to describe. We quickly got cleaned up, Bev did a load of laundry, and then we walked to a nearby store to pick up a few supplies. On the way back to the hotel we stopped at a Whataburger restaurant, of which there were seemingly thousands of locations throughout Texas, for a couple of milkshakes. We still felt physically drained, but our mental outlook was continuing to improve.

Shortly after leaving Comstock, Larry had taken my bike, as well as that of Ted, who had been riding a spare bike since shortly after leaving Fort Davis, to a bike shop in Del Rio for repairs. Shortly after 4:00 p.m., Larry drove Ted and me to the shop to pick up the two bikes. When we walked into the shop, we were greeted by a somewhat disorganized mishmash of spare parts, new and used bikes, and cycling clothing, and we realized that this was a quintessential "old-school" bike shop, organized in a manner perhaps only the self-taught mechanic understood. Both bikes were finished, and I asked for the cost of the repair (plus another tube of Chamois Butt'r). The mechanic responded with what I thought was a very reasonable price, particularly given what we were used to paying at our local bike shop back in Kansas City, and I gladly paid. When Ted asked to pay for the repair of his bike, the mechanic told him that the price I had paid was for both bikes, making the repair charge even more reasonable. For the remainder of the tour, neither Ted nor I had any more significant mechanical problems with our bikes. While I had appreciated being able to ride Larry's bike for the past two days, a bike with far more advanced components than I was used to, it was good to have my old reliable Trek model available for the next day.

We had our team meeting at 5:15 p.m. and then adjourned to the hotel bar. With our room keys, the hotel had provided each of us a coupon for a complimentary margarita or beer. The bar opened at 5:30, hence the later-than-usual 5:15 team meeting. The margaritas were good, and it was a nice change of pace to have some relaxed social time talking with the other riders. After a couple of rounds we moved into the hotel restaurant for dinner, where Bev ordered the salmon and I had the bacon-wrapped chopped sirloin, all with large helpings from the salad bar. It was the end of an enjoyable Friday evening in Del Rio, Texas. As Bev was the only female in our group of eleven, the nice gentleman serving us gave her a little bouquet of paper flowers he had quickly created. It was a nice touch.

Everything is relative, and the Del Rio Ramada Inn and Resort would never be confused for a Four Seasons or Waldorf Astoria hotel. But having ridden through barren stretches of West Texas for the past week, to the nine riders and two support guys this was tantamount to lodging at its finest.

• • •

Since leaving Clint, Texas five days earlier, each morning we had relied on the support guys for breakfast, eating instant oatmeal, muffins, bananas, and other similar staples, which was serviceable but over time increasingly monotonous. So, it was particularly enjoyable to fill up at the hotel breakfast buffet, its eggs, bacon, sausage, and biscuits and gravy a much-appreciated treat. We kind of hated to leave Del Rio and this hotel, but we had a long eighty miles to get to Camp Woods, our destination town on the edge of Texas Hill Country. As we checked the inflation of our tires and prepared to depart, the sky was heavily overcast, and though the sun had risen the atmosphere was particularly dark and dreary. Standing by our bikes in the parking lot, another rider said, "Look at all those birds." Previously unnoticed, in the trees and on the power lines next to the hotel were countless birds, occasionally squawking but otherwise just seeming to watch us as we prepared to leave their domain. It was reminiscent of the playground scene from Hitchcock's "The Birds," though luckily we all made it out of Del Rio unscathed.

As we left the hotel, it was muggy and the wind was lightly blowing. Then before we had ridden five miles, we encountered a heavy mist, not quite rain but enough to get our jerseys wet and make my glasses, without which I could barely function, an opaque mess. The road was smooth for the first time in several days, a nice but wet surface that continued until we got about a half mile past the entrance to Laughlin Air Force Base, a prominent installation where fighter pilots are trained. (On weekdays, the Laughlin airfield has more take-offs and landings than any other airport in the United States, though at this early Saturday morning hour and with the wet and overcast sky, we didn't see much action.) It was to be an eighty-mile day, and from just past the Air Force base to the end of the ride, around seventy-five miles, the road was a very rough "chip-and-seal" surface. Known to some as a "poor man's asphalt," this crude form of pavement is often utilized in small towns and villages that lack the finances to afford anything better. But we were riding on U.S. 90, a major east-west thoroughfare with a speed limit of 75 mph. Tractor-trailer rigs and oversized pickup trucks were traveling at least that fast, and the shoulder was maybe three feet wide, but even rougher than the actual highway surface itself. Traffic was heavy for a Saturday morning, but Bev and I would sneak out onto the actual driving lane where a smoother groove had been worn over time, and then when we saw an oncoming vehicle in our mirrors we would quickly slide back onto the shoulder. Though the skies had brightened and the mist had dissipated, it made for a jarring ride.

The first SAG stop of the day was in a small roadside rest area, the highlight of which was the impromptu toilet facility that consisted of a tree and fence row at the back of the property. The second stop was in the little town of Bracketville, where the support guys had set up on a side street. Across from the SAG stop was a convenience store with a Subway restaurant, so Bev and I walked over to grab a sandwich. As we entered, we met another rider who was leaving and noticed an older gentleman in line waiting for the salad he had ordered. It was a frustratingly slow one-person operation, but when this older man got ready to pay for his salad, the young lady at the cash register told him that the person in front of him had paid for his order. Evidently, he had allowed the rider, Ted, to order ahead of him, so Ted had quietly paid for this gentleman's meal before leaving. This older man had been rendered speechless by this gesture, but as we were leaving and realizing we were associated with the man who had paid for his lunch, he asked us numerous questions about what we were doing, where we were going, etc. Ted's gesture had clearly made his day, but to Bev and me it had simply reinforced our perception of just how good of a person our teammate was. We happily left the Subway with a couple of sandwiches and big smiles.

Leaving Bracketville, we rode for the next fifty miles or so on isolated state highways and ranch roads alongside hunting properties and large ranches. We had transitioned out of the desert and into much greener environs, with the Texas Hill Country beckoning. But we were still on a very rough chip-and-seal surface, which made for another bone-jarring and seat-bouncing but otherwise uneventful ride. After several days of riding on what we were learning were typically rough Texas roads, it was as if our bikes were slowly being rattled to pieces.

We stayed that evening at the Woodbine Inn in Camp Wood, Texas, another small but clean older motel in which Trans-America Cycling had booked most of the rooms. We had never heard of this tiny town, but for the past several days we had been hearing about this amazing barbecue spot that was a favorite of Larry's. Living in the Kansas City area, considered by its residents to be the epicenter of the barbecue world, it would take a powerful experience for us to consider it a top-notch barbecue restaurant. With the lowest of low-key atmospheres, we were in for such an experience. After the team meeting, we walked through downtown Camp Wood (not a long process) to "Two Fat Boys Barbecue", a little hole-in-the-wall joint that produced truly amazing food. We walked in and the menu was handwritten on the wall, evidently subject to change, though it was doubtful any alterations had occurred in recent memory. In turn, everybody walked up to the counter and gave the cashier their order, and within thirty seconds they walked away with a heaping plate of food in their hands. Bev and I each had the "large plate" with ribs and brisket and sides of coleslaw, potato salad, and beans. For the next twenty minutes or so along the extended table where the eleven of us were sitting, there was virtually no conversation except for an occasional, "Could you pass me the sauce?" It was simple but exceptionally good barbecue, every bit as tasty as Larry had advertised. It had been a long and fairly hard day, and everybody had been hungry as we had headed to "Two Fat Boys", so after dinner, some broke off in search of a beer, while others, including Bev and me, stopped at the local diner for some ice cream. It was Blue Bell, a brand which wasn't at that time available in our part of the country, but which was immensely popular in Texas. After all of that barbecue and the clean plates we had left behind, Bev had a cone and I had a scoop of vanilla and chocolate in a cup. What an evening!

• • •

Except for shorter days, we were typically on our bikes for seven to ten hours. And though each of the nine riders generally began their ride within ten or fifteen minutes of each other, different individuals had varying levels of ability and different paces. Some stopped at SAG stops for longer periods and others barely stopped at all, some stopped for lunch, and some stopped several times each day to take photos. By the end of each ride, there might be fifteen or more miles between the first rider to arrive at the hotel for the night and the last ones, most often Bev and me. While the two of us always rode together, we only very occasionally rode for short periods with other riders, so for most of the tour, it was just the two of us working together to put miles behind us. And for safety reasons, we rode in single file along the side of the road or, when available, on the shoulder. So, we had hours and hours to ourselves each day, something that I didn't find to be nearly as challenging as I might have anticipated.

Though I can't speak about Bev's thought processes, there were always issues to keep my mind occupied. As I typically rode in front, I was always on the lookout for broken glass and other debris that might cut or puncture a tire. And I was always concerned about making sure we didn't miss a turn on the route. Some days were quite simple, calling for a left turn out of one hotel parking lot and then after ninety miles a right turn into the next. But on days with multiple turns, I wrote the distance between each of the turns on a piece of paper, which were typically close to accurate but seldom exact on the Apple Watch I used to compute distances. As such, I then needed to compute the accumulated distance until the next turn. For example, there might be an estimated 5.8 miles to the next turn and the route mileage at the last turn was 35.6 miles, so I'd compute in my head that we would make our next turn at around 41.4 miles. As such, I would try to keep repeating to myself, "41.4, 41.4, 41.4," until we made the next turn, and then I would start the whole computational and memory process all over. It sounds overly simplistic, and there were no doubt better solutions to this issue (such as an advanced bicycle computer). But over the course of a 3,000-mile ride through parts of the country and on roads we had never before experienced, we never missed a turn. And as a missed turn could add a frustrating number of miles to an individual route, this was no small issue.

But even with worrying about navigation and the location of SAG stops and hotels and other ride-related issues, there was still an inordinate amount of time left for random thinking. It was during one of the many rides of this tour that I began to envision this book, a travelogue of our cross-country trek interspersed with the many life lessons that were learned or reinforced in the process. But other times my mind tended to wander, and often it gravitated to some song that became lodged in my mind, causing me to sing it quietly or otherwise. Often the song selection had no rhyme or reason, but other times it seemed a bit more logical. For example, after crossing from New Mexico into Texas, I kept thinking about the classic Marty Robbins hit "El Paso." This song stayed with me for a couple of days, and one afternoon in a secluded section of the route, with Bev too far behind me to hear, I found myself singing this song in my best Marty Robbins voice (which was pretty good, if I say so myself). The morning after we fought the brutal headwinds on the route to Comstock, Texas, as we were checking tires and getting prepared to leave the motel, one of the support guys, showing a bit of sadistic humor, played Bob Seger's classic "Against the Wind." So of course, I couldn't rid myself of that song for the next several hours.

I always tried to stay positive and in the moment, but occasionally circumstances admittedly pushed me into the realm of negativity. On the day we dealt with continuous teeth-chattering rough roads from Del Rio to Camp Wood, similar to but still worse than the roads we had encountered earlier in the week, I started thinking of newer and more appropriate state mottos for the state of Texas. The official motto for the state is simply "Friendship," a quality we observed in many of the Texans with whom we interacted. But in my tired and "chipped-and-sealed" state of mind as we approached the end of that jarring day, the best, most accurate, and appropriate motto I could think of, one that was probably not quite billboard-ready, was "Texas . . . Sh*#ty Roads, But At Least Our Taxes are Low." Our crossing of Texas, not yet even half-completed, was clearly beginning to weigh on us.

• • •

For our Sunday morning ride into the Texas Hill Country from Camp Wood to Ingram, the route notes in our rider's notebook described four major climbs, some very steep with no shoulder, twisting turns, and equally steep descents. The notes concluded this section by suggesting, "For safety reasons, riders that do not consider themselves strong climbers should elect to SAG (bypass) this portion of the route." Though we had made great strides during the three completed weeks of the tour, neither Bev nor I considered ourselves to be "strong climbers," though given good road conditions and shoulders and sufficient time, I believe we could at this point handle all but the most difficult climbs, as we had proven in California. But we were, and still are to a large extent, self-professed "white-knuckle descenders," meaning we lacked the experience, skill, and confidence to undertake long, winding downhill sections without genuinely fearing we might have some sort of mishap. As we would learn, the downhill sections of these four climbs were several miles long, and a bike builds up tremendous speed and momentum flying down a 5% to 10% descent. Likewise, it takes skill to effectively use the brakes and maintain control of the bike, skill we didn't believe we had yet attained. Just like the earlier section in Arizona, the support guys (who had been spot-on in their assessment of that route) suggested that once we had committed to these climbs we would need to follow through, because, as had been the case earlier in the tour, there would be little cell service and few places for a vehicle to stop and pick up riders and their bicycles while going up or down. We trusted Larry and Chuck and their comments about this section of the route. Consequently, as the other riders dispersed, Bev and I spoke briefly and quickly concluded that we should heed the warnings in the route notes and bypass the initial section of the route. One other rider made the same decision.

After the six other riders had left the motel in Camp Wood, the three of us loaded our bikes onto Larry's pickup and climbed in to be shuttled for much of the day's eighty-one-mile route. As we rode up and then down the first large hill, we confirmed we had made the correct decision for the two of us. The route was reminiscent of a mountainside road in Colorado, not as long but perhaps a bit steeper. There were many parts of the route with no shoulder, tight turns with guardrails, and very steep sections. We would have welcomed riding the entire route, and I still have some nagging regret that we didn't, but we were glad we had again chosen correctly, at least for the two of us.

As a result, the first half of the day was rather relaxing. We stopped in the little town of Leakey, where the support guys set up the first SAG stop. As we waited for the riders to arrive, Bev and I walked over to a little market that was just opening on this cool Sunday morning. As we paid for our coffee we spoke with the proprietor, a very nice gentleman who asked us where we were from and told us he had a daughter in Baxter Springs, Kansas, a little town in the southeast corner of the state near the Missouri border. The second SAG stop was at a crossroads in the valley between two large climbs. The support guys set up in the parking lot of the Lost Maples Country Store, a rustic outpost that seemed to offer a little bit of anything a Hill Country traveler might want or need. Bev and I each had a nice BLT sandwich, which we took out on the large front porch, where we sat on a bench, ate our lunch, watched the occasional passing traffic, and waited for the riders to arrive. We wanted to be riding and felt more than a little disappointed that we weren't, but were otherwise enjoying the day.

In time, we departed and made the short drive to the final SAG stop, around thirty miles from our hotel in Ingram, Texas. We unloaded our bikes and, having been ready to ride for some time, we quickly headed toward our motel for the evening. Though nothing like the first part of the route, the last section was at first very hilly before leveling out as we followed the Guadalupe River, which we crossed numerous times. As we rode past beautiful ranches and riverfront resorts, the lush, green landscape was just beautiful. While riding along in the still-rural countryside, we came across the "boot fence," an iconic landmark that was more famous than we realized at the time. For a short distance along both sides of the road, on each fence post had been placed boots of different kinds—work boots, cowboy boots, hiking boots, etc. It was a welcome diversion.

In time, we began to experience increased traffic, and then more commercial development, and around 3:00 p.m. we arrived at our motel for the evening, the Hunter House Inn in Ingram, another older but clean and functional motel. For Bev and me it had been in some respects a good day, albeit a bit disappointing. While we weren't necessarily second-guessing our decision to bypass the first part of the route, we had felt like bystanders on a trip we were a part of. Hence, less than satisfying.

• • •

When we were still in California, somebody had posed the idea of everybody pitching in $10, and the last person to not have had a flat tire would win the pot. Eight riders had decided to participate, and most (like Bev) were out of the running before we exited our first state. Since around the time we entered Texas, the contest had been down to Allan from Denmark and me. He and I had jokingly discussed how we hoped we would end up tied when we reached the Atlantic, meaning neither of us would have to deal with a flat for the duration of the tour. Given my history (and the sealant I inserted into my tire tubes), I was fairly confident I wouldn't get a flat (I did not), and I genuinely hoped that Allan wouldn't either. As we waited at the Lost Maples Country Store for the last riders to come in, we got word that Allan had hit a piece of plastic that gashed one of his tires, causing more damage than a simple nail or other puncture. Allan soon got back on the road and would have several more flats before we reached St. Augustine, but evidently I had won the pot.

At the team meeting, Larry, who had been the keeper of the "flat tire cash," asked Allan to make the presentation of the $80 to me. It was a less-than-poignant moment, in part because I had "won" the contest on a day I bypassed much of the route. In retrospect, I wished I had suggested that under the circumstances we simply continue the contest until the next flat. But I didn't come up with that response in a timely manner, and instead announced that the liquor bill at dinner that evening would be on me.

We ate at a nice Italian bistro in nearby Kerrville, Texas called Bella Vita. Alan from Scotland had previously mentioned his taste for a good California Zinfandel wine, a varietal that he suggested was hard to find in his native country. So Bev, Alan, and I (and even Chuck) shared a nice bottle of Renwood Old Vine Zinfandel, which paired nicely with each of our meals. It was a very enjoyable dinner.

The Hunter House Inn didn't offer a complimentary breakfast, and I think most of us were growing a bit tired of the instant oatmeal, muffins, bananas, etc. that the support guys had been providing. We were therefore happy when it was announced that the support guys would provide breakfast the next morning in the restaurant attached to the motel. As we walked to the restaurant it was still dark and very cold, with temperatures down into the '30s, the lowest we had experienced thus far on the tour. As we were all seated around a long table, Larry and Chuck stood up and began to sing a song to the tune of "Happy Birthday," instead inserting the phrase "Happy Halfway." Most of us hadn't realized that at the end of this short forty-two-mile ride to our rest day destination of Fredericksburg, Texas, we would have completed half the days of riding and half the total miles. For me, this little surprise brought mixed emotions. It was so hard to believe we had ridden halfway across the country, particularly given our genuine doubts at the start about being able to complete this challenge or even get out of California. But on the other hand, the day we had dipped our back tires in the Pacific Ocean in San Diego, just a little more than three weeks earlier, seemed so long ago. At the age of 60, Bev and I had matured, had grown stronger, and were far more confident than we had been just three weeks earlier. And oddly, instead of worrying about how we were going to complete the next ride, we were beginning to wonder how difficult it was going to be when, in a little over three weeks, there would be no more rides to complete.

LIFE LESSON #3
When your needs are simpler, you have a much greater appreciation for what you have.

"You have succeeded in life when all you really want is only what you really need."

—Vernon Howard

I t had been an excruciating day as we battled strong headwinds, a sandstorm, rain, and a two-hour climb to end the seventy-two-mile ride from Clint to Sierra Blanca in West Texas. As we rode our bikes into the parking lot of the motel for the evening, the only accommodations in this little town, it was clear that this establishment would at best provide a clean bed and a shower, and if we were lucky, some internet access and a TV. As we quickly got settled and cleaned up in time for an early dinner in the only open restaurant in town, we found that our earlier estimation was correct: the beds seemed clean and the water in the shower was plenty hot. As for the other amenities, the wi-fi signal was sparse and we never even turned on the television. So in this room, we had a bed and a shower, making for rather meager accommodations on this night following a particularly challenging ride. The irony, though, is that this room in a rather rundown motel provided pretty much all we needed.

Bev and I had worked hard to reach the point in our lives where we could live comfortably, though certainly not lavishly. But we were no doubt sometimes guilty of concerning ourselves with what some call "first-world" issues, such as becoming irritated when the satellite radio in one of our vehicles was temporarily unavailable. Or when a restaurant was a little stuffy on a particularly hot day, the air conditioning units unable to keep up with hot and humid Midwest conditions. Or having to wait more than a few minutes to be seated at that restaurant when we had gone to the trouble of making a reservation. And then, the ultimate and rather irrational concern so common in our society: irritation over slow internet access or a poor cellphone signal. Though I am an easygoing individual, I have been guilty of concerns like these on more occasions than I would like to admit.

Regarding hotel rooms, our standards had become somewhat high, seeking large, clean rooms in establishments with numerous amenities and at an affordable price. We might be disappointed if the view from the room was obstructed, or if the complimentary breakfast selection lacked foods we preferred, or if the exercise room lacked an elliptical machine. Common chains like Motel 6, Super 8, or Econo-Lodge had been traveling staples for us in our younger and poorer days, but as we aged and became more affluent, we gravitated to more upscale offerings. As for this rather rundown motel in Sierra Blanca, under any other circumstances, we wouldn't have exited the interstate for such accommodations.

But so much had changed a third of the way into our cross-country tour, and the shower in that rather rundown motel felt awfully good. And the mattress on the bed (which had also seen better days) served my exhausted body quite well. In other words, at this particular point in our lives we didn't need much, and this lodging establishment met those limited needs just fine.

It was striking just how simplistic our lives had become since leaving San Diego. Our routine on the tour had become very predictable and our needs so simple. Rather than closets full of clothing, we were each living out of two small duffle bags that carried all of our cycling and non-cycling apparel, as well as all of our personal effects. We rotated through three or four cycling jerseys and shorts (and probably could have done quite well with only a couple of each). We similarly had four or five outfits that we wore each evening, and on rest days, a greater variety due to the anticipated seasonal changes as we progressed eastward. Choosing what to wear from such a small wardrobe became a veritable non-issue, and for the first time since childhood, I cared little about what I wore. All of our worldly possessions made little difference beyond what we carried in those small duffle bags. As a result, the contents of those bags became so much more important and much more appreciated.

After the first few challenging days of the tour and as we settled into our routine, some of the mundane pleasures of life, many of which we had previously taken for granted, took on new meaning. Limited to one cup of regular coffee each day by concerns about dehydration (as well as untimely urges to find a toilet), that singular beverage became a far more special treat. While riding down a secluded highway on a cool, cloudless morning, we came to appreciate the intense rays of the sun perhaps like never before. Sitting on a folding chair at an early afternoon SAG stop, unlike with the literally thousands I had almost unconsciously eaten previously, I savored the flavor and nourishment provided by a hastily assembled peanut butter and jelly sandwich. At the end of a challenging day, our bodies caked with a combination of sweat and road grime, a hot shower transcended its daily ritualistic quality to become a much-anticipated pleasure. It became an almost joyful activity to which we looked forward, a symbolic action signifying the completion of the day's ride. Similarly, a tallboy can of cold beer represented a treat we had earned, the frosty liquid appreciably slaking our hard-earned thirst. Nightly dinners, often of virtually no culinary significance, were savored, satiating real hunger born of long, hard days, a genuine longing and need for food we had not experienced in years.

These were simple joys, but we were truly living a simple life. Our days were at times very challenging, but Bev and I were both incredibly happy. Compared to our regular lives, we really had little—just our bikes, a few sets of clothes, and a few personal items. With such simplicity, our focus somehow changed and our minds became uncluttered.

Factors such as the excitement of what we were striving to accomplish, our almost constant exposure to glorious sunshine, and our enjoyable interactions with our fellow riders and the support guys undoubtedly clouded any direct correlation. But an odd version of what statisticians call an "inverse relationship" had developed: we were functioning with far fewer luxuries and material possessions, but we were somehow happier. What an unexpected and powerful concept!

As I reflect on these days long after our cross-country tour ended, I think we learned a critically important lesson. We found that when you don't have much, your appreciation for what you do have actually increases. And just as important, the little things in life take on a whole new meaning.

CHAPTER 4
WILL THIS STATE NEVER END?

The rides leading to rest day locations tended to be relaxed and almost festive affairs, and this short, forty-two-mile ride to the Texas Hill Country town of Fredericksburg was no different. Buoyed by the celebratory breakfast (and the lyrical sounds of Larry and Chuck, such as they were), we left Ingram, Texas in cold conditions that would in time turn into a beautiful day as we completed one of the most enjoyable rides of the tour.

The first ten miles of the route followed surprisingly busy city streets and then state highways through the large towns of Ingram and Kerrville before turning onto a series of "ranch roads," paved rural thoroughfares that in places were little more than one lane wide. Shortly after turning off a state highway onto one of those roads, we encountered likely the steepest hill of the entire tour, an incline of around one third of a mile that some of the riders with GPS devices suggested was a 17-18% grade, very steep. About halfway up, I glanced down at my Apple Watch to see that my heart rate had spiked to a level I couldn't, or at least shouldn't, sustain for very long. So I stopped and waited for Bev to arrive, and after catching our breath, we had little difficulty navigating the remainder of the incline. After that the hills were gently rolling, there was virtually no traffic on the narrow roads, and the pastures and fields were still green and beautiful on this sunny mid-October day. The ranch road on which we were riding passed through the front yard of different homes, with residents having to walk across the road to get to their garage. It was open range country, and we rode by different breeds of cattle grazing lazily alongside the road. I was wearing a red jersey, and though I can't attest to the veracity of the notion of bulls charging people wearing red, I was glad none of the ones we passed showed any interest in me or my attire. All in all, our ride through this rural portion of the Hill Country was relaxed and pleasant.

We arrived at our home for the next two nights, a Comfort Inn on the outskirts of Fredericksburg, at around 12:30 p.m., giving us one and a half days in this great location for some time off the bike. The motel was a bit isolated, around a mile from downtown, but with their attention to service, the support guys offered to shuttle us back and forth from the Main Street area, where most of the restaurants and attractions were located. Rest days were such a joy for a variety of reasons. Of primary importance was the opportunity to take a day off from riding, giving our bodies a little extra time to recover. Some riders were able to sleep later than usual, though Bev and I seemed to largely follow the same early-to-bed, early-to-rise schedules we had firmly established.

Riding through open range outside of Fredericksburg, Texas

Just as significant, however, was the return to a relatively normal existence that a rest day provided. For one day, we didn't have to pack our bags and move to the next hotel room. We could eat a leisurely lunch in the restaurant of our choice, and if we wanted we could enjoy more than the two beers to which we had limited ourselves on the days before we rode. Similarly, I could drink more than my customary one cup of regular coffee, the limit I had established due to concerns about dehydration. And on rest days we could just lounge around and do nothing if we wanted, though that seemed to seldom occur. In essence, our purpose was to ride across the country, but it was such a treat to not have to do so. Oddly, by the end of the actual rest days, we were typically becoming anxious to get going again.

Located around seventy miles north of San Antonio and eighty miles west of Austin, we found Fredericksburg to be a charming small city of around 10,000. Established in the 1840s, the German influence remains strong in the town's restaurants, museums, and architecture. Among the families of prominence in Fredericksburg was that of Charles Henry Nimitz, who built the now-famous Nimitz Hotel in the downtown area. The elder Nimitz is perhaps best known as the grandfather of Fleet Admiral Chester Nimitz, who famously served as Commander of U.S. Forces in the Pacific theater during World War II. The Nimitz Hotel has been restored and now houses the Admiral Nimitz Museum, which tells the story of the town's most famous resident. Even more notable is the striking facility built next to the hotel that serves as the home of the National Museum of the Pacific War.

After getting settled in our motel room and cleaned up, Bev and I walked a half-mile to Andy's Diner, an impressive breakfast and lunch spot that would soon be closing for the day. After a large lunch and a piece of pie, we began our leisurely walk back to the motel. It was a beautiful day, we had that morning completed a most enjoyable ride, and we had learned that we were closer to the end of the tour than to the beginning. Physically, we felt amazingly good, and as we strolled through this well-kept neighborhood, Bev and I felt a profound sense of happiness.

Back at the Comfort Inn, while Bev did some laundry, I spent some extended time cleaning and lubing both of our bike chains. Dinner was on our own for the next two nights, so that evening we were shuttled to the downtown area and had a very nice dinner at the Fredericksburg Brewery. We each had a different type of schnitzel, very prominent fare in this German-influenced town, and I had a couple of pints of a particularly good local pale ale while Bev had some wine. We met up with Ross, always an interesting dinner companion, and afterward we stopped for some frozen yogurt before catching a ride back to the motel. It had been a really good day.

After a particularly good night of sleep, we made a quick run to Walmart, where our main purchase was three bottles of Woolite, the detergent Bev used to hand-wash our cycling shorts and jerseys. We were then shuttled into town for the afternoon, where we sat on the shaded patio of a sports bar and shared a chicken schnitzel sandwich and an avocado salad, each a little unique and both very good. We took our time in this very relaxed setting because we had nowhere we had to be and nothing more to do to get ready for our next ride.

We eventually made our way to the National Museum of the Pacific War, a fascinating and truly world-class museum that, in our opinion, rivaled the National World War I Museum in Kansas City and the National World War II Museum in New Orleans. In addition to enjoying the countless quality exhibits that were offered, it was good to immerse ourselves for a couple of hours in something other than cycling. We concluded our tour of the museum complex with a walk through the beautiful Garden of Peace, a tranquil setting that had been gifted to the museum by the people of Japan. We left both impressed and amazed at such a high-quality museum in this small town in central Texas.

For our last dinner in Fredericksburg, we found a patio table at a small, upscale establishment called Otto's German Bistro. As the sun descended on a mid-autumn evening, the cooling temperature made us question our decision to eat outside, though the lush trees and chirping birds made for an idyllic setting. Bev ordered the Red Pepper Gnocchi and I the Wurst Plate (which I was informed was pronounced "verst plat"), an assortment of German sausages, sauerkraut, and different mustards. I wouldn't typically order such a dish, but as they say, "When in Fredericksburg . . ."

We returned to the motel rested and anxious to get back to riding. Fredericksburg had been such a neat location for a rest day, and quite honestly, we kind of hated to leave.

• • •

We left the Comfort Inn at around 8:00 a.m., the edge of the Hill Country ahead of us on a very hilly seventy-seven-mile route to Austin, the state capital. It was a challenging ride, with over 4,000 feet of climbing up long and at times steep hills followed by equally long descents, riding mostly on backroads. After one of the SAG stops in a state park, we came to a sharp descent to a "low-water bridge", which was basically a low spot where a small stream flowed over the road. We had been forewarned that water would be present, that the surface was "slimy" and thus slick, and that we should be particularly careful. Dutifully adhering to the support guys' warnings, Bev and I very carefully walked our bikes the fifty feet or so across the water, which was a little deeper than we had anticipated. Our cycling shoes and socks were soaked, though our shoes were cleaner than they had been when we left San Diego. We watched as a rider behind us decided to ride through the water and fell hard as he was crossing, uninjured though very sore the next day.

The route was for the most part simple except for a couple of critical turns, one of which I almost missed, not realizing we had reached the new road until we were almost past it. A couple of riders behind us missed that turn and ended up having to ride on a very congested highway to get to the hotel for the evening. We were able to remain on the route, but had to merge onto that same highway about a mile from the hotel. Traffic was heavy during the early part of the Austin rush hour, and driving lanes and the shoulder were constricted due to road construction. It was hectic, and after weaving around construction pylons for a longer distance than we anticipated, we were very happy to see Larry standing at the edge of the hotel parking lot waving us in.

Our lodging for the evening on the outskirts of Austin was a Hampton Inn, one of the nicest hotels we stayed in during the tour. Compared to some of the other chain motels and hotels we had been frequenting, Hampton Inns were a bit more upscale, and we enjoyed the larger rooms, nicer linens, and better breakfasts such establishments provided. After finding our room, we followed the ritual we had established before the rest day, with Bev getting cleaned up while I went in search of a couple of tallboy cans of beer. There was a convenience store just across the highway from the hotel parking lot, but the "official" pedestrian crossing was a good half-mile down the road. We had just finished a hot and hilly seventy-seven-mile ride, and I wasn't about to walk an extra mile to get to a convenience store that was maybe 100 yards away. So with rush hour traffic on the highway largely stop-and-go, I weaved across all six lanes of vehicles, made my purchase in the convenience store, and weaved back across those same six lanes. By nature, I am a risk-averse "rule-follower," someone who, before this adventure, would have probably walked the distance to and from the crosswalk. But I completed this admittedly mundane crossing without giving it much thought. In subtle ways I didn't even realize at the time, this journey was changing me.

Instead of going out to dinner, the support guys took our orders and had Italian food delivered. Though one might not connect the phrases "take-out," "Italian food," "Austin," and "quality" together, as we gathered around a large table in the breakfast area of the hotel, we found these meals to be surprisingly good and a nice change of pace. After enjoying Bev's penne pasta primavera and my chicken

Parmesan, we excused ourselves, and after a long and challenging day we were both in bed by 9:00 p.m.

Three of the other riders got to bed a little later that evening. Bev and I had traveled to Austin before, exploring the downtown area and its many sights and attractions, but on this trip, we wouldn't get close to the city center. The three riders, two of whom were from Europe and might never again have the chance to experience this unique city, decided after dinner to take an Uber to explore the bars and music halls along the famous Sixth Street, listening to a variety of musical acts and no doubt drinking a few beverages. They found the music to be outstanding and got back to the hotel after 1:00 a.m. A good time was no doubt had by all three, but at least one rider was noticeably hungover as the ride began the following morning. I have found myself in the throes of a hangover a few times in my life, but never in that condition did I get up early the next morning and ride a bicycle for eighty-two miles.

• • •

As we approached the end of the first month of our tour, our evening routine had become fairly established. After the team meeting, usually at 5:00 p.m., we almost always went to dinner as a group and were back to the hotel by around 7:00 p.m. We then checked our email accounts and took care of any preparations that needed to be completed for the following day's ride. We reviewed the upcoming route, and unless that route was particularly simple, I wrote down turn-by-turn directions and traced the route on Google Maps so I could visualize the sometimes complicated turns. Bev and I didn't watch a great deal of television on this trip, and there were several hotels in which we didn't even turn on the TV. We did, however, often individually watch shows on our iPads, though that often didn't last long because Bev was typically asleep by 9:00 p.m. and I typically followed no later than 10:00.

In my "regular life", I have found that I function best when I get at least six hours of sleep each night. Logic might suggest that riding a bicycle six to ten hours most days would create the need for more sleep, but on this tour, I mostly maintained my six-hour routine. As a result of my atypically early bedtime, I seldom slept later than 4:00 a.m., and it wasn't unusual for me to be awake by 3:00. With Bev typically sleeping until around 6:00 a.m., I oddly came to enjoy these early morning hours. Almost every morning I made my one cup of regular coffee for the day and then, depending on the amount of available time, I checked the internet sites I follow (*Kansas City Star, New York Times, Washington Post*, etc.), read whatever e-book I was reading on my iPad, and maybe caught up on the handful of TV shows I followed. Strangely, if I woke up particularly early, at around 5:00 a.m. or so I occasionally took a little nap, which I realize likely seems a little odd. I was initially bummed out by my early rising time, but those early morning hours became one of my favorite times of each day.

• • •

Our eighty-two-mile ride from Austin to La Grange, Texas was long, tough, and hectic. The support guys delayed the trailer opening to 8:30 a.m., late for such a long day, but a good call that allowed us to avoid much of the rush hour traffic. In recent decades, Austin has experienced dramatic growth, approaching one million in population and surprisingly, to me at least, becoming the 11th largest city in the nation. Though we remained on the outskirts of the city, the streets and highways on which we were riding were very congested. As a result, though we avoided the peak of rush hour, riding on the still-busy city streets was a bit hectic. The previous evening, I had listed all of the turns on the route and the list was more than a page long, so we were happy to get out of the city without getting lost.

We gladly left the hustle of city traffic and were soon riding on back roads and state highways. The second and third SAG stops were at the entrances to Bastrop and Buescher State Parks. We were given the option, "if we liked hills," of riding a little longer on a very hilly route between the two parks; we politely declined. After the second state park, we departed the highway at what was referred to as the "Smithville exit." This was of interest to Bev and me for two different reasons. First, we have for many years lived in the Kansas City suburb of Smithville, Missouri, and had never before been in another town with that fairly distinct name. Additionally, one of our favorite movies while our children were growing up was "Hope Floats," a film in which the character played by Sandra Bullock returns to her hometown of Smithville, Texas after having been publicly jilted by her husband. As we approached the exit, we were amused by a billboard that promoted Smithville as the "Home of Hope Floats."

It was another challenging day, made far more difficult by a strong and persistent southerly wind that, as we were riding primarily in an easterly direction, was seldom in our faces, but was a constant presence that kept pushing us all over the road. We eventually made our way to the Best Western on the outskirts of La Grange, Texas. For dinner, we were shuttled to the La Fuente Mexican Restaurant in town, another fine establishment that offered quality Tex-Mex food. The meal was good, but the highlight of the evening was the entertainment—karaoke in the adjoining bar area. Most noteworthy was somebody's (not sure if it was a male or female voice) rendition of the classic Commodore's hit "Brickhouse," recognizable only because of the background music. I had to give the singer credit for the courage being demonstrated, but it was reminiscent of one of those deliberately bad acts on the old version of "The Gong Show." I felt fortunate that this rendition of that song didn't dominate my thoughts on the following day's ride.

Team dinner in La Grange, Texas

In the early weeks of the tour, I was convinced I was maintaining my weight simply because of the quantity of food I was consuming each day. Whenever we checked into a hotel with a fitness room, another rider went looking for that facility, not to work out but rather to see if there was a scale. For probably the last fifteen years or so I have weighed myself each morning on the same scale in our bathroom. As such, I avoided checking my weight until I returned home to that same scale. Regardless, I was convinced I wasn't losing any weight. Then, about a month into the tour, another rider commented that my face looked thinner, intimating that I must be shedding pounds. Having been at least a bit overweight most of my adult life, I appreciated these comments, though I was still skeptical. When we returned home forty-nine days after leaving in late September, on the first morning in our house I finally weighed myself and found that I had lost fifteen pounds, or around a pound every three days during the actual tour. Bev lost weight as well, though she was already much closer to her ideal weight when we began the tour.

Such a pace of weight loss is not atypical, and amounts to a little more than two pounds each week. This seemed fairly natural, given the huge number of calories we were expending almost every day. I always wore an Apple Watch, using it primarily to keep track of mileage for navigational purposes. But in the background, the device was tracking calorie expenditures, and on the particularly long days of more than 100 miles, the workout summary indicated I had burned more than 5,000 total calories. Electronic devices tend to overestimate calorie expenditures, though with its different metrics I suspect the Apple Watch is more accurate than most. Still, riding such distances over hilly terrain, often into a headwind, would for a male weighing more than 200 pounds result in a massive expenditure of calories.

So, losing fifteen pounds over the course of a forty-six-day cross-country bike tour would seem reasonable—except for the enormous (and I do mean enormous) quantities of food I was consuming each day. At the typical hotel breakfast, I would have a large serving of whatever egg dish was being offered, a couple of pieces of sausage or bacon, a couple of pieces of toast or a biscuit and gravy if available, a piece of fruit, and some yogurt. On numerous occasions after such a breakfast I told Bev, "I think I'll have a waffle," and proceeded to make and consume a large waffle drenched in syrup. At each SAG stop, I typically consumed a granola bar of some sort, a banana or apple, occasionally a small bag of trail mix, and often a peanut butter and jelly sandwich. If there was a café or even a convenience store available around lunchtime, we typically had some sort of sandwich in addition to what we consumed at SAG stops. More days than not we had some sort of ice cream, often milkshakes with as much as a fourth of the calories we consumed on a typical day in our non-touring lives. Most days, at the end of each ride, we each had a large can of beer and often a bag of some sort of salty snacks. For dinner, I had huge chicken-fried steaks, large platters of Mexican food, and in general, large helpings of whatever item I selected for the evening. My point in this dietary description is not to highlight my massive, largely unhealthy diet, but rather to suggest that I lost, on average, a pound every three days while consuming such huge quantities of food. Bev's diet was healthier and less massive in quantity, but even her food consumption was rather impressive. In other words, we ate everything and as much as we wanted . . . and still lost weight.

After the tour, we returned home a week before Thanksgiving, so after the holiday season and by the first few months of the next year I had largely returned to my pre-tour weight. This even though in the year after we completed our cross-country ride, I didn't have a single chicken-fried steak . . . and not one milkshake.

• • •

We were a little excited for our next ride because the route from La Grange to our destination in Navasota, Texas was a relatively short sixty-six miles. (In retrospect, it seems amazing now that a sixty-six-mile route was considered a "relatively short" ride.) When we took our bikes to the trailer, we quickly realized we were in for a much more challenging day than we had anticipated. It was cool and overcast, as it would be most of the day, and the wind was howling from the northeast, meaning it was at best hitting us on our left sides all day long. After dealing with the wind all day and then crossing a series of shoulderless bridges on our way into town, we made it to the Best Western in Navasota around 3:15 p.m. After the team meeting, we walked to the Las Fuentes Steak and Grill, where Bev and I each had a small ribeye steak and a glass of wine. It was a substantial meal with the baked potato and salad bar, but as we walked back to the hotel, we stopped at a McDonald's for an ice cream cone. Again, and amazingly, a lot of calories in, but even more calories out.

· · ·

We woke up the next morning in Navasota to chilly temperatures in the upper thirties, overcast skies, and blessedly, for the first time in days, only slight breezes. We were in for one of the best riding days we had experienced in a couple of weeks. Before leaving, I had the last Texas-shaped waffle of this trip. Only in Texas had I ever seen waffles in the shape of the state, but this was the fourth such waffle iron we had experienced in our two weeks in the state, a rather odd way Texans showed their obvious pride in their heritage. The waffles tasted the same, but it was a neat novelty, nonetheless.

The first SAG stop of the day was in the parking lot of a Baptist church, one of seemingly hundreds of Baptist churches we passed as we rode through Texas. At the tour they had sponsored the previous spring, the support guys, who were always sensitive about these matters, had asked the custodian at this church if it would be permissible to park their two vehicles in the parking lot for an hour or so to support a group of cross-country cyclists and were told it would be okay to do so. Shortly afterward, a deacon of the church drove up and questioned Larry and Chuck about why they were parked in the church parking lot. When told they had received permission from the custodian, the deacon told the support guys that the custodian wasn't authorized to grant that permission. This wasn't a very large church, and who would have guessed it had such a complex organizational hierarchy? But this was an ideal spot for a SAG stop, so this time the support guys made sure to contact the appropriate authority (i.e., the deacon) ahead of time.

For the next twenty miles or so, we rode on the "Texas Forest Highway" through the Sam Houston National Forest. The road was flat and winding, with a minimal shoulder but also light traffic on this Saturday morning, and with huge stands of evergreen trees lining each side. With these tall, majestic trees and the sun not yet completely overhead, the road was largely shaded; it was truly a beautiful setting. In time, we made it to the second SAG stop in the quaint little town of New Waverly. When we reached the stop in the middle of town, we had just missed a parade of horses pulling covered wagons, a novel concept to us but evidently a not-so-rare event in this part of Texas. The temperature was still a little cool, so the support guys had purchased for each rider a cup of what the convenience store advertised as "Mexican Hot Chocolate", which was cocoa mixed with a little cinnamon. It was okay, and from my taste something to have at least once, but still a nice gesture on the part of Larry and Chuck. We still had around thirty miles remaining on the route, and the last twenty miles or so into our destination of Cleveland, Texas was slightly downhill and with a slight tailwind. It was a glorious way to end a Saturday ride.

We reached the Holiday Inn Express in Cleveland at around 3:15 p.m. and were told our room was not yet ready. While Bev sat in the lobby with our bikes, I walked a short distance to a convenience store to purchase a couple of tallboy Coronas (which was becoming our post-ride beer of choice). The act of walking to a convenience store wasn't out of the norm for me, nor was purchasing two large cans of beer. But as I strolled into that little convenience store in this small town in rural East Texas, I was still wearing cleated cycling shoes, black tights, and an iridescent yellow jacket designed for cycling, meaning it had a short waist and long tail. I literally glowed, and though no one said a word to me, the folks of Cleveland likely thought I looked more like an alien from outer space than one of the locals that typically patronized their store. In time we were able to get into our room, and after the team meeting we were driven to a little storefront restaurant called Bradley's BBQ. Bev and I each had a combo platter, mine with ribs, smoked turkey, chopped beef, beans, and potato salad. For a cafeteria-style barbecue joint, it was rather good.

•　•　•

On cool days, at each SAG stop riders were given the option of removing jackets, tights, hats, etc. that were necessary at the beginning of the ride but were no longer needed as the day got warmer. Each article of removed clothing was placed by the rider in a laundry bag and then redistributed at the team meeting later that evening. At the meeting in Cleveland, someone asked where the bag of discarded clothes was located, and Chuck, who kept the bag in the van he drove, indicated that he didn't know where it was. Both support guys indicated that they would find the discarded clothes and distribute them at dinner. Shortly thereafter we noticed Chuck leaving quickly, and as Larry drove us to the restaurant in the first of two groups, we sensed he was visibly shaken.

For the most part, the cycling clothes that Bev and I wore on the tour were purchased on sale from REI or at a Pearl Izumi Factory

Outlet, largely selected with value in mind. On the other hand, some of the jackets and tights the other riders wore were much more exclusive, often fitted specifically for them, with some costing hundreds of dollars. And we were several hundred miles from the nearest bike shop large enough to carry these items. In other words, here in eastern Texas, the value of the items in the missing laundry bag would be difficult to determine, but in the middle of a cross-country tour, many of them were priceless. After dropping us off at the hotel after dinner, Larry let us know that the bag of clothes was still missing, that Chuck had gone back to the location of the last SAG stop to look for it, but that it would likely not be found. He was very apologetic, said Trans-America Cycling would reimburse everyone for what was missing, and offered to take anyone to Walmart to purchase warm clothing to get them through the next few cold days. It had stayed cool enough all day that neither Bev nor I had removed any clothing, so we weren't impacted. And almost a month into the tour, the riders had developed such an appreciation for the efforts of Chuck and Larry to meet our every need that no one was particularly upset by what had transpired.

About a half-hour after we got back to the hotel we received a text message from Chuck, a touching missive in which he profusely apologized for losing the bag of clothes. These two guys had worked to properly plan every aspect of the tour, and this unanticipated episode had shaken the two support guys far more than any of the riders. Bev and I were particularly saddened about the pain Chuck was apparently feeling as a result of this seeming oversight, recognizing again the quality of individual he was. Then, about a half-hour later, we received a second text message indicating that the bag had been found (apparently, Chuck had forgotten he had placed the bag in his own luggage) and that the clothing would be delivered to the rightful owners. "No harm, no foul," as the saying goes, but Chuck and Larry had aged appreciably as this scenario played out.

In the four weeks we had been touring, we had grown close to several of our fellow riders. At the same time, we had developed a similar closeness with and deep appreciation for our two support guys.

• • •

As we entered the breakfast area of the hotel in Cleveland the next morning, we quickly noted that something seemed different. Other than Bev and me and the handful of riders getting their breakfast, everybody else seemed to know each other. They greeted one another, in some instances asked about family members, and even called each other by their first name. And then we noticed an older couple drinking coffee and reading a newspaper, and the gentleman was wearing a Walmart vest and name tag. We wondered aloud why someone would be staying at a Holiday Inn Express while working at a nearby big-box store, and then realized that we had entered a community of individuals who were actually living in this hotel.

Though we didn't realize it at the time, Cleveland was less than fifty miles north of Houston, and we passed through this area just two months after much of the southeastern part of Texas had been pummeled by one of the most destructive hurricanes in the history of the nation. Though Cleveland hadn't been hit particularly hard by Hurricane Harvey, its proximity to the devastated Houston made it a prime location to house families turned homeless by the storm, and these folks were being housed in this hotel by the Federal Emergency Management Agency, or FEMA. We would witness evidence of the tremendous destruction of this hurricane as the day progressed.

On this Sunday morning, our last full day in Texas, the trailer opening was delayed until 8:45 a.m. due to the forecast of cool temperatures, and as we walked out of the hotel, we quickly realized the forecast was correct. With the thirty-two-degree temperature to start the ride, Bev and I wore tights, long-sleeved base layer tops under our jerseys, jackets, and long-fingered gloves to start the day. It was truly cold, but temperatures warmed up quickly, and by mid-day we had shed our extra attire, confident that after the previous day's episode our discarded items would be well cared for.

With a sixty-nine-mile ride ahead of us, we were as usual the first to leave the hotel. Though a bit chilly, it was a nice morning to be riding on a road with wide and smooth shoulders and little weekend traffic. About five miles into the ride I heard Bev yell from behind me and looked back to see that she had another flat tire, again on the back wheel, which is the most challenging to change. About the time I had removed the punctured tube, Larry drove up in his truck, and then Chuck soon followed, staying with us until we were back on the road. With only some minor excitement, the remainder of the ride was largely uneventful.

That minor excitement occurred on a four-mile stretch of country roads where we encountered the first concentration of loose dogs we had faced on the tour. For bicycle riders with minimal protection (and clothing), dogs can pose a particular danger, and the larger and more aggressive the dog, the greater the potential peril. We had been wary of canine issues since leaving San Diego, but four weeks into the tour we had encountered just a handful of dogs, and Bev and I had not been directly targeted. That changed on this sunny afternoon in East Texas. We were riding through a largely impoverished area, and it seemed like every house had multiple large dogs running loose. It was reminiscent of the Bumpus dogs in the movie, *A Christmas Story*. A group of riders had immediately preceded us, no doubt getting all these mutts riled up, so they were ready for us. Our primary defense mechanisms against marauding dogs included trying to ride faster than they wanted to run (effective, depending on the motivational level of the chasing dogs) but especially yelling at the dogs, me with my deepest and loudest voice. This latter strategy seemed to work best, at least with these hounds. We survived unscathed, though not without about ten successive adrenaline rushes.

The last SAG stop was about ten miles from the hotel in Silsbee, and around a quarter-mile further down the road we came to a Dairy Queen. Needing to find a restroom, we stopped, and as a show of loyalty to the DQ brand, we naturally ordered milkshakes.

• • •

As we rode from Cleveland to Silsbee, Texas on Sunday, October 29, 2017, just over two months had passed since Hurricane Harvey had completed its destructive path through this part of Texas and nearby Louisiana. We had watched with great interest from our far inland home in Missouri as the hurricane slammed into Texas, departed back into the Gulf of Mexico, and then made landfall again, stalling and dumping staggering amounts of rainfall on the Houston area. Watching the loss of life and property was sobering, though it wasn't until afterward that we joined the rest of the country in grasping just how devastating this storm had been. It was even later that we began to ponder whether the effects of this hurricane might impact our cross-country tour, a truly minuscule issue compared to what people in this part of Texas were dealing with. Other than some anxiety these issues caused for the support guys, who had meticulously planned the route, meals, and especially lodging, the effects of Harvey did not impact our progress on this part of the tour.

That's not to say that our contact with the human and physical effects of the hurricane didn't leave an indelible mark on each of us. For those of us living in inland parts of the country, our knowledge of hurricanes has been largely derived from watching coverage on news channels like CNN. We have learned about the destructive impact of gale-force winds and storm surge, and Hurricane Harvey had plenty of each. But the greatest destruction of this storm came when it stalled while still pumping massive amounts of water from the Gulf of Mexico. Houston was drenched, but the greatest amount of rain fell in areas east and north of the city, just south of where we were riding. The greatest amount of rainfall was measured in Nederland, Texas, less than forty miles south of Silsbee, which was our destination for the day. During the four days of hurricane-related weather, this small Texas city endured over sixty inches of rain, a massively destructive amount of precipitation. Though this was the greatest measured amount, the entire region had experienced devastating rains.

As we left Cleveland on this crisp, cool October morning just weeks after the area had been ravaged, we at first saw minimal physical evidence of what had occurred. But as we approached Silsbee, we began to encounter sights we would not soon forget. We saw homes and other buildings with apparent water damage, and then eventually rode by homes in low-lying areas that appeared to have been largely submerged. Now uninhabitable, these structures would no doubt have to eventually be torn down. Even more striking were the scenes along streams, ravines, and other low-lying areas. We saw debris, trees, appliances, and occasionally even vehicles that had been carried by the massive flow of water, only to be randomly deposited as the waters eventually receded. And strangely, perhaps the most memorable sight for me was a chain-link fence with the fencing and support poles bent almost horizontal by the force of the rushing water. Chain-link fencing is largely permeable, meaning under normal conditions water can flow through it. But with no debris evident, the force of flowing water itself had apparently been sufficient to damage the fence in that manner. It was an odd recollection, but that chain-link fence showed us as much as anything the power of the destruction the folks in this area had experienced just two months earlier. And as Bev suggested, though the sun was shining, it felt like the entire area still had a dark and depressing storm cloud hovering over it.

But those were just the physical effects; we began to comprehend the human impact when we arrived at the motel in Silsbee. We had been forewarned by the support guys that this motel was another one of those lodging choices that represented the best available option. As we rode into the parking lot of a motel that outwardly looked much like some of the other establishments we had stayed in—not luxurious, but serviceable—another of the riders who had arrived before us walked by and commented, "I think we've reached a new low." We walked our bikes over to the trailer where Larry was unloading luggage and I noticed that his every move was being shadowed by a young boy. I initially thought that with his persona as a former middle school teacher, Larry had attracted this young boy of maybe ten or eleven to assist him. I joked to Larry, "It looks like you've got some good help." But we quickly realized that this boy, like many others staying (actually living) at this motel, was simply bored and enthralled by a set of new faces.

Larry had been given the keys to all of the rooms to be utilized by the group (keys rather than key cards, possibly providing our first evidence of how much this motel needed upgrading), and with our key in hand, we went in search of our room. After unlocking the door with the key we had been given, I opened the door and then heard the television and noticed a variety of items on the floor. A bit on edge anyway, and suddenly concerned about the possible reaction to our entering an occupied motel room, we quickly backtracked, closed the door, and soon found Chuck, who was distributing luggage. After hearing that we thought the room we had been assigned was occupied, he knocked on the door. A young lady in perhaps her twenties or thirties answered the door, and it appeared that she, perhaps her mother, and a child were occupying the room. This young lady and her family were living in this small, decrepit motel room. As I stood behind Chuck as he apologetically conversed with this individual, I was struck by how resigned she was to what was being thrown at her, indicating that incidents like what had just occurred were perhaps not that uncommon. I never learned about this young lady's story, where she had lived, and what specifically had befallen her. But we gained a sense that she and her family had lost all of their material possessions in the storm, had been forced to live in this downtrodden motel room, and that even this modest lodging didn't provide them with a sense of privacy and sanctity.

As Bev watched our bikes I walked with Chuck to the lobby, where he explained the situation to the lady at the front desk. She seemed neither surprised nor particularly concerned, and in handing him the key to another room simply said, "Here, try this one." We walked back to our new room next door to the one we had mistakenly been assigned, and opened the door to our accommodations for the evening. The room was dark and in disrepair, with broken furniture and peeling paint, and just terribly stark. However, we quickly checked the bedding and bathroom, both of which we had learned were key measures of motel sanitation, and found them to be adequately clean. While Bev showered, I walked next door to a gas station in search of beer and got a good look at our surroundings. This motel had been transformed into a makeshift apartment complex. Young kids were hanging out in the parking lot, searching for something to occupy their time. People were mingling outside their rooms, and trash, broken furniture, and old appliances could be seen all over the complex. These people had lost virtually all their material possessions and these decrepit motel rooms represented the only shelter available to them. It appeared that the dark and depressing cloud Bev had described had followed us to this motel. As I commented to Larry, "This is so sad, but at least we get to leave tomorrow morning. These people have to live here indefinitely." The human toll of this hurricane was real, tragic, and downright heartbreaking.

Dinner was on our own that evening, and Bev and I walked across the street to a Mexican restaurant called Casa Ole, where we were joined by two other riders. More of a gourmet than me, Bev had a spinach-stuffed chicken breast while I ordered another chicken-fried steak, which I considered appropriate for our last dinner in Texas. Equally fitting, the steak came on a separate platter, filling the entire plate and covered in gravy. Needing to maintain my strength for the next day's seventy-six-mile ride into Louisiana, I made sure to again clean my plate.

Waking extra early the next morning, I was particularly anxious to get going and to put this motel, Silsbee, and Texas behind us. Not surprisingly, there was no coffee maker in the room, so a little before 6:00 a.m. and with Bev still sleeping, I quietly left the room and walked the three blocks to McDonald's (on a dark highway with no sidewalk, which we had found was not uncommon in Texas). I got a variety of breakfast items for each of us. With no breakfast offered by the motel, this was far preferable to the instant oatmeal we would have had otherwise. We left the motel at 7:45 a.m., and for most of the day as we concluded our time in Texas, we faced flat roads, a slight tailwind, and decent surfaces, making our last three days in the state the best riding we had experienced since entering El Paso over two weeks earlier. Just a couple of miles after the last SAG stop of the day we rode across the Sabine River, which serves as the boundary between Texas and Louisiana in these parts, and with that, we had crossed our fourth state. With three other riders, we stopped for photos in front of a "Welcome to Louisiana" sign, and in general, with a rest day facing us the next day and this huge state mercifully behind us, we were feeling pretty good.

• • •

For the most part, everyone was glad to have Texas behind us; I know I was. I left Texas with decidedly mixed feelings about this huge, historic, and in so many ways amazing state. We saw some truly interesting sites—in El Paso, in areas just a few hundred feet from the border with Mexico, certainly during our time in Fredericksburg and the Hill Country, and other scenery along the way. Still, I may have been jaundiced as a bike rider by the bad roads, the rude drivers, and the abject poverty that seemed to permeate so much of the state, as well as the 75 mph speed limit on two-lane highways (and 80 mph on interstate highways). And though we interacted with some very nice Texans, we often noticed a subtle underlying current of superiority that was difficult to fathom. We admittedly steered clear of Dallas, Fort Worth, Houston, San Antonio, and most of the other cities that are viewed by many as the "Crown Jewels" of Texas, so we traveled through the lesser-known underbelly of the state. Nevertheless, we are glad we were able to experience this huge state in the manner we did, and we will never forget our extended time there.

We were happy to enter Louisiana. And though the completion of our crossing of Texas, more than two weeks and 1,000 miles, represented a milestone on this tour, we still had another thousand miles ahead of us before we would reach our destination in St. Augustine. First, though, our initial stop in this new state would present us with what in many respects was our most profound challenge of the entire forty-six-day tour.

LIFE LESSON #4
If you don't trust the goodness in the people you might encounter, you'll never get on the bike.

"In this world there is always danger for those who are afraid of it."

—George Bernard Shaw

don't know what brought forth the anger in the young man, no doubt never will, and he may not have really understood the reason himself. We were riding on some deserted state road in the middle of nowhere in the eastern part of Texas, encountering little traffic in this area dominated by large farms and ranches. It had been a pleasant day when a young man in an old pickup truck passed us, screaming words we couldn't discern but which were no doubt negative comments. As he stared at me with piercing eyes as his truck sped in front of me, he gave me what we now realize is the universal sign of disdain for cyclists: the middle finger. This obscene hand signal brings forth in some people a desire to retaliate, but for me, it simply raised my guard, a concern that this angry young man might double back and somehow do more to Bev and me than give us an insulting gesture. But after not seeing that beat-up old truck again for the next couple of miles, our pleasant afternoon ride continued without incident.

During our forty-six-day tour, we were passed by thousands, perhaps even tens of thousands, of vehicles, and the number of these obscene gestures directed toward us (at least that we noticed) could be counted on one hand. And at no point on this journey were we legitimately put in danger by the intentional actions of any of these drivers. Still, these incidents of being "flipped off" gave us pause, put us on guard for at least a little while, and at times caused us to wonder about the thoughts and motivations of the individuals on the other side of those middle fingers. The first occurred on a lonely federal highway in California in the early days of the tour, a day that caused me to ever-so-briefly focus on our vulnerability as we cycled our way across the country.

On the day Bev and I struggled as we traveled up and down the "bunny hop hills" in eastern California, we had encountered countless people without truly interacting with any of them. Riding through this barren, desert-like terrain with no other riders in sight, cellphone coverage that was spotty at best, and only isolated signs of civilization, we encountered sparse traffic that at times would back up due to what might be called "bottleneck" conditions. On this day, those bottlenecks were most often caused by us. With a very narrow shoulder on this two-lane highway, we were forced to ride on the edge of the actual driving lane. As we climbed any of the never-ending hills, most of the many cars, pickups, and tractor-trailer rigs patiently waited for us to crest the hill before passing. The lone exception was an angry young man who gave us a menacing look and the aforementioned middle finger as he passed. Otherwise, none of the drivers seemed, at least outwardly, to be too incensed by the resulting inconvenience.

Typically in this setting, as it would often be in other locales as we crossed the country on narrow roads, cars and the occasional large trucks would simply give us a little room and pass without much reduction in speed. But on rare occasions on this day in California, vehicles passed us a little closer and a little faster than we would have preferred. Not surprisingly, this caused my thoughts to stray in odd ways on this long, dry, and isolated day. With no visible signs of civilization for miles in any direction, there were no riders or support guys behind us, and on this winding highway with sparse traffic and a 65 mph speed limit, there was nothing to protect us from the unknown drivers we encountered. Bev and I were riding one behind the other, and any of the hundreds of cars and trucks that passed us could have run us over, perhaps purposely, and no one else would have known what had happened to us. It was admittedly a morbid and rather macabre thought, but riding a bicycle on a largely shoulderless highway with plenty of time to think can cause the mind to wander in strange directions.

Miraculously, or likely not so miraculously, not one time that day were we in any way threatened by any of these potentially homicidal drivers. When so many of them had the opportunity to pick off two pesky old bicycle riders, why were we able to survive the day unscathed? From my perspective, the answer to this only partially sarcastic question is fairly simple, but is also one that, in this day and age, runs counter to what we are sometimes led to believe: *almost all of the people we encounter in life are caring, and decent, and good.*

Particularly as a former history and government teacher, I am somewhat of a news junkie (just ask Bev). And though I don't profess to be the sharpest knife in the drawer, I am usually smart enough to discern what I am hearing on the local and national news broadcasts and channels. Unfortunately, not everyone is equipped with the filters needed to put everything they hear in its appropriate perspective. This is so important, because if I took to heart all of the bad news I heard every day, I might never leave the house. And even that could prove dangerous, given the ever-present threat of marauding thieves looking to break down our front door, kill us, and take all our stuff (which presupposes that anyone would actually want our stuff).

There are no doubt people outside of urban areas who believe that if they were to travel into the core of a major American city, they would probably get robbed if they were fortunate enough to not get murdered. Some internalize what they hear on the news to the point they are convinced that large groups of criminals want to come into our country similarly bent on wreaking lawless havoc on our society. These apprehensive people aren't necessarily bad folks; perhaps just narrowly-informed and maybe in some instances a bit prejudiced. To a large extent, they can't see beyond the negative side of human nature, particularly in people who may look or act differently from them.

Do murders occur? Obviously yes, though statistically, despite recent increases, the murder rate is lower today than when I was growing up. Does crime occur? Certainly, though again statistically, the violent crime rate in most parts of the country has largely continued to decline over most of the past quarter-century. Do we need to use common sense and keep our eyes open in situations that might be potentially more dangerous than others? Absolutely. But more importantly, do we sometimes assume, or fear, the worst in people and allow that assumptive fear to limit the scope of our lives and interactions? Yes—and that is so unfortunate. From my perspective, while no doubt there are unscrupulous, unsavory, and even dangerous individuals among us, that does nothing to dispel my belief that the vast majority of people in this world are fine and upstanding individuals with a much greater inclination to help me than to harm me. I strongly believed this before riding a bicycle from coast to coast, and that belief was only strengthened by my encounters with countless individuals in the process of completing that journey.

Which brings us back to our ride on that isolated, narrow, and undulating highway in the California desert. At that time, we were just five days into our forty-six-day trip, and Bev and I were still getting comfortable riding so close to high-speed highway traffic. My brief musings about a deadly encounter with some nefarious driver were fleeting, and I was soon able to focus my thoughts and efforts toward getting up and over all those damned bunny hop hills. We rode as far to the side of the road as we could and kept an eye on oncoming traffic through our eyeglass mirrors when possible, but otherwise operated under the assumption that those drivers passing us would do nothing to purposely harm us. If we had genuinely thought otherwise, then we should have remained barricaded in our home back in Missouri.

CHAPTER 5
RIDING THROUGH THE HEART OF THE DEEP SOUTH

I will forever remember DeRidder, Louisiana, our first stop in the state, primarily for three reasons: it was the location of the third of our four rest days; it was where we had a very memorable Cajun meal; and it was where, for a few intense hours in the middle of the night, I became deathly ill.

With a population of around 10,000, DeRidder is a rather nondescript town that is the birthplace of country music star Chris Cagle and novelist Jennifer Weiner. We wound our way through the western Louisiana town to find our hotel for the next two nights, the Best Western Plus DeRidder Inn and Suites. After our previous night in Silsbee, this genuinely nice and clean hotel might as well have been a part of the Ritz-Carlton chain (though Ritz-Carlton hotels aren't typically located next to a Walmart, as this hotel was).

At the team meeting, Larry and Chuck suggested that since we were now in Louisiana, we needed to have some Cajun food, a particularly new experience for the riders from Scotland and Denmark. So, we piled into the support vehicles and rode to Cecil's Cajun Café, a really neat restaurant in the downtown area of DeRidder. With no ride to worry about the next day, we had one of the most pleasurable meals of the entire tour, enjoying exceptional regional fare and relaxed conversation with a group that had really bonded over the previous month. Bev had a combination platter of various seafood dishes with a glass of wine and I had a large, pan-fried tilapia filet covered in a crab sauce and a large glass of Abita Amber, a noted Louisiana beer. It was excellent food served in a fun atmosphere, a truly memorable meal.

With few local distractions our rest day was particularly relaxing, working on our bikes, making a supply run to Walmart, and otherwise just lying around the hotel; it was, after all, a rest day. By this point in the tour, we had ridden nearly 2,000 miles, which was more than many cyclists ride in an entire year, certainly more than our typical yearly mileage. We had brought with us an extra set of tires, and with the tour two-thirds completed, we used the extra time to change out all four tires. With a good cleaning and lubing of our chains, we were ready for the last thousand miles to St. Augustine.

As we often did on rest days, we used this opportunity to take stock of how our bodies were handling the rigors of the long daily rides, particularly now that we were much closer to the Atlantic than to the Pacific Ocean. Astonishingly, we seemed to be holding up amazingly well. We both were dealing with sore rear ends, but with Chamois Butt'r and A&D Ointment as needed, we were preventing full-blown saddle sores from erupting. Bev in particular seemed to be adapting very well to the daily grind, and some of the other riders had commented on how well she was doing. By this third rest day, I had lost much of the grip in each hand from holding on to the handlebars for the six- to ten-hour riding days we had been experiencing. I also had a couple of what biking enthusiasts call "chainring tattoos," a common malady caused by clumsily getting off the saddle and having the front chainring on the bike rip a string of sores on the back of one of my calves. Such a wound is considered by some cyclists to be a badge of honor, but it represented to me a daily reminder of just how much of a klutz I could be. All in all, compared to what we might have feared when we left San Diego a month earlier, we were doing amazingly well. In some respects, though, that was about to change for one of us.

•   •   •

On our last evening in DeRidder, we walked across the highway to the Double D Steakhouse, one of those quaint little restaurants that offered on each table a bucket of peanuts in the shell. In addition to the peanuts, Bev and I each had a small steak filet, potato, and salad; a tasty dinner, but nothing too exotic. That would become a more relevant fact as the evening progressed. Afterward, we returned to the hotel to prepare for the next day's ride, a ninety-five-mile route to the small Louisiana town of West Bunkie. The forecast called for heavy rain all the next day, which would be our first really wet ride, so for the first time on this trip we broke out our rain gear.

It was October 31, and about an hour after returning to the hotel there was a knock on our door. We opened it to find Larry and Chuck delivering Halloween-themed cupcakes. Both cupcakes were angel food, but one had orange icing, which Bev quickly grabbed, and the other had deep, black, very thick icing. Very unfortunately, this would also become a more relevant fact as the evening progressed. We weren't particularly hungry, but it was a holiday, and the support guys had gone to all of this trouble . . . so we ate our cupcakes. I was struck by the intense black color of the icing. It's probably best not to know just how much food coloring was used to attain such a dark tint, but I ate my cupcake.

I went to bed around 10:00 p.m. with a touch of heartburn, but otherwise felt fine. Around 12:30 a.m. I woke up with what seemed like worsening heartburn, so I went into the bathroom for some antacid. I wasn't feeling great, but I had no idea what was about to quickly ensue. Without going into excessive grotesque detail, what ensued was diarrhea, and then dizziness and an absolute sense of fatigue. When Bev found me I was sprawled out on the bathroom floor, too weak and dizzy to get up. I was unable to lift my head enough to get to the toilet bowl (about a foot away) when I threw up what Bev would describe as a dark black mess. (Happy Halloween!) I felt much better, though Bev had to clean up the mess that I had made, likely ruining the white bath towels that were available. With my condition so much improved, I took a quick bath to make sure I was cleaned up, and then went back to bed. At that point, I thought I might even be able to ride the next morning. At 3:30 a.m., however, we went through the entire sequence again, though a handy trash can allowed me to avoid the sort of mess I had made earlier. I finally made it back to bed, totally depleted and barely able to move, and just like that my ride the following day would not happen. I'm not sure if I suffered from some sort of bug, or as Bev suspected, a bout of food poisoning, but at that point it didn't make much difference. I do know that I was so grateful that Bev had been there to take such good care of me.

When we woke up the next morning, Bev called Larry to let him know what had transpired and that neither of us would be riding that day. It was raining hard as the other riders left the hotel, and we genuinely felt bad for them. We hadn't necessarily been looking forward to riding in a downpour, but I know I would have preferred a long, ninety-five-mile ride in the rain to what I had experienced the night before. I was still feeling particularly weak, barely able to walk without using whatever wall was available for support. Following our unwritten agreement that if one of us didn't ride, neither would ride, Bev rode in the support vehicle with Larry as well. I was glad she was there to watch over me, forcing me to drink Powerade all day. (I drank multiple bottles, and had become so dehydrated that I never needed a toilet until the end of the day.) Riding in the reclined front seat of Larry's truck, we were mercifully able to get in our room at the Howard Johnson's in West Bunkie a little after 1:00 p.m. Still feeling spent and exhausted, I immediately crawled into bed and slept for a couple of hours.

• • •

For the riders, it was a long, wet, and horrendous day, with weather conditions varying only by the intensity of the rain. Navigating a complicated route can be challenging on a sunny day, and the steady rain made following the map much more difficult. One rider missed a turn and ended up riding an extra ten miles, and another made a wrong turn that added fifteen miles to the ninety-five-mile route. But to their credit, all the riders made it to the hotel unscathed. The incessant rain that finally stopped in the afternoon had wreaked havoc on everyone's bikes, so as all the riders cleaned and lubed their chains, Larry and Chuck took care of Bev's and my bikes. What great support guys!

After the team meeting, the riders walked to dinner at a nearby truck stop/casino. (We were now in Louisiana, after all.) I was beginning to feel better following a long nap, but I still wasn't ready to venture too far from the bed. Bev attended the meeting and dinner, and had told me she would bring back something bland for me to try to eat. She brought back a grilled cheese sandwich and a baked potato, and after eating all the sandwich and half of the potato, I was continuing to feel better. We decided that barring any setbacks, we would plan on riding the next day, a seventy-six-mile route from West Bunkie to New Roads, Louisiana.

• • •

As we began our ride the next morning there were overcast skies and some light fog, and I was feeling much better; not nearly back to normal, but hopeful that I would be able to complete the day's ride. Luckily, the day was largely uneventful, with almost completely flat roads, though some in poor shape, and occasional headwinds. As we rode from one parish to the next, we seemed to be experiencing the essence of the true Louisiana. We rode by vast fields of sugar cane, a crop we hadn't realized was so prominent in the state. We saw standing water virtually everywhere, and no doubt associated with that water, we also saw huge mosquitoes. Though they didn't bother us as we rode, we were quickly swarmed whenever we stopped. We were riding through poor areas, with far more rundown homes than nice ones, and at times as we rode through the countryside it seemed we might ride through Bon Temps, the fictional Louisiana setting of the HBO series "True Blood."

Though the support guys assured us that there was no hidden meaning, the first SAG stop was situated in front of a funeral home in the little town of Simmesport. The second stop was situated in front of a senior citizen's center in Inness, an appropriate setting given the age of most of the riders (as well as the way some of us felt). After that second stop, we crossed the Atchafalaya River on a huge but narrow bridge that seemingly went straight up (not really, but it seemed that way at the time) and then straight down, the largest hill we would face that day.

SAG Stop in Innis, Louisiana

It was a warm day and very humid (the days of 8% humidity in the desert seemed so far behind us), and by the time we got to the Cypress Inn in the small city of New Roads, we were tired and dripping with sweat. But we had made it, a feat that had seemed so doubtful just a day earlier. There was a Sonic Drive-In next to the hotel, and in a reversal of roles, while I got cleaned up, Bev walked over and got me a milkshake and her a large iced tea. The restorative powers of a chocolate milkshake were impressive, and my recovery from whatever had ailed me two nights earlier continued as a result.

After the team meeting, we walked a short distance to a large, shed-like building with a brightly lit sign in front advertising the establishment as "Hot Tails." Though Hot Tails sounds more like the name of a strip club, it was actually a Cajun restaurant with a sign above the door that proclaimed, "Hard Core South Louisiana Cuisine."

And it was. Not wanting to tax my still-delicate stomach, Bev and I both ordered the gulf shrimp over sautéed vegetables. While the shrimp were spicier than I had anticipated (it was a Cajun restaurant, after all) and the vegetables were a little heavy, both were very tasty and filling, and happily, my tender insides didn't revolt. Not wanting to press my luck, I had water with my meal while Bev enjoyed a local beer. As we walked back to the hotel, I felt better than I had since that fateful night in DeRidder.

• • •

A McDonald's was located a couple of blocks from where we were staying, and because the hotel didn't offer breakfast, I was there just after the restaurant opened at 6:00 a.m. We had a big day ahead of us, a hilly ninety-two miles to Amite, Louisiana, and we felt we needed a bit more fuel than would be provided by the instant oatmeal and muffins offered by the support guys. We were approaching the final stages of this long tour, and we realized that although there would be back-to-back eighty-five and eighty-six-mile rides in Florida, the next two days would be the last truly formidable challenges. This day's hilly ninety-two miles would be followed the next day by the longest ride of the tour, an equally hilly 110 miles that would take us into Mississippi. After that, we had a couple of relatively short days leading up to our last rest day destination, a Gulf-front hotel in Orange Beach, Alabama. But first, of course, we had two particularly tough days to get through.

As we left New Roads just after sunrise, it was a little misty and very foggy, with the Mississippi River very close to where we had stayed. We were glad to have flashing taillights, though the highway on which we rode had a smooth, wide shoulder. About ten miles into the ride we came to the James J. Audubon Bridge, a modern, two-mile span across the river. At its peak, the cable-stayed bridge was over seventy-five feet above the Mississippi, with two sets of massive towers rising at least twice that high above the bridge surface. As we approached the span, we encountered thick fog, but sensed we were about to climb a massive structure. At the peak of the bridge, we couldn't make out the top of the towers because of the fog and could barely see the river below.

The first SAG stop was in the small town of Jackson, Louisiana, a little burg of less than 4,000 that reeked of history. Founded in 1815, early in its history Jackson had a reputation as an educational center, earning the name "The Athens of the South." According to local legend, Andrew Jackson and his troops camped at this location after the Battle of New Orleans. Chuck had proven himself to be a master of miscellaneous and eclectic information, and on this day he told us that we were riding on the birthday of the Earl of Sandwich, and that to commemorate such a momentous occasion, Subway restaurants were offering buy-one, get-one-free sandwiches—and that there was a location on the route as we were leaving town. When we reached the local Subway, we stopped and bought a couple of sandwiches to have later in the day; we simply couldn't pass up a BOGO deal that would honor the Earl of Sandwich in the process.

We would find that on this long day, we needed those sandwiches. After several days of riding on flat roads we had to get reacclimated to the constant rolling hills we faced on the long route to Amite, as well as the 110 miles to Wiggins, Mississippi the following day. As a result, it was a long, hot, and very humid day, and by the time we arrived at the Amite Comfort Inn, we again were both exhausted and soaked with sweat. It had been a day of backroads and many turns, each of which represented an opportunity to get lost. Add in some detours around road construction, and it was a particularly challenging day. We had devoted quite a bit of time the previous evening to studying the route and writing down each turn and the estimated distance on each road, so we were able to avoid any wrong turns. Not so for one of the other riders, who got lost twice—the second time ending up in Mississippi. He was shuttled back to the route each time, but his ride had been terribly frustrating. He rode with us much of the way into the last town; I suspect he felt that with us, he might have a better chance of not getting lost a third time. He had a great attitude about his rather wandering ride, but it had been an especially tough day for him.

Amite, Louisiana was like the countless other small towns and cities we stayed in on this tour, one in which our experiences were largely limited to eating and sleeping. And in this instance, a little unwanted middle-of-the-night excitement. Dinner was "rider's choice," meaning we could eat wherever we wanted. Bev and I were both exhausted and not interested in any elaborate dinner plans, so we walked to a nearby Wendy's and brought back to the hotel for each of us a large salad, chili, and a hamburger. It was a lot of food, but with a couple of Blue Moons, we were able to eat it all. We were tired and had the longest ride of the tour ahead of us, so in need of a good night of sleep, we both went to bed earlier than usual.

Our sleeping plan was progressing quite well until around 2:30 a.m., when we were awakened by the shrieking sound of an alarm. We dutifully put on some clothes and took the stairs to a side door, then congregated with several of the other riders in the parking lot, watching as the Amite Fire Department arrived in full force. It was luckily a cool but dry evening, as we weren't allowed back in the building for what seemed a longer time than it actually was. We would learn that in a first-floor room a bag of microwave popcorn had been overcooked, creating enough smoke to trigger the alarm. We were eventually allowed to reenter the hotel, but time and excitement precluded a return to sleep. While Bev tried to get a little more rest, I resumed my early morning routine while lamenting that I wouldn't begin this longest of long days with as much sleep as I had hoped.

Leaving Amite, Louisiana on the longest ride of the tour

With the longest ride of the tour ahead of us, we left the hotel at 7:30 a.m. It was again foggy and soupy, and after riding a mile or so, our glasses were covered with water. Bev is far-sighted and can ride without glasses, but my extreme nearsightedness makes riding without glasses a distinct hazard. We assumed that at 7:30 on a wet and foggy Saturday morning, traffic would be minimal for the twenty-six miles to the first SAG stop in the little town of Franklinton. But as we left Amite, cars and pickups were bumper-to-bumper on the road on which we were riding. We soon learned that this was the date of the annual "25-Mile Yard Sale" between Amite and Franklinton, and as any yard or garage sale veteran can tell you, the best bargains go to those who get there early. And they did, with hordes of ardent shoppers. Cars and trucks were all over the place, and in some stretches, yard sales seemed almost continual. Despite the fog and mist, traffic (car and pedestrian), and lack of a shoulder on which to ride (due to parked vehicles), this slow, two-hour ride ended up being a neat experience, in some odd respects almost a cultural phenomenon. Despite the dreary conditions, we saw some good people attending an event many had eagerly anticipated since the last first Saturday in November. As we rode by one of the countless groups walking along the road on their way to the next yard sale, a youngish woman pointed her finger at us and said with what we hoped was mock sternness, "Now, y'all make sure you're careful out there." We assured her that we would. We had never experienced anything approximating a "25-Mile Yard Sale," much less on bicycles and in the mist and fog. It made for a surreal memory and was an odd highlight of the tour.

Shortly before the first SAG stop, the mist stopped falling and the fog lifted, though it would mercifully remain cloudy until the early afternoon. The second SAG stop was in a commercial area of Bogalusa, on the far eastern border of Louisiana. It was around lunchtime on this longest of days for us, so Bev and I walked the short distance to a Hardee's restaurant, where we again looked for the healthiest item on the menu. We each had to settle on the grilled chicken club sandwich with cheese and bacon. We had a sense of déjà vu, thinking back to the Carl's Jr.-induced heartburn at the end of the first day of the tour, and as such were unsure whether this lunch selection would create challenges for us as the ride continued; fortunately, it did not.

Shortly after leaving Bogalusa, we crossed the Pearl River and entered Mississippi. We had completed the crossing of our fifth state and now entered our sixth, but it was otherwise an inauspicious event. The remainder of the afternoon, almost sixty miles of riding, took place on an intricate network of backroads and county highways. I had written down each turn and distance, filling an entire page, and many of those turns were poorly marked and in obscure parts of the Mississippi countryside. Luckily, we never got lost on this incredibly long day that was made worse by the humidity and later in the afternoon by the return of sunny skies. But the roads were good for the most part, traffic in most areas was light, and in some parts the scenery was impressive. This was a large logging area, and we rode through huge, impressive stands of evergreen trees that seemingly created a narrow ribbon of road to pass through. There was a surprising number of huge lakes fronting large, beautiful homes that reflected on the water's surface.

It was a day of interactions, both with dogs and with the people of Louisiana and then Mississippi. We dealt with several dogs, including one in particular that kept coming at me as I tried to speed away from him. Earlier in the tour, I had jokingly commented at dinner with the other riders that if we got chased by a large dog, I didn't have to ride faster than the dog—I just had to ride faster than Bev. (I think Bev found this to be at best mildly humorous.) This dog, though, was tenacious, continuing to bark and growl as he nipped at my heels. He finally gave up, and I felt a sense of relief as I slowed to catch my breath. But then I realized that Bev, who was riding behind me, would probably be the next target of this large, pesky mutt. I stopped and turned around, ready to ride back to help her, but watched with a combination of relief and befuddlement as the dog barely gave her a disinterested look as she rode by.

I got an admiring whistle from a couple of young women in an old pickup truck, though I am confident it was meant more as a joke than the result of being impressed by the sight of this grandpa in a pair of tight cycling shorts. We were "flipped off" by a young man in an old, beat-up car, evidently incensed only by our presence on the narrow shoulder. Still, being the brunt of such resentment out in the middle of nowhere was momentarily unsettling. But even this was greatly overshadowed by our interaction with the two gracious older women at a stoplight as we were leaving Bogalusa. One rolled down her window and asked with a big smile, "Where y'all coming from?" When Bev said, "San Diego," this nice lady responded with amazement, "Oh, my word!" These two nice ladies wished us safe travels as they sped off to continue their day. On a challenging day, interactions like this one sustained us for several miles.

We plodded on, taking our time and trying not to push too hard, and after ten hours of riding, 110 miles, and around 3,000 feet of up-and-down climbing, we finally made it to the Hampton Inn in the Mississippi town of Wiggins. We were exhausted, justifiably more tired than we had been at any other time on this trip, but we were elated to have arrived at our destination for the evening and to have completed the last truly daunting obstacle of the tour.

It was approaching dusk as we arrived at the hotel, so we quickly got cleaned up and settled, attended a quick team meeting in which everyone seemed particularly tired, and then were shuttled to a McAlister's Deli for dinner. To commemorate our second and last "century" ride, the support guys included with the meal for everyone a dessert of their choice. Bev leaned over to me and demurely asked, "Do you want to share one?" I politely but firmly responded, "No." So we each had a large piece of cheesecake topped with strawberry sauce. Altogether, it was a huge amount of food that we both were able to consume fairly easily. Heading back to the hotel, despite feeling full after such a large meal and sore enough to struggle to get in and out of the truck, all in all we were feeling surprisingly good. While we weren't anxious for this grand adventure to end, we were now confident we were going to make it to the Atlantic.

• • •

As Sunday, November 5 arrived in Wiggins, we reverted to standard time as daylight savings time ended. The good news was that we had theoretically gained an extra hour of sleep; for me, though, it simply meant that I woke up even earlier than usual. The hour that we "gained" would be "lost" again as we entered the Eastern Time Zone as we worked our way across the Florida panhandle.

Ahead of us was a relatively short sixty-nine miles to Pascagoula, Mississippi. Tired and a little sore from our just-completed 110-mile ride, this day would prove to be far more challenging than we might have anticipated. As we left the hotel and headed south toward the Gulf coast, it was foggy, very muggy, and virtually windless. The roads were good, with little traffic on this sleepy Sunday morning, and in no time the fog had lifted, though the overcast skies helped diminish the effect of the rising temperatures, at least until later in the afternoon. About halfway into the ride, as expected, the terrain became more suburban and the roads busier, in part as we watched well-dressed Mississippians driving home from church in the early afternoon. In time we passed under Interstate 10 (which we had been riding alongside off and on since California) and noticed a dramatic increase in traffic as we entered Ocean Springs, a waterfront community across the bay from Biloxi. We needed to make a left-hand turn onto U.S. 90 (which we had been following since Texas), and to do so we needed to cross three lanes of backed-up traffic, which at this point seemed daunting if not impossible. But it had to be done, so we worked our way to the turn lane and moved onto the highway that we would follow to Pascagoula. We soon found the source of much of the traffic as we passed what was proclaimed as the "Largest Arts Festival in Mississippi and the Gulf Coast," which was impressive almost on the scale of the 25-Mile Yard Sale.

We rode the last twenty miles on the very busy U.S. 90 through an area that in many parts had an almost urban feel. The highway was flat, straight, busy, and long, and in time we became more fatigued (a result of the past few long days, and for me, maybe a minor byproduct of the illness earlier that week). We decided we needed some good ice cream and began looking for a Dairy Queen, our ice cream venue of choice on this trip. When after a few miles we hadn't come across a Dairy Queen, we decided we would welcome any good ice cream. Our standards falling as our need for an energy boost continued to increase, we ultimately pulled into a McDonald's for an ice cream cone (Bev) and a chocolate shake (me). That was the boost we needed, and soon we were riding on the causeway leading to the ship-building city of Pascagoula, Mississippi.

Just after passing a sign honoring Pascagoula's most famous son, Jimmy Buffett, and right before entering the downtown area, we came to a huge, impressive bridge spanning an inlet from the Gulf of Mexico. Not uncommon in the Gulf area, this bridge was very tall and peaked at the top to allow large vessels to pass under. It was a very steep incline, but we quickly handled it with little difficulty. At the top of the bridge, some areas protruded from the structure to allow pedestrians and bicycle riders to view the shipbuilding facilities and the Gulf further in the distance. As I approached the top of the bridge, I started to look for a good place to stop to take some photos from such a stunning vantage point. Moving slowly, I didn't notice a large drainage grate with openings that ran parallel with the highway. Before I realized what was occurring, my bike suddenly stopped and I felt myself doing a quick, crude somersault over the handlebars with the bicycle ending up on top of me. I quickly realized that my front tire had slipped into one of the openings on the grate. I was clearly at fault, as I should have been watching the road in front of me rather than the distant scenery (though admittedly I have yet to discern the functionality of a drainage grate at the apex of an extremely steep bridge). Bev was riding right behind me and watched all of this transpire, and later said it was like watching me fly over my handlebars in slow motion. She got to me almost instantly. Two men in two pickup trucks also saw this occur, and in a very caring gesture, stopped their vehicles and turned on their emergency blinkers to ensure no oncoming traffic came near us. We thanked them profusely for their care and concern. I was rattled, but other than some scrapes and scratches and then stiffness and soreness the next day, I was okay. I quickly realized just how lucky I was, as I could have easily broken a bone or landed on my head, causing a concussion or some other injury, ending my tour just as we were preparing to enter our final state. But we had lived to ride another day. We quickly checked my bike, and finding it still in good working condition, we rather timidly rode the last mile to our hotel.

• • •

When we arrived at the Hilton Garden Inn in Pascagoula, another of what had been a string of really nice hotels, our rooms weren't yet available. Still a little shaken from our incident on the bridge, we were both in need of an adult beverage. While Bev watched our bikes, I asked someone at the front desk where the nearest con-venience store was located. He replied that there was a store about a quarter-mile from the hotel (it was probably closer to a half-mile), so in biking shorts and jersey and cleated cycling shoes, and with a little dried blood still on my elbow, I walked there along the side of the road in this little Mississippi city. With a couple of cold Dos Equis tallboys in hand, I made it back to the hotel to find that our room was ready.

The support guys took restaurant and lodging selections very seriously, and for past tours, they had taken riders to a restaurant they considered to be just "so-so." As the riders were riding into Pascagoula, Larry was checking out a new spot that had been rec-ommended to him by the locals. After a quick team meeting, we all climbed into the support vehicles and rode through what seemed like a particularly depressed part of town to a nondescript business called Bozo's Market and Grill. In this concrete building, we had the most memorable dinner of the entire tour. We never found out who Bozo was, and though there was a little market, we didn't see anything that had been grilled. But we found out that this rather odd place had recently been named one of the "top ten seafood dives" in the United States and had been featured in a review in *USA Today*. In a region known for seafood, it clearly had its bonafides. We walked in with a bit of amazement, and though a traditional long table in the center of the restaurant had been reserved for our group of eleven, most of the other tables were crude and had a large, round hole every few feet or so, with a trash barrel under each hole into which shells and other trash could be thrown. The atmosphere was fairly raucous and the diversity of clientele was impressive. In this very unique establishment, we walked up to a young lady seated at a card table who took our order and wrote it down on a white paper bag, and then we took that bag to another young lady at the cash register at the front of the building. As we weren't sure how all this worked, Bev and I each made what we thought would be a safe selection and ordered the seafood platter, which we assumed included a little bit of every seafood item they offered. When our names were called, I walked up to the window to get our food, which had been placed in the same white paper bag on which the order had been written. Our food had been jammed into extra-large (really huge, larger than we had ever seen) compartmentalized white Styrofoam containers, packed so full that masking tape had to be used to keep it from bursting open. When we did open the containers, we found mounds of deep-fried shrimp, fried oysters, different kinds of fish, and deep-fried crab clusters. Underneath the fish and some wax paper were coleslaw, baked beans, fries, and hush puppies. Of course, there were all kinds of different sauces in crude dispensers on each table. It was a massive amount of food, which Bev couldn't finish but which I did. It was amazing, authentic, and a real taste of the Gulf Coast. To honor the setting, Bev and I each had with our meal a can of Pabst Blue Ribbon beer.

As we huddled just outside the restaurant's front door in the cool Mississippi air, waiting for the others to finish their meals, we were filled both with fried seafood and memories of a meal that was extraordinary in so many ways.

• • •

Though still a bit full from the seafood bounty of the previous evening, we were able to consume a nice cooked-to-order breakfast in the hotel's lobby as we prepared for the sixty-eight-mile ride to our rest day location in Orange Beach, Alabama. Though we didn't realize it at the time, we were embarking on one of the best riding days of the entire tour, one that was relaxed, stunningly picturesque, and very memorable. After departing Pascagoula, we rode through the Mississippi backcountry toward the first SAG stop in the fishing town of Bayou La Batre, crossing into Alabama in the process. This town of around 2,500 is best known (at least to me) as the hometown of Bubba Blue, the large-gummed Army friend of the title character in the movie "Forrest Gump." It was also the location of the headquarters of the Bubba Gump Shrimp Company, for which Forrest served as a "shrimpin' boat captain." Bayou La Batre is a neat little hamlet that reeks (figuratively and literally) of the fishing heritage that still serves as its lifeblood. To provide a little local flavor, at the SAG stop the support guys offered "MoonPies," a southern favorite that combines marshmallow, graham cracker, and chocolate. Strictly to show my appreciation to Larry and Chuck for their thoughtfulness, I ate a MoonPie, a cultural experience I won't now need to repeat.

Leaving Bayou La Batre, we rode on a beautiful tree-lined coastal highway, then along the edge of a peninsula, and finally on an elevated causeway with views of Mobile Bay surrounding us. We crossed another steep and impressive bridge similar to the one we had crossed into Pascagoula and then onto Dauphin Island, Alabama, a neat little barrier island with Mobile Bay to the north and the Gulf of Mexico to the south. It is perhaps best known for its bird sanctuaries and Fort Gaines, a fort built in the 1800s that was first captured by Confederate forces early in the Civil War, then recaptured by Union forces during the Battle of Mobile Bay in 1864. In that battle, Union Rear Admiral David Farragut purportedly gave the order, "Damn the torpedoes, full speed ahead," or something similar to this famous phrase, just a few hundred yards from the shore of Dauphin Island.

There are just two ways to travel on to and off of Dauphin Island: the causeway on which we had just ridden and some sort of boat. At the team meeting for this route, the support guys had stressed that we needed to make sure we made it to the tip of the island by 12:30 p.m. to catch the ferry that would transport us across the bay to the peninsula on which we would ride to our hotel on Orange Beach. Literally not wanting to miss the boat, we arrived a good hour before the departure time, sitting in the shade as we ate the sandwich Bev and I had purchased at a convenience store on the island. The ferry arrived on schedule at around 12:15 p.m., and after several vehicles disembarked, several others, including those driven by Larry and Chuck, drove onto the large vessel. With all of the cars and trucks parked and secured, the nine riders walked our bikes onto the ferry, which soon after departed the island to cross Mobile Bay to Fort Morgan (strategically the counterpart to Fort Gaines), where our ride would continue. It took around forty minutes for the ferry boat to make its way across the bay, and on a beautiful day, it was a nice and welcome respite from riding. We saw large oil rigs in the bay, huge cargo ships, and dolphins playfully swimming alongside the ferry. It was a truly special experience.

Mobile Bay Ferry on Dauphin Island, Alabama

In time we docked at Fort Morgan, disembarked, and after the second and last SAG stop, departed for the last twenty-five miles to the hotel on Orange Beach. Bev had been experiencing some issues with her bike, and the folks at a local bike shop had told Larry that they could guarantee the bike would be fixed the next day, our rest day (in time for us to leave the Gulf Coast the following day) only if we brought it in before they closed. We pushed the pace to make sure we arrived at the hotel with ample time to get the bike to the shop. We rode on a stretch of road called "Alabama's Coastal Connection," passing by countless Gulf-front homes through areas that seemed almost rural. We have always found spending time at the ocean (or the Gulf of Mexico) to be restorative, easing any stresses we had been feeling. As such, the sea breezes cooling us on this warm and humid day made for a pleasant riding environment. In time, the population became denser and the traffic more hectic, and eventually we made the turn onto Perdido Beach Boulevard. With a protected lane for cyclists along much of the route, we saw gorgeous views of the Gulf, passed by parklands with trails and sand dunes, and as we entered the resort town of Gulf Shores, passed restaurant after restaurant, touristy shops, and high-rise condos and hotels. Though it took longer than we had anticipated, we eventually entered Orange Beach and made our way to our hotel for the next two nights, a Hampton Inn with balcony rooms overlooking the beach and the Gulf. It was a wonderful location for a rest day.

Along with another rider who was having some minor mechanical issues, Larry drove us to the bike shop with plenty of time to spare, and both bikes would be ready as promised the following afternoon. We returned to the hotel, and after a quick team meeting, Bev and I headed across the highway to a bustling restaurant called Ritollo's Pizza. The next two nights were "rider's choice" for dinner, and as we walked through the hotel lobby we noticed another rider, so we invited him to join us. We asked for a large patio table and ate under a beautiful clear sky on a gorgeous night on the Gulf Coast. Soon another rider joined us, and then another, and then two more, and eventually seven of the nine riders were eating pizza and drinking beer around that outside table, making for a very enjoyable evening under the stars. We finally excused ourselves, with many of the remaining riders ordering one last round. As we made our way back to the hotel we passed a Dairy Queen and stopped to get some ice cream to top off an enjoyable evening.

Touring the National Naval Aviation Museum, Pensacola, Florida

The morning of our rest day we woke up at a characteristically early hour, and as most of the hotel's inhabitants were still sleeping, Bev was able to do a couple of loads of laundry. Afterward, we had a nice and very leisurely breakfast on the back patio overlooking the Gulf. It was such a beautiful and memorable setting, with the sun still low in the sky and breezes blowing in from over the water. Orange Beach is located just a short distance from Pensacola and the Pensacola Naval Air Station, home of the Blue Angels, one of the most famous precision flight teams in the world. The team was in town for an air show the following weekend and had scheduled a public practice session for 11:00 a.m. on our rest day. After breakfast, the two support guys and five of the riders drove to Pensacola, only to find when we arrived that due to weather, the practice had been moved to 2:00 p.m.—too late for us to stay. But also on the base is the National Naval

Aviation Museum, a huge and impressive collection of aircraft dating back through the history of air operations of the U.S. Navy. Visiting the museum with us was Jim, retired from the Air Force, who was a wealth of information about many of the aircraft we viewed. A highlight was a retired version of "Marine One," the helicopter utilized by the President. Larry took a photo of Bev and me as we exited the copter, waving to our constituents. We watched an interesting IMAX film entitled "Aircraft Carrier," sharing the huge auditorium with groups of school-aged kids on field trips to the museum. As retired educators, spending time around children on a school day always reminded Bev and me of our previous careers, and in this instance, of how fortunate we were to be spending our days riding our bicycles across the country, rather than dealing with a plethora of frustrating issues and problems as we had in our professional lives.

We left the naval base in the early afternoon after spending several hours at this impressive museum. After picking up Bev's bike, we made our way back to the hotel. I cleaned and lubed my bike chain and then we took a walk on the beach, again feeling a great sense of gratitude to be at this place at this time in our lives. We walked across the street to a nice restaurant called Gilbey's Seafood and Steaks, where we each had a relaxing meal. On this "rider's choice" evening we had dinner by ourselves for the first time on the tour, and while we enjoyed our time together, we honestly missed dining with the other riders. We were increasingly realizing how, in just over a week, it was going to be difficult to leave these nine people to whom we had grown closer than we might have ever anticipated.

• • •

As we prepared to leave Orange Beach after our final rest day, we had eight days and just under 500 miles ahead of us as we made our way across Florida. All the riders had looked forward to spending two nights on the beach at a beautiful hotel overlooking the Gulf. But as we prepared to enter our final state, the mood among the riders was changing. We had been riding for almost six weeks, and the novelty of the daily grind had largely worn off. We were mostly ready to finish this epic journey, but a small part of each of us dreaded that inevitable ending.

Contrary to earlier rest days, we had a sense of confidence that we would make it to St. Augustine, knowing now that we could reach that ultimate destination simply by putting the miles behind us each of the next eight days. Just four days later, that sense of confidence would be instantly and tragically shattered in an accident that would completely redefine our cross-country tour.

LIFE LESSON #5
A rough and almost unrideable road often becomes much smoother when you cross into a new county or state.

*"I cannot say whether things will get better if we change;
what I can say is they must change if they are to get better."*

—Georg Lichtenberg

As we traveled along some otherwise nondescript county road in Mississippi, our greatest challenge beyond making it to the hotel for the evening was to avoid the ever-present potholes interspersed in the crumbling asphalt. It was one of the worst stretches of road on which we had ridden, which, given some of the decrepit surfaces we had experienced, was saying something. We continued dodging the potholes for a few more miles when suddenly, the road abruptly became smoother—not a perfect riding surface, but so much better than it had been. When we stopped for a drink of water just a short distance later, Bev smiled at me and matter-of-factly said, "New county." As had happened so often previously when riding on a rough road, crossing into a different county, municipality, or even state brought a distinct improvement in riding conditions. Whether it was because of different paving techniques or availability of funds or simply a sense of pride in providing nice roads, we didn't care; our riding was easier and more enjoyable, and each pedal stroke was more efficient and productive. On those many occasions, a simple change in location, setting, and environment had made all the difference.

This is yet another example of how cycling can be a fitting metaphor for life. So often we find ourselves seemingly stuck in relationships that have grown sour, in jobs that are unfulfilling, or in communities that don't share our values. In these all-too-common situations, our roads of everyday life are proverbially rough and pocked with potholes that slow our progress and make our existence miserable. Those around us can often surmise our need for new surroundings, but in many instances, we have become too used to our misery to understand that it's not our natural state.

But unlike how a cross-country bike tour forces us to proceed to new locales, everyday life can weigh us down if we allow it to, creating a type of inertia that seemingly impedes or prevents the relocation or reset we so desperately need. It's as if we are too busy living to live happily, a notion that on the surface may seem silly, but that is likely far more common than we realize. Completing a significant life change is often hard, exhausting work, and when we are so deeply unhappy, we may not have enough in reserve to make the moves we know are needed.

Those major life changes often require courage, and in the eyes of many, the known is far more preferable to the unknown, even if the "known" is feeding our unhappiness. As the adage goes, "Better the devil you know than the devil you don't." As an example, we may hate our job, our boss, or our co-workers, but at least we're employed and know what we're dealing with. We may know the relationship we're in is unfulfilling or toxic, but at least we're not alone. And if we were fortunate enough to eventually find someone new, there's no guarantee the new relationship would be any better. We may find our job to be mind-numbing and far from stoking our passion and our boss to be an overbearing cretin, but if we could actually get another job, it might end up being even less fulfilling and the new boss even worse than the old one. We know what we know and often fear what we don't.

In each of these instances we're in a bad place, we know it, and yet we still avoid the steps needed to move us forward. Like on that road in rural Mississippi, proverbially crossing over into a new county could make all the difference.

To be clear, there were times on our tour when we crossed into a new county and the road was just as choppy and the potholes just as prevalent as they had been before. And on a few occasions, they seemed even worse. But without exception, if we kept moving, road conditions invariably improved and our riding again became more enjoyable and less arduous.

If circumstances are making us unhappy and we decide to make a move, in whatever manner we think we need to, there is no guarantee that our life will improve. Conversely though, if we don't make a move, we can be fairly assured that nothing will improve, including our level of happiness. And whether we want to believe it or not, we deserve so much more.

CHAPTER 6
TRAGEDY AND TRIUMPH IN THE SUNSHINE STATE

Eight days and 500 miles of riding were all that remained between us and the Atlantic Ocean, and by now we had little doubt we would be able to get to St. Augustine and we were anxious to complete the tour. Still, it was more than a little difficult to leave such a wonderful Gulf-front setting in what some derisively call the "Redneck Riviera." For us, as we neared the end of a long bicycle trip, it had been an idyllic spot for a rest day.

We woke up to overcast skies, not a bad thing for cyclists as long as conditions remained dry. We ate our breakfast on the outdoor patio, taking a little longer than usual, and then lingered on our balcony as we watched the sun filter through the clouds. We finally left around 8:00 a.m. and rode through the still-quiet Orange Beach on a dedicated bike lane with a gentle breeze blowing off the Gulf. After about five miles, we came to the little community of Floribama and we logically sensed we were nearing our eighth of eight states. Sure enough, we soon came to a large sign that proclaimed, "Welcome to Sunny Florida . . . Open for Business." A couple of other riders ahead of us were getting ready to leave, so we asked them to take some photos. It sounds more festive than it truly was on this cool morning, as like the other riders we were already transitioning into a more workmanlike mode. Our last rest day was over, we would soon leave the Gulf behind, and as the day progressed, we would enter nondescript terrain that would largely continue until we reached the Atlantic. From that point forward, we were focused on simply putting more and more miles behind us.

Entering our eighth and last state

Shortly after entering Florida, we turned away from the Gulf, its beautiful vistas, and the touristy establishments we had been passing and headed toward Pensacola. We followed backroads and highways until we entered a quaint downtown area where the SAG stop had been set up adjacent to a small park. It was a hip-looking area, likely catering to the personnel stationed at the Naval Air Base. After leaving downtown, we rode for about ten miles along the Pensacola Cliff Drives Scenic Highway, a hilly but very picturesque stretch of road offering views of the Gulf, then Pensacola Bay, and finally around Escambia Bay as we worked our way toward the little town of Milton, our destination for the evening.

As we rode along U.S. 90 with a couple of riders just ahead of us, in the distance we saw golden domes that to me looked like one of those older car washes that had been constructed with a castle motif. As we got closer, we realized this was an actual residence, a large compound fronting the highway with the back overlooking the bay. Another rider had stopped to take photos and commented that with a sort of Asian theme, the huge residence looked like a place where the Dalai Lama might reside. With the gold Rolls Royce in the driveway as a sign, I don't suspect this was the home of His Holiness, but it made for an interesting and memorable diversion.

After crossing a series of long bridges over different arms of Escambia Bay, we departed the water for the last time until we reached St. Augustine. As we rode through the communities of Pace and Pea Ridge, we noticed the traffic beginning to pick up. It was just after noon, and with just a few miles to our hotel we suspected our room likely wouldn't be ready, so we stopped for lunch. Sitting at an outside table at a Firehouse Subs, we had a most relaxing lunch then lounged around for a while longer, leisurely checking emails until we left to complete the last six miles to Milton.

We finally made it to the Regency Inn and Suites around 1:00 p.m. and by that time our room was ready. Again the best available option in the area, the hotel was clean but very dated and in need of renovation. The previous evening, I had mentioned to Larry how much we had enjoyed staying at the Hampton Inn on Orange Beach. He responded by requesting that we remember the quality of the last lodging establishment when we arrived at the hotel for the following evening. Still, our room in Milton was clean and functional, and as such met our basic needs.

After getting cleaned up and settled, we had some extra time with our early check-in, so we explored the area within walking distance of our hotel, such as it was. As might have been predicted, we ended at a nearby Tastee Freez where we had a couple of chocolate shakes. Dinner was "rider's choice," and as had often occurred previously on these evenings, all of the riders ended up at the same restaurant. After the team meeting, all nine riders walked down the highway to a Texas Roadhouse, where Bev and I each had a nice filet steak. It was all very good in a restaurant that was surprisingly crowded for an early Wednesday evening on the Florida panhandle. To accommodate our large group, we were split into two groups and placed in large booths. Bev and I shared a booth with Steve, as well as Scottish Alan and Danish Allan. This entire tour took place during a period of extreme political strife and divisiveness in the country, and for the most part from the time we left San Diego, talk of politics had been avoided. As a result, the political leanings of most of the riders and the support guys had been difficult to ascertain. But on this evening as Steve, Bev, and I dined with two riders from Europe that we liked and respected, the conversation turned to issues like Brexit, the European Union, and immigration, and the views of these two citizens from different European nations were fascinating.

Rainy start in Milton, Florida

With a relatively short ride of sixty-seven miles to DeFuniak Springs ahead of us, and with a forecast of rain, the trailer opening was delayed to 9:00 a.m. The hotel didn't offer breakfast, so a little after 6:00 a.m. Bev and I walked across the parking lot to a Waffle House restaurant, a staple throughout the South. This chain of restaurants has gained a less-than-stellar reputation among some parts of society, but I have always found them to be clean establishments with good, unpretentious food and friendly workers. Our very hearty breakfast that morning in Milton, Florida was no different and provided a good start to what would be a cool and wet day. By the time we walked back to the hotel it was raining, so we put on our rain gear and prepared to deal with elements that would end up lasting for a couple of hours. For the first six miles of the route, we rode on a nice, paved trail, and then the next twenty or so on very isolated country roads. We encountered little traffic, almost no civilization, and felt like we were traveling through the true backcountry of the Florida panhandle. We finally made it to the first SAG stop, which the support guys had set up next to a little diner. They had arranged for everyone to enter the dry confines of the diner and get a cup of hot chocolate. In the cool and damp conditions, the hot cocoa tasted especially good.

Leaving the Taft Diner, we turned onto U.S. 90, a road on which we had experienced a variety of conditions and situations since West Texas. There were some rolling hills, but the shoulder was wide and the surface was smooth, and with the overcast but now dry skies, we had a more enjoyable day than we had anticipated when we left a rainy Milton. We reached our motel, an Econo-Lodge on the edge of DeFuniak Springs, at around 3:00 p.m. Following our typical routine, I made a beer run (two tallboy Rolling Rocks this time) while Bev got cleaned up, and then she did a load of laundry while I cleaned and lubed our drenched bike chains. Later we drove to a storefront restaurant called 4C Family BBQ, where Bev and I both had the "Sampler Platter" that included pork, brisket, and ribs. A highlight of the meal was the large flag of Scotland hanging over the bar, providing a little taste of the homeland for Scottish Alan.

• • •

As we prepared for the sixty-five-mile ride to Marianna the next morning, temperatures were in the forties, and for the first time in several days, we faced headwinds. We bundled up with a base layer top, tights, a jacket, and long-fingered gloves, most of which we would discard by the early afternoon. We again spent most of the day on U.S. 90, so we were treated to more wide shoulders and smooth surfaces, though the winds made the day more challenging than normal. The terrain this Friday wasn't unlike what we had experienced on Thursday, as well as what we would experience much of the next day. It wasn't that the countryside was necessarily boring (though it kind of was), but we were at the point in the tour where we simply wanted to get to St. Augustine. As I wrote an email to members of our family, I had to look in the guidebook to remind me of the town in which we were staying. It's sort of funny in that in the early stages of the tour, we always knew where we had been, where we were, and where we were going. Then as the routes piled up, we knew the town in which we were staying, but had to give some thought before remembering where we had been the previous night. At this stage, with just a few more riding days ahead of us and with one town looking so much like the last, all of the riders were focused on just continuing to move east, with the towns in which we were staying simply serving as way stations on the route to the Atlantic.

It was a largely uneventful day as we finally made it through the surprisingly hectic traffic of Marianna to the Quality Inn, our hotel located alongside Interstate 10. At the team meeting we found out that it was Ray's birthday, and to celebrate, the support guys provided beer for all interested riders and Ray a card and sweatshirt signed by all the riders. We found Ray, a recently retired physician, to be an interesting individual, a good family man, and an outstanding recumbent cyclist, pushing that odd-looking bicycle at speeds we could never maintain. Though at an age when many avoided recognition of their birthdays, he was appreciative of having this day celebrated. Dinner was at a nearby Ruby Tuesday, where we each had a huge helping from the salad bar as well as another large entree. To complete Ray's birthday celebration, the support guys provided dessert (cheesecake for Bev and Oreo Cream Cake for me). It was a nice, relaxed meal. Very full, we returned to our room, where I laid back in bed trying to read a book on my iPad. I realized I had dozed off when the device fell and bonked me on the nose. So I decided to just go to sleep for the night, though at 8:45 p.m. it might have been the earliest I had gone to bed since I was a child. The rigors of riding six to ten hours each day, as we had now been doing for almost six weeks, was apparently catching up with me. In this instance, however, earlier to bed also meant earlier to rise, as I was up and out of bed before 3:00 a.m. the next morning.

Particularly given the lack of interesting scenery the past few days, we had noticed a real sense of focus among the riders, a genuine desire to get this tour completed, and Bev and I shared that focus. We had five days of riding remaining, including the upcoming sixty-nine-mile ride into Tallahassee, and while at this stage we were far from bored with the tour, we would have gladly traded boredom for the tragically shattering event that was about to unfold.

• • •

It was cool and blustery as we left Marianna at around 8:00 a.m. on an otherwise pleasant Saturday morning, so Bev and I again bundled up with extra layers we would gradually shed through the course of the morning. The first thirty miles were on U.S. 90, the predominant road of the entire tour, with the customary smooth surfaces and wide shoulders, though we again had to deal with pesky headwinds early in the day. We crossed the Apalachicola River and at that point entered the Eastern Time Zone, our fourth and last of the trip. (A rather odd fact: this was the first trip Bev and I had ever taken in which we flew the same direction—east to west—to begin our journey as well as end it, thus gaining an hour or two each time. Crazy, huh?) After crossing the bridge over the Apalachicola, we climbed a long and fairly steep hill into the small town of Chattahoochee, the site of the first SAG stop. At this point, we were just a short distance from the Georgia state line.

For the past several days there had been talk among the riders about making a detour into Georgia, and in that process "picking up another state," as some proposed. As we prepared to leave the SAG stop, three other riders indicated they were planning to divert from the route for a half-mile or so to enter Georgia. Bev and I weren't necessarily enamored with riding extra distance simply to add another state to our itinerary, but the route that day would be a little complicated, especially once we entered Tallahassee, and particularly as one of these riders had a Garmin navigational device, we were glad to tag along. Being with these riders would become much more important as the afternoon evolved. After taking several photos at the "Welcome to Georgia" sign, we returned to the route and headed toward Quincy, the location of the second SAG stop. Shortly after getting back to the main highway, we noticed in the distance two riders headed toward us, traveling in the opposite direction back toward Chattahoochee. At first, I thought we were seeing the rare Florida bike riders out for a Saturday ride, but we soon realized it was Scottish Alan and Danish Allan. Not knowing what they were up to, we gave them a rather befuddled wave and they enthusiastically waved back. Wondering where they were headed, we continued riding in the customary easterly direction, not realizing we had possibly seen Scottish Alan for the last time.

• • •

When we arrived at the stop in Quincy, we quickly realized that something was amiss. Chuck, the driver of the "Chuck-wagon" with the food, water, tables, and folding chairs, was always at each SAG stop, but he was nowhere to be found. Larry was there with enough food and water to support the riders, and though he was calm, we sensed that something had occurred. He quickly informed us that there had been an "incident" in Georgia, that Alan from Scotland had been hit by a car, that his injuries were serious, and that he was being transported to a hospital in Tallahassee. Larry was a stickler about following privacy guidelines, but it was clear he was sharing all the information he had at that time. Chuck had followed the ambulance to the hospital, and we would see neither he nor Larry again until the following morning.

Steve, Jim, Bev and I were at this SAG stop all at the same time, and each of us was shaken by the news we had received. And as often happens, the lack of additional information created even greater unease among the other riders. As the afternoon and evening continued with no additional information, our level of anxiety only increased. How seriously was Alan injured? Would he need surgery? Was his life in danger? We assumed Danish Allan was at the hospital; had he been injured as well? And with a Sunday ride of sixty-five miles next on the schedule, would we continue? These were just a few of the pressing questions that dominated our thinking that afternoon, with uncertainty causing those thoughts to become increasingly pessimistic.

Despite everything, we still had to get to Tallahassee. Given the circumstances, the four of us decided to ride together to the hotel for the evening, with Jim using his Garmin device to navigate. We were appreciative of Jim's efforts, particularly given the many turns as we rode through the congested parts of the city around Florida State University. We rode past Doak Campbell Stadium, and the traffic was heavy even though the Seminole football team was playing in Clemson that afternoon. We traversed a section of the city called College Town, an area dominated by restaurants and bars that were already busy by mid-afternoon. Physically tired and emotionally drained, we would have loved at that point to simply walk into one of those patio bars, order some appetizers and drinks, and try to put the occurrences of the day in their proper perspective. But we still had some riding to complete, traversing commercial and residential areas until we reached the Econo-Lodge, another rather sparse but clean motel located right on the route. This lodging establishment from another time seemed almost out of place, given the upscale appearance of the neighborhood and the numerous restaurants within walking distance.

Before heading to the hospital, Larry had left room keys at the front desk to be picked up by each rider. After finding our room, Bev and I quickly showered and got dressed for the evening. We still hadn't received any additional news regarding Alan's condition, and at this point, the adage suggesting that "no news is good news" did not seem to apply. Harkening back to the raucous bars we had passed in College Town, I suggested to Bev that we find a nearby restaurant for drinks and an appetizer. Next door to the motel was a Chili's Bar and Grill, and over drinks and an order of chips and guacamole, we tried to make sense of what had occurred. The food and drinks were good, and we felt a little better when we left, but our concern for Alan only seemed to increase.

We returned to our room, and after laying around for an hour or so and having received no more information from the hospital, our despair was starting to return. We were craving commiseration with our fellow riders, so Bev sent a text to everyone asking if they wanted to meet up to go to dinner together. Several did, so six of us were soon sitting around a large table at a nearby Miller's Ale House. Bev had the jambalaya and a couple of different wines. I had a small steak and one of the best and most interesting beers I had on the tour. It was a local beer with the very clever, if not particularly beer-centric name of "Hopline Bling," a takeoff on the Drake song that had been so popular a couple of years earlier.

It was a good meal, and it was good for us to spend time with four of the other riders, but the atmosphere was somber. We quickly realized that the other riders were struggling with the situation just as we were. Ted and Steve, who had often ridden with Alan and had probably developed a closer relationship with him than anyone other than Danish Allan, his roommate, seemed particularly gloomy. The sentiment among many around the table leaned toward not riding the next day if we didn't get information about Alan's condition or if he was going to be in surgery during the day. We simply didn't know what was going on, and we were worried. Eventually, Ray, the retired doctor, sent a text to Larry and Chuck explaining how everyone was concerned, that several were considering not riding the next day, and that we simply needed information about how Alan was doing. Given HIPAA restrictions and the likelihood that they weren't learning much from the doctors, we didn't blame the support guys for not providing us with updates. Just a little information, however, would do much to ease our minds. It wasn't long until we received a text message from Danish Allan informing us that Alan had two broken legs and was currently in surgery. Shortly thereafter, we received a text from Larry indicating that we would have our pre-ride team meeting the next morning at 7:30 a.m. Our minds were slightly relieved, as we now knew a little about Alan's condition, would probably learn more the next morning, and the tour would continue.

After returning to our room, I was tired but still a bit jacked from the emotions of the day, so I told Bev I was going to get ice cream. Familiar only with the restaurants right around the motel, I started walking toward a nearby commercial area, believing there had to be fast-food joints in the vicinity. There were not, because despite my walking a longer distance than I had hoped I found nothing. But I was on a mission, and on this day getting ice cream seemed to be something I could control, so I kept walking and looking. Getting a bit frustrated, I eventually came to a Dollar Tree store, and though I had previously stepped foot in one of these establishments perhaps once in my life, and never to look for groceries, I decided to give it a try. Walking to the back of the store I found a cooler with frozen foods, and in it quarts of ice cream for—you guessed it—a dollar. From the limited selection, I picked cookies and cream, but then realized we had no utensils with which to eat the ice cream I had finally found. I remembered I was in a Dollar Tree, so I found a pack of 30 plastic spoons for, yes, a dollar. It wasn't Ben and Jerry's or even Blue Bell, but when I got back to the motel Bev and I devoured our $1.00 ice cream using our $1.00 plastic spoons. It was a surprisingly tasty ending to an otherwise very trying day.

• • •

As we gathered the next morning in Larry and Chuck's room for the pre-ride meeting, our thoughts weren't on the route for the day, but rather on what had occurred the day before. We were happy to see Danish Allan, who shared the truly frightening story of how the accident had unfolded. As Allan detailed the events, he and Scottish Alan had decided to ride for a few miles in Georgia, and when we met them traveling backward on the route, they were headed to the road into Georgia on which we had just briefly ridden. Scottish Alan had been experiencing some issues with his handlebars, and after cresting a hill, the two of them stopped so Alan could work on his bike. There was a minimal shoulder, and as he was working on his handlebars, part of Alan and his bike extended onto the edge of the roadway. An elderly man driving at a considerable speed topped the hill and apparently didn't see the two riders until it was too late to completely miss them. Luckily, it wasn't a direct, full-on collision, because as Danish Allan suggested, Alan likely would not have survived such an impact. Even being struck by the corner of the front end and side of the onrushing car, the injuries were devastating. Alan had sustained severe breaks to both of his ankles, several broken ribs, a punctured lung, and in addition to numerous cuts and abrasions, a very deep gash on his leg, causing his doctors great concern about potential infection. Though he was lucky to be alive, Alan had multiple surgeries and months of arduous rehabilitation ahead of him. But he was alive and had a positive prognosis, erasing a fear we had all faced the previous day.

An unsung hero was Danish Allan, who with a background in law enforcement in his native Denmark had jumped into action and provided initial treatment to his friend and riding partner. A motorist stopped to assist, and with a belt this individual provided, Allan was able to apply a tourniquet to stem the heavy bleeding from Alan's leg. It was at least a half hour before the ambulance arrived at this remote location, so the initial care Danish Allan provided was critical. Additionally, the elderly gentleman who had driven the vehicle that struck Alan was so distraught after the accident he could barely function, and in addition to caring for his injured friend, Allan had to console this man who had caused the accident. Adrenaline had kicked in for Allan, and he didn't initially grasp that he had sustained a severe cut to his midsection, but by the time he reached the hospital he realized he needed assistance. In the hospital's emergency room, Allan had to convince the nurses that he required immediate attention, having to exhibit his wound to provide the evidence that was evidently required to get medical care. He ended up receiving eight stitches in an area of his midsection. In the six weeks of the tour, we had come to like and greatly respect this quiet, modest, and occasionally very funny Dane, and his actions in the face of this tragedy did not surprise us.

Scottish Alan would soon post on Facebook a photo of himself lying in his bed in the intensive care unit. He looked like he had been beaten with a baseball bat, but seemed to be in little pain and, under the circumstances, in surprisingly good spirits. It was obvious his cross-country tour was over, but his prognosis for a full recovery seemed good. It was also obvious that he would remain in the hospital beyond the coming Wednesday, when our ride was scheduled to conclude and the team would disperse and return home. As a result, none of us would have the opportunity to give him our best wishes in person and tell him goodbye. Alan had joined us for dinner the night before we departed from San Diego and we had enjoyed getting to know him, watching as he questioned some admittedly odd American customs and discussing with him football and our hometown Kansas City Chiefs. With his determination and positive attitude, we knew he would recover over time, but Alan had a long, hard road ahead of him, and as we rode away from Tallahassee, we assumed we would never see him again.

• • •

After the meeting concluded we took our bags to the trailer and prepared for our sixty-five-mile ride to our hotel near Madison, Florida. It was beginning to soak in that for the final four days of riding, we would be a team of eight rather than the original nine, but we had collectively and individually decided that we needed to see this tour to its end. It was a fairly cool autumn day on the Florida panhandle, though by early afternoon the skies had cleared and temperatures had become seasonally warm. After leaving the commercial area around the hotel, we turned onto Old St. Augustine Road (the irony not lost on us), a "canopy road" we followed for around ten miles. On this overcast November morning, those ten miles with moss-draped trees covering the road were beautiful and very memorable. It was still early on this Sunday morning, and though there was minimal shoulder there was also minimal traffic. As a result, it was a good way to begin the ride following the stressful challenges of the previous day. After that the day was largely uneventful, at least for us, with the highlight of the route being a SAG stop in Greenville, Florida, the birthplace of the iconic singer Ray Charles. The support guys had set up the stop alongside a city park, and we all took obligatory photos standing by a bronze statue of Ray at the keyboard. It was otherwise another day of covering the miles needed to get us to the Atlantic Ocean.

By mid-afternoon, we made it to the Day's Inn south of Madison. Following our tradition, as Bev was getting cleaned up I went looking for a couple of cans of beer. After walking a half-mile or so and finally finding a convenience store that carried beer, I walked up to the checkout counter with a couple of tallboy cans of Budweiser and a small bag of popcorn. The young lady at the cash register looked at what I had placed on the counter, and in a profound southern drawl told me, "We can't sell liquor on Sundays in this county." She wasn't mean in her response, more matter-of-fact, and I got a sense that this was far from the first time she'd had to make that statement. As this was 2017 and these "blue laws" were considered archaic in most of the country, I responded, "Really?" As Bev and I had discussed, outside of Pensacola, Tallahassee, and the beach towns along the Gulf, the Florida panhandle seemed much more like Alabama and Mississippi than the rest of Florida, and this county-based "blue law" was yet further proof. As it wasn't the young lady's fault she couldn't complete the sale, I took the beers and popcorn back to their rightful place and pondered my options. There was a Dairy Queen next door and I was able to take a couple of Blizzards back to our room instead, so all was not completely lost. But again, I thought, "Really?" After the team meeting, we walked next door to a Denny's diner, where Bev and I both ordered the turkey and dressing dinner, which in the week before Thanksgiving was both festive and tasty.

●　●　●

At the team meeting that Sunday morning, as Danish Allan shared what had happened with the previous day's accident, we began to surmise the toll it had to have taken on him, both physically and mentally. Bev and I always had a sense of who had not yet left the hotel each morning as we departed. That morning we had been the first to leave the Econo-Lodge in Tallahassee, and as we made our way to the first SAG stop, the other riders all eventually passed us . . . except for Danish Allan. In addition to the psychological trauma anyone would have experienced in such a situation, he had sustained a serious cut to his midsection. As we were all sort of looking out for him (as if he needed our supervision), when he didn't pass us, Bev and I became concerned that Allan was struggling, or even that he had decided not to ride that day.

Our concern was so misplaced. When we got to the first SAG stop, we asked about Allan, and the support guys told a story that spoke volumes about his character and tenacity. Our Danish friend had been the one who had placed the most emphasis on riding each and every mile of the tour, going as far on one occasion as to backtrack on the route when road construction had required that riders be shuttled a short distance. So, we shouldn't have been surprised to learn that after the team meeting, Allan had asked the support guys to drive him to the spot on the route where he and Scottish Alan had turned north to ride into Georgia. He intended to complete the remainder of the previous day's route that he had missed and then ride the route for that Sunday. He had to have been exhausted physically and emotionally after what he had endured the previous afternoon. But instead of taking the day off, as would have been justified, with his eight stitches he rode more than 100 miles. We greeted Allan as he entered the hotel parking lot, and he humbly and simply stated, "I had to do that."

• • •

We both woke up early on the last Monday morning of our tour, just three riding days from St. Augustine. Because the hotel offered only a meager breakfast, and because we had a long eighty-six-mile ride ahead of us, we walked across the parking lot to the nearby Denny's for a more fortifying meal. Bev ordered one of their "Grand Slam" offerings with meat, eggs, and pancakes, a combination she would never order in our regular (i.e., non-cross-country-bike-riding) lives. I ordered my typical diner breakfast selection of two eggs (over medium), meat (this time ham), hash browns, and wheat toast. When the order came, it consisted of a pile of fried eggs, a slice of ham, and two pieces of toast, but no hash browns. I am somewhat of a connoisseur of hash browns, and I was a bit disappointed that they were missing from my order. I tactfully told our waitress that I still needed an order of hash browns and added that I thought I had been given an extra egg. She informed me that I had been given *four* fried eggs and that she would get me the missing hash browns. Now, any rational person would put one, maybe two of the eggs aside, with issues of gluttony and heart disease coming to mind as potential reasons. But I had been raised to not waste food, and because we had a long ride ahead of us, and because, well, I like fried eggs, I ate everything on my plate(s) and enjoyed every bite. I also realized that when we arrived back home in four days, my eating habits would have to significantly change, lest I end up weighing 300 pounds.

After packing, loading our luggage in the trailer, and checking the inflation in our tires, a daily routine we had been following for the past six and a half weeks, we left the hotel. We rode on a series of back roads until, for the last time, we turned onto U.S. 90. We had been riding on this highway since our travels through West Texas, and since leaving that state, the riding surface had typically been good and the shoulder sufficiently wide. If you can actually "miss" a road, we were going to miss U.S. 90. We eventually left the highway for the final time, traveling on various county and state roads. We crossed the beautiful and somewhat famous Suwannee River (as in the song, "Way down upon the . . ."). We passed a series of Florida state parks, and at the end of a long eighty-six-mile day, we finally made our way into the small Florida hamlet of High Springs. Our destination for the evening was the High Springs Country Inn, an older "motor hotel" that decades ago had probably been considered prime lodging for travelers on their way to Gulf and Atlantic beaches. We noticed several other people at the motel drying out their wet suits and soon learned that High Springs is informally known as the cave-diving capital of the world, with natural springs offering diving in clear water flowing year-round at a temperature of seventy-two degrees. After a quick team meeting, we drove to a downtown Mexican restaurant called El Patio, where appropriately we sat outside on the patio. It was a beautiful evening in Central Florida, and the camaraderie of the close-knit group in one of our last meals together was in evidence. Contributing to the positive vibe was the support guys' offer to buy the first round of drinks. (I had a margarita and Bev a beer.) As we drove back to the next to last motel room of the tour, I thought about how much I was going to miss the day-to-day routine we had established, as well as the fellowship of these other men. As we might have anticipated, we were ready for the daily rides to end while simultaneously wishing the tour would continue indefinitely.

• • •

We left High Springs at 8:00 a.m. on an eighty-five-mile ride to our last overnight stop of the tour in Palatka. It was a challenging day for a variety of reasons, including several riders getting lost as they navigated their way through Gainesville, the bustling little city that is the home of the University of Florida. We traveled on busy state highways as we approached the city and then followed a series of urban trails and city streets as we made our way to the first SAG stop in a large park on the outskirts of the city. As we rode into this beautiful park with landscape dominated by moss-draped trees, I was struck by two distinct realizations: first, that the only rider at the stop when we arrived was Danish Allan. We soon learned that all of the other five riders had become lost as they tried to reach the stop, with three bypassing the SAG stop altogether. Second was that, after over six weeks of riding in areas we had not previously experienced, this park seemed oddly familiar. For several years Bev and I had traveled in late February to spend some time on the Atlantic beaches, most typically in Daytona. The February before this mid-November SAG stop, we had spent a night in Gainesville, and on the following morning had sought an area trail on which to run. As I looked around the park after getting off my bike, I quickly realized that just a few months earlier, we had parked in this same parking lot and then walked to the nearby trail which on this day we would be riding. Just as the next day we would enter St. Augustine, a historic city with which we had become very familiar, the unexpected revisiting of this neat park was yet another subtle reminder that we would soon be returning to familiar life routines and environs.

We soon left this picturesque park, riding for sixteen miles on the Gainesville-Hawthorne Trail. This paved trail was impressive and beautiful, allowing us to ride through dense pine forests, along swamplands, and eventually into the small town of Hawthorne. We sort of hoped to see an alligator as we rode by bogs and swamps, but at the same time lamented how we might react if we were to encounter one. After eventually leaving the trail, we rode on some choppy roads as we made our way to the second and last SAG stop of the day in the village of Melrose. (Bev and I both believed it was only fitting that on our last long day of riding we would encounter both rough roads and headwinds, harkening back to our seemingly endless trek across the state of Texas.)

Shortly after that last stop, we entered our third and final trail of the day, the Palatka-Lake Butler State Trail. After we had gone just a couple of miles on this paved trail, we noticed three riders a short distance ahead of us leaving the trail and getting back on the highway. Danish Allan noticed us riding toward him and waited to let us know what they had encountered. Allan spoke impeccable English, but with a distinct Danish accent. When he told us that the trail was flooded, and that he didn't know how deep the water was on the trail, but that it was in what he called an "alligator-looking area," he had our attention. If the trail was unsafe in the eyes of Allan, the seemingly fearless law enforcement official from Denmark, well, that was more than good enough for Bev and me. So we thanked him, called the support guys so they could inform the riders behind us, and rode on Highway 100 the twenty miles or so into Palatka. It was kind of a dreary day on what had been a long ride and we were getting tired, making the last several miles seem endless. As we entered Palatka, we stopped at McDonald's for milkshakes to celebrate completing our last long day; it just seemed fitting.

• • •

Replenished, but still ready to end a long day, we finally made it to the Quality Inn right on the banks of the very wide and surprisingly beautiful St. Johns River. Just a few months earlier the Palatka area had been impacted by the remnants of Hurricane Irma, a powerful Category 5 storm that devastated parts of the Caribbean before making landfall in Florida. As we approached the hotel, we could still see some of the damage the property had recently sustained. (In fact, as we were packing to leave the next morning, power was cut off to the entire facility as an electrical transformer was being replaced.) At 5:00 p.m., we met for the last team meeting to discuss what would occur on the atypical final day of riding. Afterward, Bev and I met three other riders, Ross, Ted, and Steve, for a drink in the bar at the hotel restaurant. We still enjoyed swapping stories with these three guys we had gotten to know very well through the course of the tour. Though we had continued to get stronger as the mileage continued to pile up, we were physically drained and mentally tired of the daily grind. But we were really going to miss these three guys and the other riders and support guys.

Larry and Chuck had reserved a meeting room where we gathered at 6:00 p.m. for a presentation they had dutifully put together. They started out performing a "rap" in which, donning sunglasses and sideways caps, they lyrically congratulated us on completing the tour, ending their hip-hop rendition by dropping their mics (actually water bottles). While I'm no fan of or expert on hip-hop music, these two artists were less "Straight Outta Compton" and more two semi-retired guys from Northwest Arkansas, but their musical efforts were both amusing and greatly appreciated. They then presented each rider with some gifts, most notably a t-shirt, a cycling cap, and of greatest importance, prints of some of the more significant photos of each of us they had taken through the course of the tour. They then presented each rider with an award. Bev was proclaimed a "badass" and presented the well-deserved "Queen of the Hills" award. I received the "Best Negotiator" award for talking Bev into doing a cross-country bike trip. (In reality, there had been little if any "negotiation" required.) I also received a new tire tube for having the fewest flat tires (none). They then showed a PowerPoint presentation of a series of photos chronicling our journey since leaving San Diego. Both support guys had been diligent about taking photos, and Chuck had done the heavy lifting in putting the presentation together. Accompanied by subject-appropriate classic rock music, watching this series of photos was oddly powerful and a little emotional, bringing back memories of days and locations and events we had already almost forgotten. All in all, it was a genuinely nice ceremony.

As the festivities concluded, with the focus of the ceremony placed clearly on the riders, I felt an additional comment was warranted. I offered, "When we started this trip, we were a little uncertain as to whether or not we could actually pull this off. Now that we have virtually completed the tour, we realize we couldn't have made it without Larry and Chuck." Other riders chimed in with expressions of appreciation, but for none of the others could the statement have been truer. At best recreational cyclists with minimal mechanical skills, Bev and I had had no business attempting to cycle across the country, and attempting to do so on our own would have been asking for failure. But in addition to the support and logistical planning important to all of the riders, the support guys had gladly provided Bev and me with additional attention, from guiding me through my first tire repair and replacement to shuttling us past sections of the route that transcended our skill and comfort level to hauling Bev and me on the day I was too sick to walk, much less ride. These two guys are not only very competent at leading cycling tours, they are also good, caring people to whom we will always owe a debt of gratitude.

Afterward, we all went to the hotel restaurant, a Beef O'Brady's, for dinner, where Bev ordered a steak bowl and I had the seafood platter. It was a fun but bittersweet gathering, as I sadly realized this was the last time we would all be together for a meal. And though he was still convalescing in the hospital in Tallahassee, Scottish Alan loomed large in our consciousness.

● ● ●

The next morning I woke up at a characteristically early time, and in these pre-dawn hours I was in a reflective mood. As I tried to gain some perspective regarding what we were about to accomplish, my emotions seemed to be running the gamut. I was growing weary of long bike rides day after day, but a part of me didn't want this amazing journey to end. Similarly, I was ready to get back home, but at the same time I was nervous about how I would react to returning to our old and comparatively mundane routines, realizing that at my core, I had likely changed in multiple ways.

Perhaps of greater significance was how the scope of what we were doing was finally beginning to sink in. Since leaving San Diego, where our doubts had threatened to overwhelm any confidence we may have been feeling, we had maintained a laser-like focus on the task at hand each day. As a result, we kept our eyes on the proverbial trees and avoided contemplating the forest, or the magnitude of what we were accomplishing. But the previous few days, as that forest was suddenly right in front of us and thus unavoidable, we had begun to give a great deal of thought to what we were about to finish. I sincerely wanted to avoid arrogant thoughts, because countless people with the desire and appropriate drive could do what we were about to finish. But amazingly, we were about to complete a 3,000-mile bicycle ride across the country. It's something we had thought about and dreamed of doing for years, but deep down never really believed we would, or could, accomplish. As I lay in bed in our hotel room in Palatka, Florida, I realized that on this day, that dream was about to come true, and that Bev and I would have done it together, which made this entire experience so much more special. In the dark, with my riding and life partner still getting a little more needed sleep, my emotions bubbled to the top, and I momentarily became just a bit misty-eyed. It would take some time for the two of us, both individually and together, to process these strong feelings.

Leaving Palatka, Florida on the last day of the tour

But we still had one more ride, a forty-two-mile route that would take us to the beach in St. Augustine. With the anticipated shut-off of the electricity, we were packed up and ready to go well before the 8:00 a.m. trailer opening. It was a cool morning, and our view of the wide expanses of the St. John's River was idyllic. Our plan was to ride to the lone SAG stop of the day, the last one of the tour, and then ride into downtown St. Augustine. There we would meet up with Chuck, who would ride with us as he led us to Anastasia State Park, where we would dip our front tires into the Atlantic. After taking a series of photos in the parking lot, we departed in cool and overcast conditions that, except for a brief glimpse of sunshine, would continue all day.

In a departure from what had become our standard practice, our group of eight riders rode together along the entire forty-two-mile route, with one exception. About a mile after crossing the long and rather impressive bridge over the St. Johns River, we turned onto the first of a series of county roads and state highways. Among us were a couple of riders who often looked for alternate routes that would reduce distance or traffic or offer improved road conditions. Though those better routes were rarely available, they kept looking for them. As we were riding on a somewhat busy state highway following Ross, who was leading the group, those two riders peeled off and started riding on a paved trail that ran parallel to the road on which we were riding. Soon two other riders joined them, and the two groups of four (Bev and I stayed on the highway) rode side-by-side for a mile or so. Suddenly the trail turned into the woods, and we wouldn't see these four guys for the next ten miles. We assumed they would probably somehow make their way onto a busy highway that would take them to the SAG stop. But as we would soon learn, the trail had ended shortly after turning into the woods, and the four had had to backtrack and push hard to catch back up with us. Still, all was well, as the eight riders were back together before the last SAG stop of the entire tour.

The last SAG stop of the tour

We rode along the beautiful St. Johns River, a wide and majestic waterway that more resembled a lake than a river. The SAG stop was set up in a riverfront park in the little community of Riverdale, and the riders were in a jovial mood as we ate snacks and replenished our water bottles for the last time. In fact, there seemed to almost be a hesitance to leave. Though I never kept track, I suspect that over the forty-two riding days of the tour, there had been well over 100 of these stops, and we could attest that they literally kept us going during tough riding days, providing fuel and water but more significantly offering a short-term goal on the way to completing a painfully long ride. There were days when we couldn't think about the fifty or sixty miles left on the route, but we knew we could get to the next SAG stop, and then the one after that, and eventually we made it to the hotel at the end of the ride. After this last stop, we finally left as a group, riding largely in silence as we battled side winds on the roughly twenty miles into downtown St. Augustine.

Bev and I have visited St. Augustine on numerous occasions, and though it's not a large city, the downtown area where we were to meet Chuck is typically very hectic, with lots of vehicular and pedestrian traffic. This cool and cloudy day in mid-November was no different, and as we navigated all the traffic, Chuck was nowhere to be found. We were all decked out in our white Trans-America Cycling jerseys, as was Chuck, and in time as we scanned the downtown area we saw a familiar white jersey and a bicycle in a little park area across a busy street at the foot of the bridge we would be crossing. A little relieved, we gathered at the approach to the Bridge of Lions and took a series of photos in front of the namesake lion sculptures at the foot of this famous bridge. Soon, with Chuck in the lead, we rode across this drawbridge on the narrow pedestrian walkway, a bit nerve-wracking given the structure of the bridge and the narrowness of the walkway.

But as had occurred for the past forty-six days with almost no exceptions, we all made it across without incident.

As we left the downtown area to cross the bridge and then ride the last two miles to the beach, I wanted to savor the final moments of the tour, but after riding for an hour and a half, I needed to go to the bathroom. As we mingled before crossing the bridge, I asked Chuck if there was a restroom available; he didn't know, but told me we could stop on the way to the park where the beach was located. As we were riding, Chuck looked back and said to me, "Still looking for a bathroom?" At this point we were maybe a mile from the end of a 3,000-mile bicycle ride, everyone was anxious to get finished, and I really didn't want the entire group to stop and wait so Rob could go to the bathroom. So, as we were riding along, I suggested to Chuck that if I was the only one needing to go, we didn't need to stop. Nice guy that he always showed himself to be, he responded, "I could go," so we pulled into a convenience store. This tour was comprised largely of older men, so not surprisingly everyone needed to go, and soon there was a line waiting to use the men's room.

After leaving the Circle K, we turned into the Anastasia State Park, largely vacant on this cold, windswept day. I was in somewhat of a daze as we wound through the pine trees and then sand dunes peppered with sea oats until finally, we reached a long walkway over the sand berm that eventually led us to the ocean. Walking our bikes, we popped over a dune and got our first glimpse of the Atlantic, which for Bev and me was particularly special, given the affinity we have developed for this ocean. At the end of the walkway, perhaps a hundred yards from the surf, we took off our shoes and socks and began walking our bikes to the water. It was a scene that still seems so surreal, with a dark, cloudy sky and white-capped waves crashing on the beach, and eight cyclists trying to put into perspective the journey they were about to complete. We were soon taking numerous photos of each rider dipping the front tires in the ocean, which coupled with dipping our back tires in the Pacific, symbolized that we had completed a ride across the United States. While each of the other riders was photographed individually completing this process, Bev and I did so together, and given how closely tied we had been for the past forty-six days it seemed only appropriate.

Celebrating the end of our cross-country tour,
St. Augustine Beach, Florida

We took several group photos of the eight riders and two support guys, and two were particularly special. Scottish Alan had often worn a cycling jersey emblazoned with the flag of Scotland. Unbeknownst to the rest of us, Danish Allan had brought this jersey with him to the beach. Allan and Alan, roommates since the beginning of the tour, had grown particularly close, with that bond having become even more strongly forged by the accident just four days earlier. Allan suggested that we take a group photo with him wearing this Scottish jersey that symbolized that our injured teammate was with us in spirit. We took two photos, one with everyone facing the camera with our arms around each other and the other facing the ocean with Danish Allan's arms raised in triumph. It was perhaps the most emotional part of the whole process; we sincerely wished Scottish Alan could have been present to experience this moment with us, but were heartened by the news that back in Tallahassee, his recovery was progressing as we all had hoped. His spirit was clearly with us on that beach in St. Augustine.

Paying tribute to our missing team member at the end of the tour

Very often, the symbolic conclusion of a major life event ends up feeling anticlimactic, the journey having far more meaning than the ultimate destination. The "tire dip" moment was no different—a symbolic ceremony that had been preceded by a life-altering journey that represented the truly significant part of this story. Plus we were getting cold, with unseasonably low temperatures bolstered by bitter winds whipping off the ocean. So after around fifteen minutes of photos and congratulatory handshakes and hugs, we were all ready to find some protection from the elements, moving to a nearby shelter house. The wife of one of the riders as well as the girlfriend and a couple of other good friends of another were present for the moment and to enjoy the celebration. Chuck and Larry provided champagne (actually mimosas) and someone had brought some beer called "Southern Tier," which was fitting given that we had just finished 3,000 miles on what the Adventure Cycling Association called the "Southern Tier." After a half-hour or so the group began to disperse, a bittersweet moment, as we suspected we would never see any of these people again.

Chuck drove three of us to a local bike shop, where our bikes would be packed and shipped home. The other rider was Ray, the recumbent-riding retired physician from Minnesota who was being picked up at the bike shop for a flight out of Jacksonville later that evening. After bidding Ray a surprisingly emotional farewell, we returned to the state park to pick up another couple of riders to be dropped off at the Sleep Inn, a nearby hotel where several would be staying that night. We took our luggage from the trailer for the last time and checked into our room, and soon after received a text from Larry indicating that he and Chuck had decided to leave that evening rather than wait for the next morning, allowing them to stop at the hospital in Tallahassee to visit Scottish Alan. We understood and appreciated their desire to head home early, but we lamented not being able to express our appreciation and farewells to these two fine individuals. It was clear that ready or not emotionally, this amazing journey that had taken the last forty-six days, but which had largely consumed us for most of the past year, was coming to an end.

We had just completed the greatest physical challenge of our lives, and in the process had reached a truly lofty lifelong goal. Certainly not sad, but also not feeling the joyful happiness one might expect from such an occurrence, we seemed to be in a sort of emotional purgatory. As we sat in our small hotel room in St. Augustine, a location we had been striving to reach for such a long time, we struggled to understand why under these amazing circumstances we didn't feel more elated.

LIFE LESSON #6
Take It One Ride at a Time.

"Tell your heart that the fear of suffering
is worse than the suffering itself."

—Paulo Coelho

E arly in the tour, we were sitting around one afternoon after completing the day's ride, talking about nothing in particular beyond wind and flat tires and other topics that seem to come up when a group of cyclists gets together. Out of the blue, another rider offered, "Did you see on the next map that 8,000-foot climb in New Mexico?" I had not, but he certainly had my attention. Our cross-country tour was following a route detailed in a series of seven maps developed and printed by the Adventure Cycling Association, and the support guys had given us all seven at our orientation meeting in San Diego. When this rider commented on that future huge climb in New Mexico, we were still working through the first map and were somewhere in Arizona. He had pulled out the next map, looked ahead several days, and was stressing over what had to be a huge climb. And now I was also stressing over the same future route. Ironically, when Trans-America Cycling was developing the itinerary for this tour, Larry and Chuck had opted for a different route, one that bypassed the highest elevations in New Mexico. As a result, this rider, and now I and others, was worrying about a challenge we would never encounter.

To the extent possible, Bev and I were doing our best to not start thinking about the next day's ride until we had completed the ride we were on. It sounds so uncomplicated, but if you focus on what might happen in the future, it's really difficult to appreciate what you are doing right now. This concept may seem simple, but for most people, it is also incredibly challenging. We wanted to enjoy ourselves, and to do this we had to live in the moment; appreciating the experience, taking in the scenery, and embracing the challenges we were facing. We were always aware of any particularly long days on the schedule, and we certainly knew when a rest day was on the horizon. But for each of the forty-two rides on the tour, we never once looked at the map or pulled the information sheet for any ride until just before the team meeting the night before it was to occur. To the best of our ability, we experienced the tour "one ride at a time."

This wasn't that difficult for either of us, but it ran completely counter to the habits I had formed in my professional life. Particularly during my years as a school superintendent, I was a "thinker" more than a "worrier" (well, I did worry quite a bit). But I was thinking all the time. Sitting at the dinner table with our family, I would find myself thinking about some difficult meeting on the schedule and how I might address the concerns being expressed. Listening to the lesson in church, my mind might wander to focus on some potential problem that might impact the school district. Whether there were budget matters, personnel issues, or student performance measurements, I was always thinking about something else, meaning I couldn't (or wouldn't) focus on the task at hand, regardless of how enjoyable it should have been. I was always concerning myself with what might happen in the future, and how I could somehow prevent some possible but unlikely incident or problem from occurring. I once heard a fellow superintendent comment about how he could always "leave the job in the office;" if true, that amazed me, because the job followed me everywhere I went. As I knew at the time, and as I came to fully appreciate after retiring from that career, this was not a healthy way to live.

Bev had always exhibited a more inquisitive and outwardly spiritual side, exploring the teachings of Byron Katie, Don Miguel Ruiz, Neal Donald Walsh, and numerous others. One of those others was a rather eccentric spiritual teacher of German descent named Eckhart Tolle. Lending credence to Tolle's teachings in the mass media world of the late 1990s was his "discovery" by Oprah Winfrey. Bev had purchased his first major book, *The Power of Now*, and her comments about his teachings piqued my interest.

The concept of mindfulness, which dates back at least to ancient Buddhist traditions and which stresses the importance of maintaining attention on what is happening in the present moment, was just beginning to come into modern prominence when I began reading Eckhart Tolle's book for the first time. And within the first couple of chapters, it had the proverbial effect of slapping me across the face. As he wrote, "Nothing ever happened in the past; it happened in the Now. Nothing will ever happen in the future; it will happen in the Now." Esoteric perhaps, but these words from this German scholar truly resonated with me. Stated far more simplistically than this unique spiritual leader, from my perspective, Tolle was suggesting that the past is done and can't be relived, and the future hasn't occurred yet and can seldom be controlled or manipulated. The only real experience we can have is what is occurring right now, and if we dwell on the past or the future (like I was doing constantly), we were in essence wasting way too much of our lives. If internalized, that would be a powerful lesson for anyone.

Regarding the constant "monkey chatter" that was seemingly dominating my thinking, Eckhart Tolle suggested that one's mind was like a tool to be utilized in completing a particular task, sort of like a wrench used to loosen a bolt. When the task is completed, like when the bolt is loosened, you lay the wrench aside and move on to address other issues. But unlike the admittedly mundane example of using a wrench, we never seem to put our minds aside, continuing our thought processes in a manner that is obsessive and serves no positive purpose. "As it is," he writes, "I would say about 80 to 90 percent of most people's thinking is not only repetitive and useless, but because of its dysfunctional and often negative nature, much of it is also harmful." As I read these words, it was as though Eckhart Tolle was speaking directly to me; I suspect many readers had that same thought, the power of this simple concept being so universal.

In his book *10% Happier*, Dan Harris writes, "The voice in my head is an asshole." (Can you relate to this statement? I know I can.) Like Harris, the ABC News anchor who worked to alleviate his anxiety with a dedicated meditation practice, I found some benefit in regularly devoting fifteen minutes or so to sitting in silence. But really, a combination of the reduction in stress that accompanied my retirement as a public school administrator and just being cognizant of how rampant my mind was continually running helped me to be more present, more mindful, and to live more in the moment. I was (and still am) a work in progress when those changes were put to the test in the fall of 2012.

To put that story in context, I must first tell this one. Born in 1957, I grew up in a time when a cancer diagnosis was tantamount to a death sentence, so many of the treatment modalities we now take for granted having not yet been developed or perfected. And like most people of their generation, my parents had an existential fear of anything associated with any type of malignancy. I can recall conversations at our dinner table in which one of my parents, typically my mother, because she was more in tune with the happenings of our small town, commented that such-and-such member of the community "had *a* cancer." Not "had cancer," but rather had been found to have a foreign entity that had invaded and taken over their body. And then I recall follow-up comments like, "she was such a nice person," or something along those lines, already talking about this cancer victim in the past tense even though she was still alive. The fear of cancer in my family was that visceral, and ironically or otherwise, each of my parents would succumb to different types of cancer after living into their eighties. After growing up with such societal and familial fear of this dreaded disease, it was like it had been etched into my DNA.

Fast forward around fifty years to 2012, and I was sitting in a hospital gown as our family doctor began my annual physical. It would be an exaggeration to suggest that I enjoyed my annual trek to the doctor's office for this yearly ritual, the inevitable pokes and prods being downright unpleasant. But there was one aspect of the physical I did look forward to, and that was when our longtime physician discussed the results of the lab work I had completed a week or so earlier. Bev and I had worked diligently through exercise and relatively good nutrition to lead a life that by most measures was a healthy one. And this brief discussion of the results of a series of blood tests and urinalyses served as a simplistic reward for the lifestyle decisions we had been making. When on a couple of occasions our doctor had stated, "Your lab work is *spectacular*," I beamed inside.

But on this afternoon as he looked at the printout with the lab results, our physician just said, "Mmmm," and then began rifling back through records that detailed my medical history. Having your doctor say "Mmmm" is not a good sign in a situation like this, particularly when you were looking forward to hearing something along the lines of "spectacular." After a few moments, he said simply, "your PSA is elevated." As he continued, he told me that this level had been steadily increasing in recent years, but that this was the first time it had surpassed a threshold that indicated a potential problem. I was vaguely familiar with the PSA as a test for the possible presence of prostate cancer, but my knowledge was admittedly very limited. Our doctor spent most of our available time discussing what this meant, recommending a plan of action, and stressing that this blood test meant that I *might* have prostate cancer, but that false positives were not uncommon. For my part, I wasn't handling this bit of news particularly well. In retrospect, my upbringing had kicked in, and when our doctor suggested that I might have prostate cancer, or I might not, I heard only one word . . . *cancer*. Even without a confirmed diagnosis, my mind was racing.

I soon consulted a urologist, who on the Monday after Thanksgiving completed a biopsy of my prostate. A week later I was back in the urologist's office to receive the results of the biopsy, which indicated that I did have prostate cancer. And again, I didn't handle the news particularly well. Perhaps to make me feel better, the doctor said, "Nobody likes to get cancer, but if you have to get cancer, this is not a bad cancer to get." As I would learn, he was absolutely correct, though at the time and in my worried state of mind, that comment fostered emotions in me that bordered on anger, so deep were my fatalistic notions about the prospects of any cancer diagnosis.

A couple of weeks after Christmas, I had robotic surgery to remove my prostate, a successful procedure that was accompanied by virtually none of the dreaded side effects that can result from that surgery. All was going well when my three-month PSA showed no signs of cancer, and I was beginning to believe I had successfully concluded my battle with this disease. Then at six months, the blood test was positive, indicating that not all the cancerous tissue had been removed during the surgery. Hoping and believing that I had put this episode behind me, I again didn't handle well the notion that malignant tissue was still in my body. It was as if I had faced the same cancer diagnosis twice. Over the holiday season in 2013, I underwent daily radiation treatments for eight weeks, very quick therapies that left me feeling strangely helpless as my half-naked body was strapped to the gurney so the brief bursts of radiation could bombard the targeted areas of my midsection.

Since shortly after the completion of those forty treatments, my PSA tests have been "undetectable," meaning there has been no trace of prostate cancer. Given the nature of the disease, there is the possibility that in future years my annual tests will indicate that the cancer has returned (or rather, that it never completely left), and if it does return I will fight it with every available treatment. In the meantime, though, I'm going to work diligently to keep thoughts about that possible return out of my mind, because from my perspective, the notion of excessively worrying about a disease that might but likely won't return isn't much better than actually having it back in my body. The cancer-averse aspects of my DNA at times bubble to the surface, but I have worked hard to live in the moment when it comes to being cancer-free.

In other words, I have dealt with prostate cancer, and will deal with it again only if and when I have to. In the meantime, in this particular part of my life, I'm going to do all I can to take it "one ride at a time."

CHAPTER 7
"WHAT DO WE DO NOW?"

One of my favorite political movies is "The Candidate," a 1972 film in which, after a long and arduous campaign, the upstart candidate (played by Robert Redford) defeats the long-time incumbent to become a U.S. Senator from California. In the last scene of the movie, with ecstatic supporters surrounding him, the new-ly-elected senator breaks away from the crowds to lead his campaign manager (played by Peter Boyle) into an empty hotel room where, with a lost look on his face, he asks, "What do we do now?" Having poured everything into winning the election, now that he had won, the young politician was at a loss as to what the victory meant and what now needed to be done.

As Bev and I sat in our hotel room in St. Augustine with no preparations to make, no meetings to attend, and no long rides confronting us, in some ways that was how we were feeling, wondering in an almost numb manner, "What do we do now?"

. . .

With little to do but wait to depart for dinner, and realizing we each had a great deal on our minds, Bev and I had a long talk, sharing our emotions at the end of this amazing journey. We were both so happy and proud to have accomplished what we did, though we both agreed that fully grasping the magnitude of this accomplishment would probably take some time. As we shared with each other, one of the predominant emotions we both were feeling was a profound sense of gratitude on many different levels. We were both grateful that we had been physically able, at the age of sixty, to ride our bicycles across the entire United States. We were both grateful to have been able to complete this journey without any major mishaps or injuries, at least any directly involving the two of us. We were both grateful, to be completely honest, to have had the courage to even attempt such a feat. We were both grateful that we'd had the time and resources to undertake such an endeavor, knowing that so many did not. And we were both grateful, so very grateful, to have been able to experience this incredible trip together. Though we didn't know in what way at the time, we were both confident that this experience had profoundly changed us, likely deeply and in many ways.

We didn't complete this journey for any reason other than simply to do it. There had been no hidden agendas, no desire to "find ourselves," no underlying purpose other than to push ourselves and fulfill a long-time goal. But to our children, and in time to their children, the message associated with Mom and Dad, Grandma and Grandpa, at the age of sixty riding their bicycles across the entire country, over mountains, through deserts, through cities and completely barren areas, through rain and wind and even sandstorms, will hopefully be clear. If you set a goal or identify a dream that's important to you and work hard enough and stay focused long enough, it can come true.

But when you put your heart and soul into a task, making it your total focus for many months, and when that goal is finally reached, there is often a reckoning—a reset, if you will—and a spate of emotions that accompany the otherwise joyful ending of a long, hard, but incredibly satisfying journey. As Bev and I discussed, we were already beginning to experience an "activity withdrawal" and a "people withdrawal." When the morning after reaching the Atlantic I again woke up all too early, for the first time in over one and a half months, I didn't have something physical I had to either complete or prepare for that day. Even on our four rest days, we had always been looking ahead to the next ride, preparing ourselves for the physical demands of what was to come. Though we quickly resumed our regular exercise regimen upon returning home, we had no physical activity we *had* to complete this day or the next day, or whenever. We were so looking forward to letting our bodies heal and recover from the demands of the just-completed forty-six days, but in a weird sense, we knew we would miss the rigors of completing a long ride every day and the odd sense of order that accompanied that process. Some might very logically suggest that we could always complete a long ride every day if we so desired, and that would be true, but it would be so different from the focused, required activity to which we had grown so accustomed.

Just as important, by the evening after the tire dip in the Atlantic, Bev and I were already experiencing "people withdrawal." Over the previous six and a half weeks, we had developed deep acquaintances with each of the other riders and the two support guys, had experienced good times and challenges together, had eaten countless meals together, and had joked and kidded with each other. In other words, we had become like a family, and the accident the previous weekend had seemed to draw us even closer. As each rider left Florida and returned home, we had a foreboding sense that we would likely never see most if not all of these new friends ever again, and we found that to be even more emotionally challenging than we had anticipated. On our last evening in Florida, Bev and I walked a half mile or so to a waterfront restaurant called the Conch House, where we shared a relaxing meal. It was an exceptionally good dinner in a beautiful setting, and one of the very few meals we had experienced with just each other since leaving San Diego. Even on "rider's choice" days, people had often ended up at the same restaurant. It was really good to have a nice, celebratory meal together, just the two of us, but it felt rather odd to not have been swapping stories with at least a few of our fellow riders. We were looking forward to getting back home and reuniting with our "real" family, but the emptiness we were feeling was evidence of just how much we were going to miss these people.

• • •

In the early morning hours on the day we departed for home, with me still in a reflective mood and Bev getting a few additional hours of needed sleep, I thought about my riding partner for the past forty-six days. On the first day of the tour as we climbed the seemingly never-ending mountain just outside of San Diego, Bev had struggled mightily, as had many of us. By the second day, however, with an even more challenging route than the day before, we had come to realize the need to relax, to take as much time as we needed, and to find enjoyment in the experience, and we had had a tough but otherwise really good day as a result. Both of us had always worn little mirrors on our glasses to allow us to watch from behind for oncoming traffic. I typically rode in front, and I used the mirror to make sure Bev was staying with me as much as to watch for any approaching vehicles. It had been truly amazing to watch her continue to get more powerful and gain more confidence as the tour progressed. As another rider commented to her after watching Bev easily climb a particularly long and tough incline, "You are one tough lady." I had always known this, but as I reflected in our darkened hotel room, I realized, or more accurately had reinforced, two important conclusions about my longtime life partner: First, as if there had been any doubt before beginning this experience, Bev is an incredibly strong woman, both physically and mentally. And second, but of equal significance, I could not have been prouder of her for how she handled the rigors and profound challenges presented by the amazingly difficult journey we had just completed.

• • •

The shuttle to take us to the Jacksonville International Airport for our flight home was scheduled to pick us up at 9:45 that morning. At breakfast, we were able to tell our goodbyes to Steve, the other rider who on this tour had completed his first "century" ride and a genuinely nice guy. As we walked to the elevator to take us back to our room, we met and shared our farewells with Danish Allan, in some respects the individual on the tour with the most interesting background and a rider for whom our respect had continued to grow, particularly in the hours and days following the tragic accident of the previous weekend. We finished packing and hauled our luggage down to wait outside for our shuttle on this gorgeous autumn morning in Florida. Ross, the most cycling-focused rider on the tour and Bev's previously unknown Murray State classmate, was reading a newspaper as he also waited for his ride. We said goodbye to Ross and were soon picked up and on our way to the airport. Just like that, our time with this great group of people with whom we had grown so close had come to an end.

Our flight home was uneventful, with both of us still in a bit of a daze as we prepared for our transition back into our "normal" lives. It had been almost fifty days since we had driven a car or cooked a meal or vacuumed a carpet. It had also been that long since we had slept in our own bed, sat in our regular lounge chairs, or watched our own TV, these being just a few of the countless pleasures we had heretofore mindlessly taken for granted. We soon found that transitioning from a long and challenging bicycle tour back to our admittedly cushy life of retirement was smoother and quicker than we might have anticipated. We were glad to be home, though it took some time for the restlessness we regularly experienced to diminish. Coming home a week before Thanksgiving helped, and we were soon caught up in the revelry of preparing for Christmas with our expanding family, our granddaughter now one and a half and our daughter-in-law less than six months from delivering our grandson. With the inevitable (at least for me) eating that seems to accompany the holidays, in time I regained most of the weight I had lost during the tour. In many respects, within a couple of weeks, we were back to normal, almost as if this amazing journey had not occurred.

• • •

Except that it had occurred, and our status as one of a relatively small number of people who had ridden a bicycle across the United States was an achievement we were proud of and something that now helped to define us; an experience that would stay with us for the rest of our lives. Most people would consider this a significant accomplishment, but Bev and I tried to be relatively lowkey in sharing this experience with people we encountered. Still, anyone coming back from such a trip would likely have a little extra jump in their step; we certainly did.

Still a little tired physically and mentally from the daily grind of the tour, we eased back into our exercise routine. Before intense workouts of an hour or less ceased to provide sufficient mileage as we prepared for our cross-country trip, Bev and I had regularly completed spin classes at our local YMCA. We had often taken a Friday morning class that was particularly intense, a "Les Mills RPM" class that utilized selected music to guide riders through an extended period of high-intensity interval training. It had been months since we had last completed any sort of spin class, focusing instead on completing two- and three-hour training rides that were less intense but far more taxing. For the class scheduled on the Friday after Thanksgiving, which would be our first time on any bicycle since arriving in St. Augustine more than a week earlier, the instructor had advertised on social media that instead of the regular forty-five minutes, the class would be a more challenging one hour in length. Bev and I didn't care how long the class would be, as we simply wanted to get our legs back into a cycling motion. Weekday cycling classes often brought many of the same participants, but holiday periods typically attracted a different crowd. And this Friday morning was no different, with the studio filled with a much younger clientele, including a large number of college students home for Thanksgiving. As we walked into the studio, perhaps the two oldest individuals planning to participate in this extra-rigorous class, we sensed skepticism in the looks we received from these much younger participants. Unspoken was the likely sense of doubt in these young people that these two old folks could actually complete this class without keeling over. Bev and I both shared this sensation, and I wryly commented to her, "If they only knew . . ." She gave me a big smile in return, and we both completed the hour-long class with no difficulty. With our bikes not yet returned from Florida, it was good to get our legs pedaling again.

But that's what completing a major significant challenge does for you: it instills a quiet swagger that transcends confidence. In front of these young fitness cyclists, we didn't need to stand up and let everyone know we had just biked across the country; the only two people in that room who needed that information were Bev and me. In the coming months there would be numerous occurrences when, while questioning whether or not we could do something, we subtly reminded ourselves of what we had done during those forty-six days the previous autumn. In essence, if we could pull that off, we could accomplish nearly anything we wanted to.

• • •

So, other than the internal and, to a diminishing extent, external changes we had experienced, by the beginning of the new year, our day-to-day lives were largely back to normal. Though our discussions with others about our cross-country journey continued to decrease in frequency over time, one question that we often encountered involved our future plans, what our next adventure might be. I was typically a bit more circumspect than Bev in responding to these inquiries, saying things like, "You just never know what we're going to do." Deep down, though, we were dealing with yet another variation of the question, "What do we do now?" We both knew that, as our health and circumstances permitted, more adventures were in our future.

By this point in our lives, for a variety of reasons both psychological and physiological, we had developed an almost visceral need for this type of challenge. We had learned from all of our experiences, from running a marathon, to riding the Missouri Katy Trail, to hiking across the Grand Canyon, and finally to traversing the United States, that a major challenge provided the impetus and focus we needed to push ourselves to remain healthy, as well as to provide needed flavor in our lives. With this last and most significant of such experiences successfully completed, in addition to the desire that had been present for such a long time, we now had the confidence to tackle journeys from which we might have previously shied away.

What that next challenge might be remained unrevealed, but Bev and I both hoped and now believed that together, countless memories remained to be made.

LIFE LESSON #7
Don't expect everyone to appreciate the significance of your accomplishments.

"And those who were seen dancing were thought to be insane by those who could not hear the music."

—Friedrich Nietzsche

A s our flight left Jacksonville on that mid-November afternoon, on one level, Bev and I were anxious to get back home, resume our routines, and prepare for the holidays. But on another level, as the magnitude of what we had just finished began to sink in, we were absolutely pumped, and in our excitement we were ready to share with others stories about our journey. We both realized, however, that we would likely need to be cautious about how much and with how much enthusiasm we discussed our cross-country trip with people we encountered. We were clearly excited about what we had experienced, but to assume that everyone else (or anyone else, for that matter) shared that level of excitement would be naïve, as well as contrary to human nature, a lesson I learned at an early age.

When I was eleven, my father took me on a trip to Los Angeles, my first time flying in an airplane. The highlight of that trip was a day at Disneyland, which in my preadolescent mind was truly "the most magical place on earth." I was enthralled, and that day has remained among the most amazing and memorable of my life. I watched with utter fascination the now-rudimentary animatronics used in the "Pirates of the Caribbean" and with Abraham Lincoln reciting the Gettysburg Address, the humorous depiction of the animals in the "Jungle Cruise," and the splendor of "Main Street" with the iconic Cinderella's Castle in the background. I still get a smile thinking back on that trip, and as we flew back to Missouri, I couldn't wait to tell the other kids in the neighborhood all about my amazing adventure.

But none of the other kids in our neighborhood had been to Disneyland, and thus had no frame of reference when I described in an animated fashion how Lincoln had looked so real, or how the hippo on the Jungle Cruise had come out of nowhere to "attack" our boat, or how the Bell Telephone "Circle-Vision 360" movie had made me dizzy. Being typical youngsters of that era, these other kids had been interested in my Disneyland stories for a little while, and then they tolerated them for a while longer, and then finally they did little to feign their growing lack of interest. In time I became an even bigger bore than normal, though it took my immature and developing psyche a while to grasp the changing dynamic. While it took some time to internalize, it was an important lesson I never forgot: that just because something was fascinating to me, it didn't necessarily mean anybody else would share that interest.

• • •

In the months leading up to our cross-country tour, we had remained largely quiet about our upcoming trip, ultimately telling just a handful of family members and friends as our departure date approached. We continued this subdued approach afterward. About a week after we arrived back home, Bev posted a brief trip summary on her Facebook page, but other than that we simply responded to questions about what we had been up to for the past few months. When others learned about our trip their responses tended to vary, ranging from nonchalance to expressions of genuine amazement. On one end, some seemed to truly grasp what we had done, and in some instances expressed polite envy of our experience. In other words, as Bev and I often discussed afterward, they "got it." They asked questions, wanted more information, and in some instances said something like, "Boy, I would love to do that." On the other end, in response to our statement that we had just finished riding our bicycles 3,000 miles across the southern United States, some responded with something like, "Well, that's nice. We just got back from a trip to Branson." Others, after learning that we had ridden on our bicycles for six, eight, and ten hours each day for a month and a half, responded incredulously, in effect asking, "Why would you want to do that?" To these folks, all good people, the notion of a cross-country bike tour was tantamount to getting forty-six consecutive root canals. In other words, they didn't "get it," and what's more, they really didn't care to.

But really, why would they? What we had done was especially important to Bev and me, and part of us felt compelled to share our story with everyone. Luckily, we didn't act on those feelings. Many people have completed amazing journeys, travels, and vacations that have generated great pride and enthusiasm. While that's wonderful for them, and the pride they feel is justified, that doesn't mean I would want to spend a couple of hours looking at their vacation photos or hearing their travel stories. And the converse was true regarding the cross-country bike trip we had just completed. Just because it was important, perhaps even impressive, to us didn't necessarily mean it had much meaning to those we encountered. Besides, from our perspective, we had completed this trip for ourselves, and if our story resonated with others, then we needed to simply value the connection we had made. But to expect others to be fascinated with our story simply because we were would be a unique blend of arrogance and irrationality.

Had the eleven-year-old version of me come across another kid who had been to Disneyland (I don't think I ever did), we could have had a joyful conversation. Similarly, Bev and I stand ready to share stories from our bike trip with anyone expressing genuine interest. In the meantime, we have each other . . . and a lot of amazing memories.

EPILOGUE
A HAPPY ENDING AFTER ALL

I n time our lives returned to our pre-tour routines, and though not a day went by without recalling our countless memories, recollections of this journey came to dominate our thoughts less and less. Still, out of nowhere we might recall a memorable dinner we had on the tour, a particularly challenging ride, or some visually impressive scene. A prank instigated by Ted, a conversation about some obscure cycling event with Ross, or out of the blue, some hilarious comment from Danish Allan delivered in his distinct accent, or a particularly helpful gesture by Larry or Chuck would come to mind.

And never far from our thoughts was Scottish Alan. Our emotions immediately following the accident near Tallahassee had been dominated by deep concern about his well-being, with our initial lack of information driving fear that perhaps he had perished. After learning that he was going to be okay and that after a lengthy stint of rehabilitation he was expected to make a complete recovery, we were relieved but still filled with a sense of emptiness that Alan had not been with us when we reached St. Augustine. In time, though, our thoughts turned to curiosity about how his convalescence and rehab were progressing.

We tracked his progress through his occasional Facebook posts and were heartened and a little amazed at how positive and upbeat he remained, despite the circumstances of his injuries. After multiple surgeries and then being transported back to his native Scotland in an air ambulance, he progressed from a wheelchair to a walker, then crutches and protective boots. In time we were happy to see photos of his first time back on a bicycle, a short but consequential ride that might have occurred without his doctor's approval. In all these photos, Alan looked great, just like he did before the accident, and he continued to express his gratitude for the health care professionals who had cared for him. He seemed so happy to be alive and active again. He had purchased a new bike to replace the one that was decimated in the accident, and eventually he began riding longer distances. We hadn't been able to give him our goodbyes and considered it unlikely we would ever see Alan again, but we were delighted that his recovery was progressing so well.

●　●　●

In mid-August, around nine months after the tour had concluded, we received an email from Larry of Trans-America Cycling that was as welcome as it was unexpected. It stated that shortly after the accident, he and Chuck had told Alan that if he ever wanted to finish the portion of the tour he had been prevented from completing, they would be there to assist him. Just a few days before Larry sent this email to us, Alan had accepted their offer, saying to them that he wanted to "finish what I started." He would resume his tour at the last point on the actual route before the accident had occurred and would finish with a tire dip into the Atlantic in St. Augustine, completing his journey almost a year to the day from when the rest of us had completed our tour. In this email, Larry invited all the other riders from our tour to join them in Florida to celebrate Alan's finish, and to ride the last leg of the tour with him if we so desired.

In a bit of synchronicity, Bev and I each received this email and read it within a few minutes of each other. We both had the same reaction: we wanted to be there when Alan finished. Of equal importance, we both felt we *needed* to be there, not just for Alan but for ourselves as well. Our cross-country tour had been an amazing experience, but the one remaining loose end was the absence of Alan when we dipped our tires in the Atlantic and our inability to see him again before leaving Florida. Of tantamount importance was Alan's need for closure, but the rest of us on that tour needed closure as well. By that evening, we were making airline and hotel reservations, excited to complete this unexpected trip back to Florida.

• • •

It was a couple of weeks before I responded to Larry's email regarding our plans, and his return response intimated that Alan's tour completion plan had morphed into a much bigger celebration. While it would have been great to ride with Alan (and Larry and Chuck) on the last leg from Palatka to St. Augustine, we couldn't justify the hassle and cost of shipping and reassembling two bikes just to complete a forty-two-mile ride. We had decided we would fly to Jacksonville, travel to Palatka for the celebration and dinner Larry and Chuck had planned, and then drive to St. Augustine to be present when Alan arrived to complete his tour.

In Larry's response, he indicated that four other riders, Jim, Steve, Ted, and even Allan, traveling all the way back from Denmark, were not only planning to be in attendance, but would be riding with Alan, Larry, and Chuck for the entire 300 miles. We had wondered whether we would be the only two from the tour who would travel to Florida for these festivities, so we were surprised and pleased to learn that we would be seeing five of the other seven riders from the tour and that Alan would have good company as he completed his journey. And quite frankly, Bev and I could relate to these four riders wanting to actively participate in this ride, a desire to help Alan as well as a personal need to relive at least a part of what, for most of us, had been one of the most amazing experiences of our lives.

• • •

Four days before Bev and I were to fly to Florida, the team gathered in Tallahassee to begin the completion of Alan's tour. Like on his original tour, he was riding to raise money for Alzheimer's Scotland, and this time also the Florida chapter of the Alzheimer's Association of America. As Larry and Chuck would be riding with Alan, the group would be supported by Larry's wife Vicky and Jim's wife Sandy. Alan had been aware that Steve and Ted would be riding with the group, so it was a surprise when Jim showed up. It was an even greater treat for him to see Danish Allan, who had traveled from Europe for this important event.

Alan had suggested to Larry and Chuck that the daily rides be limited to around sixty miles, a particularly impressive daily distance for a rider who until just a few months earlier had been unable to ride a bicycle. As a result, some of the routes were adjusted and a day was added to the itinerary, making the distances a bit more manageable but still challenging.

For the first route, the group was shuttled back to the little Florida town of Chattahoochee, the location of the last SAG stop before the tragic accident. As it was not located on the original route, most of the group didn't ride past the site of the incident, possibly sparing the emotions of Scottish Alan. (Perhaps true to his nature, Danish Allan did ride past that location, likely to gain his own sense of closure regarding this traumatic event.) The team rode back to the hotel in Tallahassee, completing an uneventful but very meaningful first day. The next day, the group completed a sixty-mile ride to Madison, and then the following day another fifty-nine miles to High Springs. Through much of these rides, the team acted as much as protectors as friends, surrounding Alan as he made his way down the highway. On the fourth day, under warm conditions, the group completed a forty-three-mile route to Gainesville, and the next day followed fifty-eight miles of trails and back roads into Palatka, the last overnight stop on the route. Alan was riding well, and other than a slight fall on some loose sand, the rides had been completed without incident. Just as the rest of the team had been at this point a year earlier, Scottish Alan was a short forty-two miles from finally completing his cross-country tour.

• • •

On the next to last day of Alan's tour, Bev and I arrived at the Jacksonville International Airport in the early afternoon, picked up our rental, and headed toward Palatka. The group was staying at the Quality Inn, the same hotel where we had stayed a year earlier. Larry and Chuck had meticulously planned out the evening to recreate as closely as possible the activities Alan had missed while awaiting additional surgery in Tallahassee, most notably a celebration ceremony with awards and a video presentation (as well as a revision of the dreadfully delightful Larry and Chuck "rap"), followed by a group dinner at the Beef O'Brady's restaurant in the hotel.

Larry had stressed that other than he and Chuck, no one else knew we were coming to Florida, and that he somehow wanted to orchestrate a sort of big reveal to the rest of the group. We had been the only married couple on our tour, and Bev the only female, and as such, we had been somewhat of a novelty. But we were skeptical that our arrival would be such a big deal, though we certainly wanted to follow Larry's lead. As we approached Palatka, Bev sent him a text and he responded that everyone in the group was sitting around in his room and that we should just come there when we arrived at the hotel.

The Quality Inn and Suites Riverfront in Palatka is an interesting property, an older hotel that has seen better days but which is located on the banks of the wide and beautiful St. Johns River. Rooms open to the outside, so on the riverfront side guests can simply open their doors to majestic vistas. Larry and Chuck's room was on that riverfront side, and as we quietly approached we saw that the door was open and all kinds of laughter and loud conversations were emanating from the room. We had an eerie sense of déjà vu, a palpable feeling that we were back on the tour and the riders were sitting around drinking beer after a ride. Which was exactly what these guys were doing.

As we stepped into the room I said, "Are there any cyclists in here?" For just a second the group sat in slightly stunned silence, momentarily struggling to figure out who these two people were. Then, almost in unison, they stood up and moved toward us, offering hugs and handshakes as they showed how genuinely pleased they were to see us. The group had been back together for the past five days, and had further bonded as they accompanied Alan on each day's ride. As a result, Bev and I had wondered whether we would fit back in, two non-riders among these guys who were riding the last 300 miles of

Alan's tour. If we were concerned about this, we shouldn't have been. One rider asked, "What are you doing here?" as if we were just in the area and had decided to stop by to say hello. I joked, "I came to see you." Within five minutes it was as if we were back on the tour, swapping stories and telling jokes and lofting friendly insults and drinking beers. It was incredibly good to be back with these people.

It was the first time we had seen Alan since just before the accident, as he and Danish Allan had been riding backward on the route before making their fateful turn toward Georgia. As I said to him, "It is so good to see you." Indeed it was, and he looked great, belying the severity of his injuries and the difficult rehab he had faced for the past year. Two of our fondest memories of Alan were our conversations about professional football in general and the Kansas City Chiefs in particular, and the bottle of Zinfandel we had shared near the midpoint of our tour. As congratulatory gifts, we brought Alan a Chiefs t-shirt and a bottle of Zinfandel from one of our favorite California wineries.

After a while, we gravitated to the hotel's conference room that Larry and Chuck had set up for the re-do of the celebration ceremony. Though this wasn't officially a Trans-America Cycling event (rather "friends helping a friend," as Larry had explained in his email), these two guys provided for everyone (Bev and me included) a commemorative t-shirt and other gifts, and the original video presentation expanded to include scenes from the just-completed four days of riding. A year earlier the two support guys had presented to each rider a special award, largely comical, to highlight a special accomplishment or "power." Scottish Alan had missed out on the original award ceremony, but tonight he was presented the "4-1-1 Award." From the day we had dipped our back tires in the Pacific Ocean in San Diego over a year earlier, it had taken Alan 411 days to complete his tour. But with just one ride remaining, it was now clear he was going to finish. As the ceremony concluded, we adjourned to the hotel restaurant for a very enjoyable dinner. It was a wonderful and gratifying time spent with people who meant a great deal to us.

• • •

We were on hand the next morning as the group prepared to begin the last ride of Alan's tour. Larry had asked us to bring our Trans-America Cycling jerseys to wear for photos on this last day. The group was delayed for a few minutes as Alan and some of his fellow riders were interviewed by a reporter from the *Palatka Daily News*. My only comment to the young journalist was, "I'm glad you're doing this, because this is an amazing story." He and his editors agreed, as for good reason Alan's journey strongly resonated with virtually everyone who heard about it.

In time, the group made its way out of the hotel parking lot and then across the expansive bridge over the St. Johns River, a relatively short ride of forty-two miles facing them on this cool, overcast morning.

• • •

Supporting the riders was Jim's wife Sandy, who we had met in Louisiana during the original tour, and Larry's wife Vicki, a delightful, retired teacher we were meeting for the first time. After the riders left, Sandy and Vicki prepared to depart for the only SAG stop, located in a neat park overlooking another section of the St. Johns River. With some time to spare, we went back to our room to pack and then headed to St. Augustine.

After walking along another section of St. Augustine Beach and then killing some time at a Starbucks, we made our way to Anastasia State Park, believing we had plenty of time before Alan and the other riders arrived. We almost missed them, as favorable winds and a quick pace allowed these excellent cyclists to arrive sooner than anticipated. After parking near the entrance to the beach, we found Vicki and Sandy, who informed us that the group had already crossed the Bridge of Lions, just a couple of miles away. Soon we saw in the distance a group of cyclists wearing white jerseys passing the entrance gate into the park; after an incredible year, Alan's cross-country journey was about to come to an end.

Alan's tour completion, 411 days after leaving San Diego

As we waited for the riders to reach us where we were standing near the walkway to the beach, we weren't sure what Alan's emotional state would be when he finally dipped his front tire in the Atlantic. After all, he had been frustrated in his initial attempt to make it this far just a year earlier, and had endured months of grueling rehab just to regain the ability to walk and then to ride a bike. Many under those circumstances would find their emotions bubbling to the surface, a mixture of joy and relief as a lifelong goal was finally reached. But as he pulled up and prepared to walk his bike the final hundred yards or so to the ocean, the Scottish engineer was as calm and reserved as he had typically been during the original tour. We continued to be impressed, though not surprised, by the demeanor and workmanlike attitude Alan exhibited the entire time we were around him.

After posing for some photos and speaking with a representative of the Alzheimer's Association, Alan made his way to the long walkway on which he walked his bike before taking off his cycling shoes and heading to the water. We hung back to take pictures and got a good shot of Alan as he frolicked in the Atlantic, a big smile denoting the satisfaction he felt at finally, a year later but perhaps in an even more fulfilling fashion, reaching this milestone.

It was sunnier, warmer, and far less windy than it had been a year earlier, so everyone spent more time on the beach taking photos and enjoying Alan's moment. While it was obviously special for him, I was struck with an odd mixture of joy and relief, the latter stemming from the realization that Alan was recovering well and thriving, and that the last loose end from our tour the previous year had now been tied. We felt happy and proud for our Scottish friend.

Larry and Chuck had tried to replicate virtually everything Alan had missed, and to celebrate this milestone they again served mimosas to everyone present. Countless photos were taken, with Alan wanting to be photographed individually and in small groups with everyone present, an obvious desire to make this special moment last in perpetuity. Soon it was time for the festivities to break up and for the group to head to the hotel for the evening. All but one couple stayed that evening in the St. Augustine Sleep Inn, the same hotel in which we had stayed a year earlier. So, as the riders rode their bicycles to the hotel, Bev and I found a liquor store where we bought a case of beer for the group. It was again a treat to sit around with these good folks and have a few beers before dinner.

For dinner, we all walked the half-mile from the hotel to the Conch House, the waterfront restaurant where Bev and I had celebrated just a year earlier. Since Alan had begun the final leg of his cross-country tour just five days earlier, Trans-America Cycling had paid for his rooms and meals, just as they had for the rest of us in the last days of the original tour. When we were seated at the restaurant, Alan informed everyone that after Larry and Chuck had covered his expenses the previous five days, this meal was on him. It was a nice and much-appreciated gesture, and seemingly a way for Alan to show his appreciation for the support he had received.

The following morning after breakfast, we said our goodbyes to Chuck, Larry, and Larry's wife Vicki, and then packed and prepared for the hour-long drive to Jacksonville Beach, where we were spending the night before flying home the following day. The St. Augustine airport was on our route, so we shuttled Steve, Ted, and Danish Allan to pick up rental cars. As we dropped them off at the terminal, there were hugs all around as these three good guys expressed their farewells. Then, with more gratitude than sadness, we headed to Jacksonville, our reunion with Alan, Larry and Chuck, and the rest of the riders now concluded.

In some ways, that surprisingly emotional (at least for Bev and me) airport parting from Steve, Ted, and Allan was a metaphor for our entire trip back to Florida. We had truly wondered if, a year after originally saying goodbye to these folks, things might be a bit awkward. But within minutes of our surprise reappearance, we were all sitting together, swapping stories and playful insults just as we had done a year earlier. As a result, it had been for Bev and me a wonderful couple of days.

As I reflected on this afterward, I think I came to understand our emotions as we dropped off these three at the St. Augustine airport. When we had completed the forty-six days of our original cross-country tour, riders and support guys began to depart almost immediately, quite possibly and maybe even likely never to be seen by each other again. Plus, at the time we were still slightly shell-shocked by what we had accomplished, and that coupled with our lingering concerns about Scottish Alan gave us an empty feeling we had not anticipated.

But that month and a half of riding had bonded us together even more closely than we might have realized, a connection that was made even stronger as we dealt with the aftermath of Alan's accident as well as the brave actions of Danish Allan immediately afterward and in the days that followed. As the group had originally dispersed a year earlier, few if any had yet processed a full understanding of what had just transpired, an understanding that came only with time. By this time a year later, we had come to grips with what we had successfully undertaken, and the bonds that had been forged before Alan's tragic accident had only grown stronger in its aftermath.

As we said our goodbyes outside that airport terminal, we believed it was likely that we would not see these friends ever again, just as it had been a year earlier. But on this day it felt far different than it had a year ago, with everything viewed from a fresh perspective. For Bev and me, this reunion trip and our time with these good people had been a gift, a bonus opportunity made possible by the perseverance of Alan and the support and generosity of Larry and Chuck. Whereas we had left St. Augustine a year earlier with more sadness and confusion than we had ever expected, as we left Steve, Ted, and Allan at the airport to continue their journeys home, we had a profound sense of happiness. Scottish Alan was not only doing amazingly well physically, his condition at times making us almost forget the pain and hard work that had brought him back to this point, but he had finally finished his journey, 411 days after he had started. For the Fall 2017 Trans-America Cycling cross-country team, everything was now complete.

As we headed north toward Jacksonville Beach, Bev and I were quiet for a while, contemplating what had occurred over the past couple of days. Finally, I said, "What a good bunch of guys." Still looking off into the distance, Bev responded, "They sure are." In many ways, that about said it all.

LIFE LESSON #8
Great beauty can often be found in the most challenging moments . . . If you're willing to look for it.

"Let us come alive to the splendor that is all around us and see the beauty in ordinary things."

—Thomas Merton

The sun had just risen as Bev and I rode along a deserted highway just outside of Fort Davis, Texas. It was early, we were tired after multiple grueling days, and on this day we were facing one of the longest rides of the tour and the first century ride that Bev and I would complete. For us, it was a daunting set of circumstances, and while we weren't necessarily worried about the upcoming ride, there was lingering doubt about whether we would be able to handle such a long day. As we left Fort Davis, pondering what was ahead of us, we were workmanlike in our approach.

As we traveled down that deserted highway, the temperature cool and crisp, I looked to my left to see the majestic sight of the sun filtering through the clouds just above the top of some peaks in the surrounding mountains. It was visually stunning, with the filtered sun creating a kaleidoscope of hues and colors on the thin clouds. Perhaps I was overly tired, or maybe my nervousness from the first two and a half weeks of the tour had come bubbling to the surface, but that beautiful West Texas sight brought tears to my eyes. I motioned back to Bev that I was stopping, and from the side of the highway I took a photo of an image I can still visualize in vivid detail in my mind. On one of the longest and toughest days of a long and tough tour, I somehow grasped this most majestic image. Putting my workmanlike approach aside, I was able to see immense beauty lurking right on the horizon.

Often life seemingly works that way, providing glimpses of beauty even during some of the most trying of times. Many years ago, just moments after my mother had passed away in the predawn hours of a beautiful April morning, as the hospice nurse completed her required tasks I walked out the front door of my mother's home. It was a terribly sad day, my mother's death coupled with that of my father just a few years earlier leaving my brother and me with no parents, something certainly not unexpected but a jolting reality, nonetheless. As I stood outside on that difficult morning, I noticed how warm it was for such an early hour, how the sun was beginning to rise above the distant horizon, how the light winds were rustling the leaves on a nearby copse of trees. And then I noticed the chirping and singing of unseen birds as they began their day. On such a sad and difficult occasion, it was also an absolutely gorgeous day, perhaps a sign that the process of life was continuing, that death was a natural part of that process, and that everything was going to be okay.

Similarly, a different form of beauty can often be found in the human condition, as regular people demonstrate amazing qualities in overcoming challenging situations and circumstances. And so it was with Alan's accident, particularly in its aftermath. To be clear, there was absolutely nothing beautiful about this tragic event, and anyone on that tour would have done anything they could to prevent Alan and Allan from having to experience such a horrendous incident. But it did occur, and images still linger in my mind from the days and months that followed that evoke thoughts of splendor and magnificence.

Like the photo of Scottish Alan that he posted on Facebook the morning following the accident, a picture depicting a bruised and battered, but smiling, cyclist who had withstood the accident and in time would recover. Or the image of Danish Allan standing in a hotel room on that same morning, recounting matter-of-factly what had occurred the previous day, including a passing mention of his own injury and the steps he had taken to care for his riding partner, all with a demeanor that belied the magnitude of what he had personally experienced. Then there was the sight of that same rider later that day entering the parking lot of the evening's hotel after completing not only that day's scheduled ride, but also the extensive mileage he had been forced to bypass the previous day, all despite the stress and injury (and stitches) he had incurred during the accident. All of these images merely represented reactions to the travails of life, but from my perspective given the circumstances, they were magnificent. And beautiful. And all would have potentially been missed if we had been focused solely on the painfully negative aspects of what had occurred.

Then there were the images of Scottish Alan that followed, Facebook postings that would be rather mundane in the regular flow of life but which under the circumstances were incredibly meaningful. Such as Alan in a wheelchair, or standing with a walker, or simply standing, all demonstrating the progress he was experiencing as his recovery continued. Then there was the photo of Alan on his first bike ride since the accident, an action that some with such gruesome injuries might have avoided, but that showed the force of his resolve. Standing on their own, these images to most people would have minimal significance, but given the context of their evolution, they had great meaning and in their unique way, tremendous beauty.

To fully appreciate a Van Gogh painting, one must understand the anguish in the artist's troubled life that influenced each and every brushstroke. And while photos of Alan finally dipping his front tire in the Atlantic Ocean will obviously never approach the artistic significance of iconic works like "Starry Night," to those who know his story, the beauty in those photos of our Scottish friend was borne of the struggle that preceded it.

Yes, there is beauty all around us, often made more vivid by the circumstances surrounding it and typically available only to those open and willing to see it. So it was with our cross-country tour, a brief time in our lives that blessed us with countless beautiful images that will forever remain etched in our minds. I am so thankful we were open and willing to actually see them.

ACKNOWLEDGMENTS

There are countless individuals whose contributions made this project possible:

The Trans-America Cycling support guides, *Larry Love* and *Chuck Hanchett*, who provided assistance and guidance without which these two recreational cyclists could never have successfully traversed the country.

Our fellow riders, *Alan, Allan, Jim, Ray, Ross, Steve, and Ted*, a great group of fascinating and enjoyable individuals who made our month-and-a-half together so memorable and enjoyable. I hope I accurately depicted our journey together.

The countless individuals we encountered as we crossed the country, a diverse group of Americans that collectively reinforced our faith in this great nation.

Early readers of the manuscript whose feedback was helpful, supportive, and informative: *Bev Leachman, Ann Leachman, Sue Mauldin, Greg Mauldin, Larry Love, and Chuck Hanchett.*

Chuck Hanchett, Larry Love, and Jim Elliott who provided photos utilized in the project, and *Jonathan Leachman* who provided a graphic depicting the cross-country route.

Anna A., who skillfully edited the manuscript.

Members of our family, particularly *Jonathan, Kassie, Annie*, and *Nick*, as well as all our extended family, for their support before, during, and after our cross-country tour and through the completion of this project. And to our grandchildren, *Edie* and *Gus*, as well as any others who may bless us in the coming years: may you always be inspired to follow your dreams.

Bev, my partner in life and adventure, without whom none of this would have been possible.

ABOUT THE AUTHOR

Rob Leachman is a retired school district superintendent and university instructor and author of *One Ride at a Time: Life Lessons Learned on a Cross-Country Bicycle Ride*. An educator, author, and occasional adventurer, Rob and his wife Bev completed numerous "adventure travel" trips, including a bicycle trip across Missouri on the "Katy Trail" and a rim-to-rim hike across the Grand Canyon, before riding their bicycles across the United States. Rob earned a doctoral degree from the University of Missouri and lives and works outside of Kansas City, Missouri. He currently writes about areas of lifelong interest to him, including the history of track and field, leadership and goal setting, and what he calls "ageless adventure and fitness." He and Bev can often be seen hiking and biking on area roads and trails. He can be reached at *RobLeachman.com*.